A PRACTICAL GUIDE TO

Reimbursement in Managed Care

JOANNA B. YOUNTS, STEVEN D. HAMILTON,
FRANK B. STEVENS, MACKENZIE S. WALLACE

AMERICAN BAR ASSOCIATION
Family Law Section

Cover design by Mary Anne Kulchawik/ABA Design

Printed in the United States of America.

27 26 25 24 23 5 4 3 2 1

ISBN 978-1-63905-381-0
e-ISBN 978-1-63905-382-7

Contents

About the Authors

JoAnna B. Younts is Managing Director in the healthcare practice of Berkeley Research Group (BRG). She has worked in the healthcare industry for over 30 years where she has focused on healthcare pricing and reimbursement. She began her career with a consulting firm that was a contractor for the Health Care Financing Administration (HCFA), the precursor to the Centers for Medicare and Medicaid Services (CMS). While there, she worked on various projects related to the development and evaluation of Medicare reimbursement approaches. Since then, she has worked for many years in a strategic advisory role for both commercial payers and providers, helping them to evaluate their reimbursement approaches and rates, and their relationship to Medicare. In recent years, she has served as a consulting expert on numerous payer-provider disputes and government investigations, leveraging her expertise in Medicare reimbursement, as well as commercial payer pricing, reimbursement methodologies and rate setting policies.

Frank Stevens is Managing Director in the healthcare practice of Berkeley Research Group (BRG). He has more than 40 years of experience in the healthcare industry, including negotiating payer agreements with providers in 42 states, providing consulting services to academic medical centers, IPAs and medical groups regarding their payer reimbursement and billing compliance investigations, and conducting investigations on behalf of Health Maintenance Organizations (HMO) and regulatory agencies regarding alleged compliance violations. He has been appointed conservator of multiple HMOs, a responsible person in the bankruptcy court and the independent monitor of HMOs, physician organizations and hospitals in state regulatory actions.

Steven D. Hamilton is a healthcare lawyer in Chicago, Illinois. Mr. Hamilton is a seasoned trial lawyer who focuses his practice on healthcare litigation and regulatory issues. He represents health insurers and other healthcare entities in complex individual, multiparty and class action managed care cases in courts and arbitrations across the country. In addition, he has extensive expertise advising Medicare and Medicaid managed care organizations on regulatory and compliance issues, and representing those government-sponsored health plans in internal investigations, government investigations, False Claims Act and qui tam cases and other enforcement actions.

Mackenzie Wallace is a healthcare lawyer in Dallas, Texas. Ms. Wallace is an experienced trial attorney who represents healthcare entities and other businesses and directors in litigation matters. She represents hospitals and healthcare providers in coverage and reimbursement disputes; fraud and civil Racketeer Influenced and Corrupt Organizations Act (RICO) claims; Texas Prompt Pay Act, qui tam and False Claims Act litigation; and matters relating to the violation of federal and state anti-kickback provisions and Stark laws.

Assistance has also been provided by:
Ashton Dietrich, Associate, Thompson Coburn LLP
Ellen Chinn, Managing Consultant, BRG
Karen Chow, Managing Consultant, BRG
Catherine Latour, Consultant, BRG
Julia Moody, Consultant, BRG

The statements made and views expressed in this book are solely the views of the authors and not those of their firms or any of their clients.

Commonly Used Acronyms in This Book

Acronym	**Definition**
ACA	Affordable Care Act
ACO	Accountable Care Organization
AHA	American Hospital Association
AMA	American Medical Association
APC	Ambulatory Payment Classification
APM	Alternative Payment Model
CAH	Critical Access Hospital
CCR	Cost-to-Charge Ratio
CMS	Centers for Medicare and Medicaid Services
CPT	Current Procedural Terminology
DME	Durable Medical Equipment
DRG	Diagnosis Related Group
DSH	Disproportionate Share Hospital
EPO	Exclusive Provider Organization
ERISA	Employee Retirement Income Security Act
ESRD	End-Stage Renal Disease
HCFA	Health Care Financing Administration
HMO	Health Maintenance Organization
ICD	International Classification of Disease
IME	Indirect Medical Education
IPPS	Inpatient Prospective Payment System
IRF	Inpatient Rehabilitation Facility
LTHC	Long-Term Care Hospital
MedPAC	Medicare Payment Advisory Commission
MMA	Medicare Prescription Drug, Improvement and Modernization Act

OPPS	Outpatient Prospective Payment System
PAMA	Protecting Access to Medicare Act
POS	Point of Service
PPO	Preferred Provider Organization
RBRVS	Resource Based Relative Value Scale
RVU	Relative Value Unit
SNF	Skilled Nursing Facility
UCR	Usual, Customary and Reasonable
VBP	Value-Based Purchasing

CHAPTER 1

History of Government Healthcare Programs and Medicare Hospital Reimbursement Methods

JoAnna Younts

I. BRIEF HISTORY OF THE MEDICARE AND MEDICAID PROGRAMS

The first part of this chapter focuses on the history of healthcare pricing and payment and the U.S. government's creation of the Medicare and Medicaid programs. Then we shift specifically to the early years of Medicare reimbursement.

A. Healthcare Pricing Before Medicare and Medicaid

Prior to Medicare and Medicaid, hospitals and other health care providers, including physicians, established prices for their services and submitted bills to insurance companies and patients with the expectation that they would be paid in full. Although healthcare prices were not regulated, economic conditions and provider policies kept prices relatively low. However, many Americans, particularly elderly and low-income individuals, did not have access to healthcare services because they could not afford them. While some providers delivered charitable or free services, many people who could not afford healthcare or could not access free services simply went without. The implementation of the Medicare and Medicaid programs dramatically changed the healthcare system in the U.S., perhaps more than any other initiative until the Affordable Care Act was passed in 2010 because it provided access to healthcare for millions of people. In turn, these programs quickly became the largest source of revenue for many healthcare providers and a substantial portion of U.S. healthcare expenditures.[1] By 2021, Medicare spending was $900.8 billion, or 21 percent of total National Health

1 George W. Whetsell, "The History and Evolution of Hospital Payment Systems: How Did We Get Here?" *Nursing Administration Quarterly* (Summer 1999): 3.

Expenditures (NHE) while Medicaid spending was $734.0 billion, or 17 percent of total NHE.[2,3] It is projected that Medicare expenditures will grow from 4.1 percent of U.S. Gross Domestic Product (GDP) in 2021 to 6.2 percent of GDP by 2045.[4]

B. Introduction of the Medicare and Medicaid Programs

President Lyndon B. Johnson signed the bill that led to the Medicare and Medicaid programs in 1965 and the programs were launched in 1966. Initially administered by the Social Security Administration (SSA), the original Medicare program included "Part A," which covered hospital services and "Part B," which covered medical or professional services for individuals ages 65 and older. In 1977, a new agency called the Health Care Financing Administration (HCFA) was created to administer Medicare and Medicaid.[5] HCFA was renamed the Centers for Medicare and Medicaid Services (CMS) in 2001.[6] Medicare Part A and Part B are still in place today and are often referred to as "Original Medicare." Most people aged 65 and older can enroll in Part A Medicare without paying a premium because they have paid Medicare taxes for a certain amount of time while working. Individuals who do not meet the work requirements can pay a premium to receive Part A.[7] All individuals who enroll in Part B must pay a monthly premium. Most people pay the standard premium amount, which is adjusted on an annual basis.[8]

Over the years, Congress has made changes to the Medicare program and added coverage for certain populations, as well as specific healthcare services. For example, in 1972, Medicare was expanded to cover people with disabilities, as well as people with end-stage renal disease (ESRD). But the program remained

2 "The National Health Expenditure Accounts (NHEA) are the official estimates of total health care spending in the United States. Dating back to 1960, the NHEA measures annual U.S. expenditures for health care goods and services, public health activities, government administration, the net cost of health insurance, and investment related to health care." National Health Expenditure Data, Historical, Centers for Medicare and Medicaid Services, Centers for Medicare and Medicaid Services, Dec. 15, 2021, www.cms.gov/Research-Statistics-Data-and-Systems/Statistics-Trends-and-Reports/NationalHealthExpendData/NationalHealthAccountsHistorical.

3 "National Health Expenditures 2021 Highlights," Centers for Medicare and Medicaid Services, 2021, www.cms.gov/research-statistics-data-and-systems/statistics-trends-and-reports/nationalhealthexpenddata/nationalhealthaccountshistorical#:~:text=The%20data%20are%20presented%20by,For%20additional%20information%2C%20see%20below.

4 Congressional Research Service, "Medicare Financial Status: In Brief," (Updated Oct. 21, 2021), https://sgp.fas.org/crs/misc/R43122.pdf.

5 "Major Medicaid Payment Policy Developments," Medicaid and CHIP Payment and Access Commission, www.macpac.gov/major-medicaid-payment-policy-developments/.

6 DHHS and CMS, "Program Memorandum Intermediaries/Carriers, Transmittal AB-01-133," (Sep. 24, 2001), www.cms.gov/Regulations-and-Guidance/Guidance/Transmittals/downloads/AB01133.pdf.

7 "Part A costs," Medicare, www.medicare.gov/your-medicare-costs/part-a-costs.

8 "Part B costs," Medicare, www.medicare.gov/your-medicare-costs/part-b-costs.

largely unchanged until 2003, when Congress passed the Medicare Prescription Drug Improvement and Modernization Act (MMA), resulting in the most significant changes to the Medicare program in almost four decades. Under the MMA, Medicare expanded to include "Part C" and "Part D." Under Part C, private insurance companies could be approved by CMS to provide services to Medicare beneficiaries in managed care plans called "Medicare + Choice." These plans are now called "Medicare Advantage." Part D, which became effective in 2006, is an optional prescription drug program that Medicare beneficiaries can obtain by paying an additional premium.

The Medicaid program was designed as a partnership between the federal government and state governments, to provide coverage for low-income individuals and families.[9] Both Medicaid and Medicare are known as "entitlement" programs because enabling legislation requires that benefits be paid as long as individuals meet the eligibility requirements.[10] The federal portion of Medicaid spending in each state is called the Federal Medical Assistance Percentage (FMAP). The formula to calculate the FMAP is constructed so that the federal government pays a higher proportion of Medicaid costs in states with lower per capita income relative to the national average and a lower proportion in states with higher per capita income.[11] Although eligibility for coverage varies from state to state, Medicaid generally provides coverage for low-income families, pregnant women, people with disabilities and those in long-term care facilities, such as nursing homes.[12]

C. Early History of Medicare Reimbursement

Hospital participation in Medicare is voluntary, except for not-for-profit hospitals that receive federal tax exemptions for providing healthcare services to their communities and, therefore, are required to care for Medicare beneficiaries.[13] Providers whose services are covered under Medicare Part B, which includes physicians, are *not* required to participate in Medicare.

9 Specifically, people receiving cash assistance through a program known as Aid to Families with Dependent Children or AFDC. The program was replaced with Temporary Assistance to Needy Families (TANF) under the Personal Responsibility and Work Opportunity Reconciliation Act of 1996. Center on Budget and Policy Priorities, "Policy Basics: Temporary Assistance for Needy Families," (Updated Mar. 1, 2022), www.cbpp.org/research/family-income-support/temporary-assistance-for-needy-families.

10 U.S. General Accounting Office, "Statement of Joseph F. Delfico, Associate Director Human Resources Division before the Task Force of Entitlements and Human Assistance Programs," (1993), www.gao.gov/assets/122637.pdf.

11 The George Washington University: National Health Policy Forum, "The Basics: Medicaid Financing," (January 5, 2016): 1–2.

12 "History," Centers for Medicare and Medicaid Services, Dec. 1, 2021, www.cms.gov/About-CMS/Agency-Information/History.

13 American Hospital Association, "Fact Sheet: Underpayment by Medicare and Medicaid," (Feb. 2022), https://aha.org/fact-sheets/2021-01-07-face-sheet-underpayment-medicare-and-medicaid.

There are three categories of providers relative to Medicare participation:

1. Participating providers—Provider agrees to accept the Medicare rate as payment in full and may not bill the patient for anything other than applicable deductible, coinsurance or copayment amounts.
2. Nonparticipating providers—Provider agrees to treat Medicare patients but does not agree to accept the Medicare rate as payment in full.[14]
3. Opt-out providers—Opt-out is a contract between a provider, a Medicare beneficiary and the Medicare program where the provider or beneficiary does not file a claim to Medicare. Instead, the physician or practitioner bills the beneficiary directly.[15]

Almost all healthcare providers in the U.S. participate in Medicare.[16] This is largely because for most providers, Medicare patients make up a large percentage of their practice and revenue.

When Medicare began, hospitals were reimbursed based on their costs while physicians and other providers were reimbursed based on their "reasonable and customary charges," which, at the time, meant the prevailing fees for the same services in their geographic location. This approach was borrowed from Blue Cross and Blue Shield plans, which used a reimbursement methodology called "cost plus." Under this payment approach, physicians were compensated according to "reasonable and customary charges" that the physicians themselves set, and hospitals were reimbursed based on a percentage of their actual costs. However, these reimbursement approaches resulted in skyrocketing healthcare costs for the Medicare program because they created incentives for hospitals to increase their costs and for physicians to increase their charges in order to receive higher reimbursement.[17] This led to several efforts by the federal government to contain costs throughout the 1970s.

Congress first attempted to control healthcare cost growth by putting limits on Medicare reimbursement based on whether costs were "reasonable." Reasonableness was defined based on, "comparisons of the cost of covered services by various classes of providers in the same geographical area." In addition, there were also limits

14 For nonparticipating providers, Medicare pays 5 percent less than the Medicare Physician Fee Schedule allowed amount and providers cannot charge patients more than the "limiting charge," which is 115 percent of the Medicare Physician Fee Schedule amount. "Annual Medicare Participation Announcement," Center for Medicare and Medicaid Services, Mar. 25, 2022, www.cms.gov/medicare-participation.

15 "Opt Out of Medicare," Noridian Healthcare Solutions, (May 12, 2022), https://med.noridianmedicare.com/web/jfb/enrollment/opt-out.

16 CMS reported that as of 2021, 98 percent of providers participate in Medicare. "Annual Medicare Participation Announcement," Center for Medicare and Medicaid Services, Mar. 25, 2022, www.cms.gov/medicare-participation.

17 George B. Mosely III. "The U.S. Health Care Non-System, 1908–2008," *American Medical Association Journal of Ethics* Volume 10, Number 5 (May 2008): 324–331.

placed on charge increases for physicians.[18] The federal government attempted to implement numerous other efforts to control healthcare costs, but they were met with strong opposition from hospital associations and physician groups such as the American Medical Association, and as a result, were generally unsuccessful. At the same time, however, legislation that mandated control measures included provisions "to develop and engage in experiments and demonstration projects designed to determine the advantages and disadvantages of various alternative methods of prospective reimbursement to hospitals, extended care facilities, and other providers of services . . . in order to stimulate providers through financial incentives to use their facilities and personnel more efficiently and thereby reduce program costs."[19] Although cost control measures largely failed, the legislation to explore alternative payment approaches set the stage for a radical transition in hospital reimbursement and ultimately a dramatic overhaul of Medicare reimbursement approaches for nearly all types of healthcare providers, beginning with inpatient hospital services in 1983.[20] As we will see in this chapter, the introduction of these approaches resulted in substantial cost reductions as illustrated in Figure 1.1.

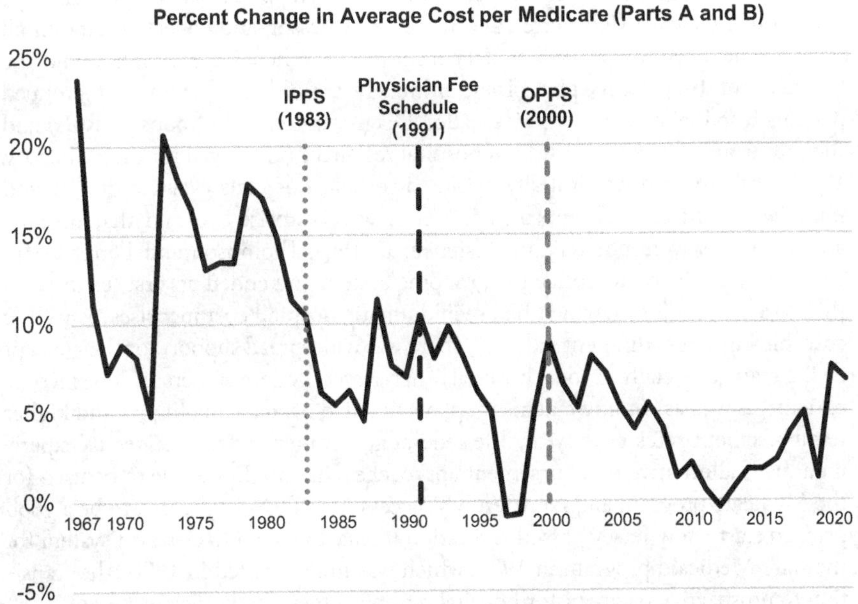

Figure 1.1 Changes in Medicare Beneficiary Costs over Time

18 Congress.gov, Public Law 92–603, (October 30, 1972), p. 1395, www.congress.gov/bill/92nd-congress/house-bill/1/text/pl?overview=closed.

19 Congress.gov, Public Law 92–603, (October 30, 1972), p. 1390, www.congress.gov/bill/92nd-congress/house-bill/1/text/pl?overview=closed.

20 Rick Mayes, "The Origins, Development, and Passage of Medicare's Revolutionary Prospective Payment System," *Journal of the History of Medicine and Allied Sciences* (January 2006): 35.

II. HOSPITAL PROSPECTIVE PAYMENT

A. Introduction and Historical Background

While federal legislation had authorized research regarding reimbursement alternatives to cost-based payment, academic researchers had already begun trying to address the issue. In a 1974 article entitled "Prospective Payment of Hospitals," University of Michigan Professor William Dowling described the concept of shifting financial risk to hospitals by paying them fixed amounts for medical services. His premise was that the cost of medical care was relatively predictable and that incentives could be created for providers to be more efficient. While he did not demonstrate *how* the prospective rates would be determined, he did set the stage for further research on the concept.

Around the same time, researchers at Yale University began working on a system of classifying inpatient hospital patients according to diagnosis codes. John Thompson, a former nurse and professor of public health and hospital administration, was trying to find out why the cost of maternity, newborn and non-maternity medical care varied dramatically among Connecticut's 35 hospitals, even though all hospitals in Connecticut were not-for-profit and had similar labor costs. Thompson teamed up with Bob Fetter, another Yale professor, and collected data on all Connecticut hospitals, as well as data from the state hospital association and the Connecticut Blue Cross plan. They ultimately created a program that grouped patients into diagnostic categories, called Diagnosis Related Groups (DRGs) and then measured the consumption of hospital resources (i.e., costs) for each category. While the program was initially designed to help hospitals evaluate quality and improve patient care, Thompson and Fetter were surprised to find that hospital administrators were not very interested in it. Thus, Thompson and Fetter began exploring other ways to utilize the grouping system and ended up first testing it in the state of New Jersey, which had seen dramatic hospital cost increases, as well as cost shifting across different payers.[21] There was widespread support for the concept in the state, especially among hospitals that served large numbers of low-income patients, as well as commercial health plans that had been paying higher and higher reimbursement rates every year. The federal government wanted states to experiment with alternative reimbursement approaches that might be able to be used for the Medicare program and New Jersey's success with DRGs appeared to be a good place to start. New Jersey passed legislation to enact a new DRG-based system for the state Medicaid program in 1978, which was implemented in 1980. The transition to prospective payment for hospital reimbursement had officially begun.

B. Creation and Structure of DRGs

New Jersey's experiment with DRGs was successful in changing the financial incentives for hospitals. As described previously, under cost-based reimbursement,

---

21 Rick Mayes, "The Origins, Development, and Passage of Medicare's Revolutionary Prospective Payment System," *Journal of the History of Medicine and Allied Sciences* (January 2006): 14.

hospitals historically received more reimbursement for providing more services, but the new system provided incentives to be more efficient with resources. Federal policymakers were encouraged by the fact that a potential alternative reimbursement system existed, because Medicare costs continued to increase at an unsustainable pace, to the point where the Medicare Trust Fund's solvency was at risk.[22] In 1983, Congress amended the Social Security Act to require the implementation of a prospective payment system for hospitals based on DRGs for Medicare patients.[23]

Fortunately, the federal government did not have to start from scratch in the development of DRGs and could build on the work done at Yale, as well as the real-world testing done in New Jersey. As the Yale researchers had demonstrated, their DRG patient classification system provided a way to identify the types of patients admitted to a hospital and then correlate each patient type to the resources they consumed. This classification system formed the basis for the prospective payment system implemented for Medicare patients in 1983. The grouping parameters and the groups themselves have been evaluated and updated several times since then but the core operational structure has remained the same.

A DRG is defined as a group of similar clinical conditions (diagnoses) as well as services (procedures) provided during an inpatient hospital stay. Each Medicare patient is classified into a DRG according to the following information that can be found both in the patient's medical record, as well as the provider bill that is sent to Medicare for processing:

- Principal diagnosis (the reason the patient was admitted to the hospital)
- Up to 24 secondary diagnoses, including complications and comorbidities
- Up to 25 procedures
- Age
- Gender
- Discharge Destination (routine, transferred or expired)

CMS reviews the DRG definitions on an annual basis to ensure that each group continues to have clinically similar conditions and use similar amounts of resources. For example, if the annual evaluation shows that a sample of clinically similar cases for a specific DRG uses significantly different amounts of resources, CMS may reassign these types of cases to a different DRG with similar resource use or create a new DRG for these types of cases.

Today, CMS uses the DRG system called Medicare-Severity-DRGs (MS-DRGs), which account for patients' severity of illness and resource consumption by assigning

22 Rick Mayes, "The Origins, Development, and Passage of Medicare's Revolutionary Prospective Payment System," *Journal of the History of Medicine and Allied Sciences* (January 2006): 24–25.

23 Centers for Medicare and Medicaid Services, "Design and development of the Diagnosis Related Group (DRG)," www.cms.gov/icd10m/version37-fullcode-cms/fullcode_cms/Design_and_development_of_the_Diagnosis_Related_Group_(DRGs).pdf.

three levels to many DRGs. The three levels of severity in the MS-DRG system are based on secondary diagnosis codes.

- MCC: Major Complication/Comorbidity, the highest level of severity
- CC: Complication/Comorbidity, the next level of severity
- Non-CC: Non-Complication/Comorbidity, this level does not significantly affect severity of illness and resource use

For example, MS-DRGs 242 through 244 recognize three levels of severity for a patient who undergoes a pacemaker insertion:

- MS-DRG 242: PERMANENT CARDIAC PACEMAKER IMPLANT WITH MCC
- MS-DRG 243: PERMANENT CARDIAC PACEMAKER IMPLANT WITH CC
- MS-DRG 244: PERMANENT CARDIAC PACEMAKER IMPLANT WITHOUT CC/MCC

Version 39 of the MS-DRGs, which was published for use in Medicare's fiscal year 2022, contains 767 unique MS-DRGs into which patients are grouped based their clinical characteristics. Each MS-DRG is also classified as "medical" or "surgical." Medical MS-DRGs include conditions such as concussion, upper respiratory infection, pneumonia and hypertension while surgery MS-DRGs include procedures such as organ transplants, appendectomy and joint replacement.

Finally, and perhaps most importantly, each MS-DRG is assigned a "relative weight" that is designed to reflect the resource intensity for the types of inpatient cases assigned to that MS-DRG. The relative weights also vary depending on inclusion of a CC or MCC classification.

The relative weights are calculated by taking the ratio of the national average charge for the previous year for each individual MS-DRG to the overall average charge for all MS-DRGs. Thus, an MS-DRG with a relative weight of 3.0 means that the average charge for that MS-DRG was three times the overall average in the previous year while an MS-DRG with a relative weight of 0.5000 means that the average charge for the MS-DRG was half the overall average charge. For example, MS-DRG 103 (Headache without major complications or comorbidities) has a lower relative weight of .8295 compared to MS-DRG 001 (Heart transplant or implant or heart assist system with major complications or comorbidities), which has a relative weight of 28.9132.[24]

Each year, when CMS adjusts and refines the MS-DRG classification system, the coding specifications are incorporated into a software program called a "grouper" in which the data from a patient's hospital bill is analyzed and the appropriate

24 "ICD-10-CM/PCS MS-DRG v37.0 Definitions Manual," Centers for Medicare and Medicaid Services, www.cms.gov/icd10m/version37-fullcode-cms/fullcode_cms/P1990.html.

MS-DRG is assigned. In order for a hospital to be reimbursed for an inpatient stay for a Medicare patient, the patient's diagnoses, procedures and characteristics must be assigned codes that are then processed through grouper software to identify the appropriate MS-DRG and relative weight. These diagnosis and procedure codes are assigned by specially trained and certified hospital coding staff based on information documented by physicians and other medical professionals in the patient's medical record during the hospital stay. Correct coding of diagnoses and procedures is critical because it determines what MS-DRG will be assigned for a patient.

The MS-DRG grouper software is used by Medicare Administrative Contractors (MACs)[25] who are responsible for paying hospitals on behalf of the Medicare program. Grouper software is also available for purchase from several vendors and is used by hospitals, health plans and other organizations for billing, claims payment and research.

C. Medicare Inpatient Hospital Reimbursement under DRGs

As we have learned thus far, in order for a hospital to be reimbursed for an inpatient stay for a Medicare patient, the patient's diagnoses, procedures and characteristics must be assigned codes that are then processed through grouper software to identify the appropriate MS-DRG and relative weight. However, to convert this relative weight to an actual payment amount, there are several additional steps that must be completed. The payment system under which Medicare uses the MS-DRG grouping methodology to reimburse short-term acute care hospitals for inpatient services is called the Inpatient Prospective Payment System or IPPS.

For a hospital to be reimbursed by Medicare under the IPPS, most hospitals in the U.S. that participate in the Medicare program are assigned what is called a "base rate." This is a fixed dollar amount that is established by CMS based on several factors and adjusted on an annual basis. Certain types of hospitals, such as cancer hospitals, Critical Access Hospitals (CAH) and children's hospitals, are exempt from the IPPS and therefore are not assigned a base rate. They are reimbursed by Medicare using other methods that are briefly described later in this chapter.

Computation of a hospital's base rate begins with the national base payment rate, which is divided into two standardized components: operating and capital. CMS then adjusts the national base payment rate for differences in labor costs in the geographic area where a hospital is located, as well as additional costs related to training residents and treating low-income patients, if applicable. There are other Medicare policy adjustments as well. See Figure 1.2.

25 MACs are private organizations such as Blue Cross Blue Shield Plans or other organizations that contract with CMS to process claims for Medicare beneficiaries. Each MAC covers a different geographic area of the U.S. and its territories such as Puerto Rico and Guam. "Who Are the MACs?" Centers for Medicare and Medicaid Services, Dec. 01, 2021, www.cms.gov/Medicare/Medicare-Contracting/Medicare-Administrative-Contractors/Who-are-the-MACs#MapsandLists.

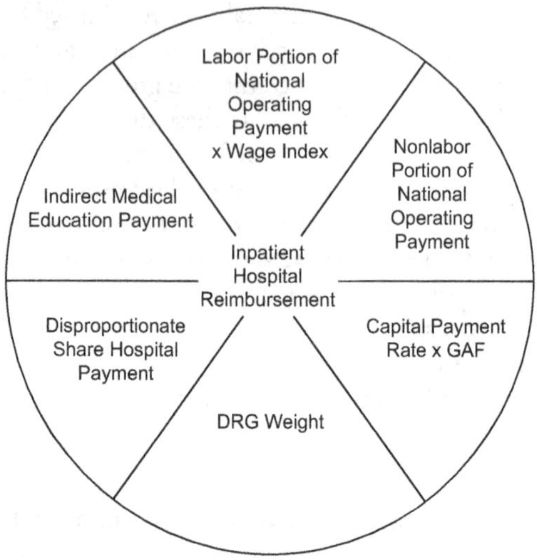

Figure 1.2 MS-DRG Reimbursement Rate Components

As shown in Figure 1.2, a hospital's Medicare base rate is composed of the following components:

- National standardized operating amount
- Wage adjustment factors
- National capital standard payment rate
- Indirect Medical Education adjustment factor
- Disproportionate Share Hospital (DSH) factor
- Other factors

National standardized operating amount: This amount is divided into a labor-related and nonlabor-related share. The labor-related share is adjusted by the wage index (see below) for the geographic area where the hospital is located. If the hospital is located in Alaska or Hawaii, the nonlabor share is adjusted by a cost-of-living adjustment factor. The labor-related share percentage is higher for geographic areas where the wage index is greater than 1.[26] The national standardized operating amount also differs slightly depending on whether a hospital has met

26 The labor-related share percentage is adjusted annually. The 2022 percentage is 67.6 percent for hospitals in geographic areas where the wage index is greater than 1 and 62 percent for hospitals in geographic areas where the wage index is less than 1 (which includes Puerto Rico).

certain quality and reporting requirements. Higher rates are paid to hospitals that have met these requirements.[27]

Wage index: The wage index factor reflects the relative hospital wage level in the geographic area where the hospital is located compared to the national average hospital wage level. CMS defines hospital geographic labor market areas based on the definitions of Core-Based Statistical Areas (CBSAs) established by the Office of Management and Budget (OMB). CMS updates the index annually based on a survey of wages and wage-related costs of short-term acute care hospitals.[28]

National capital standard payment rate: CMS establishes a single fixed payment each year that is designed to cover costs for a hospital's depreciation, interest, rent and property-related insurance and taxes. This amount is also adjusted to reflect differences in costs across different geographic areas. The wage index used to adjust the national capital standard payment rate is called the Geographic Adjustment Factor (GAF).

Indirect Medical Education (IME) Adjustment Factor: Hospitals that train residents receive an additional payment that is designed to compensate for the higher patient care costs of teaching hospitals relative to non-teaching hospitals. The IME adjustment factor is calculated using a hospital's ratio of residents to beds.[29] It is important to understand the difference between the IME adjustment factor and Direct Graduate Medical Education (GME) payments. While the IME adjustment factor is meant to compensate hospitals for the higher costs of patient care due to having residents, Direct GME payments compensate hospitals for the actual costs of their residency programs, such as resident salaries. Direct GME payments are made directly on an annual basis to qualifying hospitals rather than as part of the MS-DRG reimbursement rate.[30]

Disproportionate Share Hospital (DSH) Factor: This is an additional amount added to the base rate for hospitals that treat a large number of low-income patients. There are multiple methods used to qualify for Medicare DSH adjustment. The primary method is based on the percentage of the hospital's patients eligible for Medicaid and Supplemental Security Income (SSI).

---

27 "FY 2023 Hospital Inpatient Prospective Payment System (IPPS) and Long-Term Care Hospital Prospective Payment System (LTCH PPS) Final Rule—CMS-1771-F," Centers for Medicare and Medicaid Services, Aug. 1, 2022, www.cms.gov/newsroom/fact-sheets/fy-2023-hospital-inpatient-prospective-payment-system-ipps-and-long-term-care-hospital-prospective.

28 "Wage Index," Centers for Medicare and Medicaid Services, Sep. 15, 2022, www.cms.gov/Medicare/Medicare-Fee-for-Service-Payment/AcuteInpatientPPS/wageindex.

29 "Indirect Medical Education (IME)," Centers for Medicare and Medicaid Services, Jan. 27, 2022, www.cms.gov/Medicare/Medicare-Fee-for-Service-Payment/AcuteInpatientPPS/Indirect-Medical-Education-IME.

30 "Direct Graduate Medical Education (DGME)," Centers for Medicare and Medicaid Services, Jun. 21, 2022, www.cms.gov/Medicare/Medicare-Fee-for-Service-Payment/AcuteInpatientPPS/DGME.

Other factors: Medicare also adjusts hospital base rates or provides additional payments to hospitals to accomplish specific Medicare policies or requirements. These include adjustments for:

- Uncompensated care
- Treating patients using certain new technologies
- Acquiring organs for transplant cases
- Costs of administering blood clotting factors to hemophiliac patients
- Participation in a National Institutes of Health (NIH) sponsored clinical trials of islet cell transplantation for patients with Type I diabetes

Adjustments to a hospital's base rate are also made as a result of the following special programs administered by CMS:

- Hospital Value-Based Purchasing (VBP), where a portion of the rate is adjusted up or down based on quality measures;
- Hospital Readmissions Reduction Program (HRRP), where the rate is reduced for excess readmissions; and
- Hospital-Acquired Condition (HAC) Reduction Program, where the rate is reduced for the worst performing hospitals in terms of their number of reasonably preventable hospital HACs.

CMS also reduces MS-DRG payments when a patient has a short length of stay (LOS) and transfers to another hospital or some type of post-acute care setting such as a skilled nursing facility.

Ultimately, the hospital-specific base rate is multiplied by the relative weight for the appropriate MS-DRG in order to arrive at the final Medicare reimbursement amount.

An important note before we move to the outpatient side of the hospital: hospital and physician services are always billed separately, whether a physician is an employee of the hospital or is an independent practitioner. If a physician is employed, their services may be billed by the hospital on a separate claim form (see Claim Forms on pages 14 and 15), and they will be paid under the Medicare Physician Fee Schedule. If a physician is an independent practitioner, they must submit a claim form for the services and also be paid under the Medicare Physician Fee Schedule.

Using all of the components discussed, Table 1.1 shows the calculation for a fictitious hospital for MS-DRG 242 (permanent cardiac pacemaker implant with MCC).

Outlier cases: Acute care hospitals can also qualify for what are known as "outlier" payments for extremely costly cases. To qualify to be an outlier, an inpatient stay must have costs above a fixed-loss cost threshold amount (CMS establishes this dollar amount on an annual basis). Costs for an inpatient stay are determined by applying a hospital's cost-to-charge ratios to the billed charges for

Table 1.1 MS-DRG Reimbursement Rate Calculation MS-DRG 242 Permanent Cardiac Pacemaker Implant with MCC

Line #	*Description*	*Amount*
1	National Operating Base Rate	$6,121.65
2	Labor Portion (0.62*L1)	$3,795.42
3	Nonlabor Portion (0.38*L1)	$2,326.23
4	Wage Index	0.9239
5	Geographic Adjusted Operating Rate ((L2*L4) + L3))	$5,832.82
6	National Capital Rate	$472.59
7	Geographic Adjustment Factor	0.939
8	Geographic Adjusted Capital Rate (L6*L7)	$443.76
9	Total Adjusted Base Rate (L5 + L8)	$6,276.58
10	MS-DRG Relative Weight	3.72
11	Reimbursement Rate Before IME and DSH (L9*L10)	$23,364.57
12	IME Adjustment Factor–Operating	0.12945
13	IME Adjustment Rate–Operating	$755.06
14	DSH Adjustment Factor–Operating	0.02991
15	DSH Adjustment Rate–Operating	$174.46
16	IME Adjustment Factor–Capital	0.12
17	IME Adjustment Rate–Capital	$53.25
18	DSH Adjustment Factor–Capital	0.06
19	DSH Adjustment Rate–Capital	$26.63
20	**Total Payment Before Other** Adjustments (L11+L13+L15+L17+L19)	**$24,373.96**
21	Uncompensated care payment	$1,459.50
22	Readmission adjustment	($16.90)
23	Value-based purchasing adjustment	$17.96
24	New technology adjustment	$0.00
25	**Total MS-DRG Reimbursement Rate**	**$25,834.52**

the inpatient stay.[31] If the costs exceed the fixed-loss outlier threshold, the hospital is reimbursed the applicable MS-DRG amount plus 80 percent of costs above the fixed-loss cost threshold.

Adoption and use of inpatient prospective payment systems by state Medicaid programs and commercial health plans are discussed in Chapter 3.

31 Operating and capital costs are computed separately by multiplying the total charges by the operating and capital cost-to-charge ratios.

Key Summary Points about Medicare Reimbursement for Inpatient Hospital:

- Most hospitals are reimbursed using the Inpatient Prospective Payment System, which uses the MS-DRG reimbursement methodology;
- Each hospital has its own unique Medicare base rate;
- Base rates are adjusted for geographic location, as well as other factors, such as the number of low-income people treated and teaching status;
- Each MS-DRG is assigned a relative weight, which is multiplied a hospital's base rate to obtain the reimbursement rate;
- Base rates and MS-DRG weights are updated annually;
- Hospitals can be reimbursed in addition to the MS-DRG rate for extraordinarily costly cases that meet certain requirements. These are called outliers.

Claim Forms

Claim forms are used by providers to submit bills to payers. Standard formats are used by most payers, including public and commercial plans, and are maintained by the National Uniform Claim Committee (NUCC). While such forms were historically submitted in paper format, nearly all claims are now filed electronically using the standard forms described below.

CMS-1500: Used by non-institutional providers, such as physicians, DME suppliers and other professionals.[32]

CMS-1450: Also commonly referred to as "UB-04," used by hospitals, rehabilitation facilities, skilled nursing facilities and other institutional providers.[33]

Medicare Cost Reports and Cost-to-Charge Ratios

Institutional providers that are certified by Medicare are required to submit an annual Medicare Cost Report (MCR) to CMS.[34] The MCR is a detailed accounting report that contains facility characteristics, utilization data and, importantly, costs and charges for each department (also called a cost

32 "Professional paper claim form (CMS-1500)," Centers for Medicare and Medicaid Services, www.cms.gov/Medicare/Billing/ElectronicBillingEDITrans/16_1500.

33 "Institutional paper claim form (CMS-1450)," Centers for Medicare and Medicaid Services, www.cms.gov/Medicare/Billing/ElectronicBillingEDITrans/15_1450.

34 These reports are submitted to a Medicare Administrator Contractor (MAC).

center or revenue center) within the facility. CMS maintains the MCR data in the Healthcare Provider Cost Reporting Information System (HCRIS). Provider types that are required to submit MCRs:

- Hospitals
- SNFs
- Home Health Agencies
- Dialysis Facilities
- Hospice
- Federally Qualified Health Centers (FQHC)
- Rural Health Clinics
- Community Mental Health Centers
- Organ Procurement Organizations[35]

The costs and charges contained in MCRs are used to calculate cost-to-charge ratios, which are used in some Medicare reimbursement calculations and are also used by commercial payers, researchers, consultants, attorneys and others to evaluate provider costs relative to reimbursement rates.

Components of the Cost-to-Charge Ratio

Charges: Billed amount or price charged to payers or patients for services.

Costs: Expenses incurred to provide services, including direct (such as nursing, drugs and supplies) and indirect or overhead (such as administrative costs, utilities, and information systems). Some costs, such as rent and equipment, are fixed, meaning they do not change with volume, while others, such as labor and supplies, are variable, meaning they do change with volume.

The **cost-to-charge ratio (CCR)** is equal to costs divided by charges. CCRs can be calculated at the institutional level (total costs divided by total charges) as well as the departmental level or revenue center level (for example, inpatient, emergency room, pharmacy, laboratory).[36]

---

35 Centers for Medicare and Medicaid Services, Cost Reports, www.cms.gov/research-statistics-data-and-systems/downloadable-public-use-files/cost-reports.

36 G.T. Pickens, L. Liang and M. Roemer, "HCUP Cost-to-Charge Ratio Methodologies 2021," HCUP Methods Series, Report # 2021–05, U.S. Agency for Healthcare Research and Quality (December 17, 2021), www.hcupus.ahrq.gov/reports/methods/methods.jsp.

III. MEDICARE OUTPATIENT HOSPITAL REIMBURSEMENT

A. Introduction and Historical Background

When the Medicare IPPS was introduced in 1983, it created incentives for hospitals to be more efficient in delivering inpatient services, but it also created incentives to shift services out of the inpatient setting and into the outpatient setting. Like inpatient hospital reimbursement prior to 1983, Medicare reimbursement for outpatient hospital services was based on hospital costs, which resulted in large increases in Medicare expenditures.

In an effort to move away from cost-based reimbursement, fixed fee schedules were put into place for some outpatient hospital services in the 1980s. This occurred for clinical laboratory services in 1984[37] and for Durable Medical Equipment, Prosthetics, Orthotics and Supplies (DMEPOS) in 1989.[38] There were also separate reimbursement methods for ambulatory surgical procedures, radiology procedures and other diagnostic tests, as well as kidney dialysis and other services. Altogether, there were multiple methods in place that Medicare was using to reimburse for hospital outpatient services, which was administratively challenging and did not make a significant impact on the rate of cost increases that the Medicare program continued to experience. Thus, government officials had to start thinking about ways to change the outpatient hospital reimbursement approach as well.[39]

B. Creation and Structure of Ambulatory Payment Classifications (APC)

Interestingly, government mandates to change Medicare outpatient hospital reimbursement were in place long before a workable system was actually implemented. In fact, the Omnibus Reconciliation Act of 1986 (OBRA-86) required the Department of Health and Human Services (HHS) to develop and report to Congress on a prospective payment system for hospital outpatient services. The mandate called for the development of the system in two stages. The first stage focused on ambulatory surgical procedures, with a payment rate that included all services provided during a surgical procedure such as operating room time, supplies and drugs, but not including physician services (these payment rates were similar, in a way, to DRGs). The

37 The Deficit Reduction Act of 1984 mandated that fee schedules be established for each lab test on a regional, statewide or carrier basis. As a result, each carrier established its own fee schedule rates (hereinafter referred to as carrier rates), which are collectively known as the Clinical Laboratory Fee Schedule. The Consolidated Omnibus Budget Reconciliation Act of 1985 mandated a national limit amount (NLA) that capped carrier rates. Daniel Levinson, "Variation in the Clinical Laboratory Fee Schedule," U.S. Department of Health and Human Services, Office of Inspector General (July 2009): i.

38 "Durable Medical Equipment, Prosthetics/Orthotics and Supplies Fee Schedule," Centers for Medicare and Medicaid Services, (Dec. 22, 2021, 8:55AM), www.cms.gov/Medicare/Medicare-Fee-for-Service-Payment/DMEPOSFeeSched.

39 Barbara O. Winn, "Medicare Payment for Hospital Outpatient Services: A Historical Review of Policy Options," RAND Health (May 2005).

rates were supposed to be based on the costs of performing the procedures in hospital outpatient departments as well as ambulatory surgical centers (ASC). The second stage was to develop a payment approach for other hospital outpatient services. As part of this stage, CMS required hospitals to begin billing for outpatient services using the Healthcare Common Procedure Coding System (HCPCS) procedure codes instead of ICD-9-CM (the predecessor of ICD-10 which is used today) procedure codes in 1987 in order to prepare for the outpatient system.[40] (See the Code Sets sidebar below.) However, the outpatient hospital payment system for Medicare was not actually implemented until much later. This is largely because outpatient hospital services are highly varied and determining a way to reimburse for such a diverse array of services turned out to be more complex than originally envisioned.

Code Sets

Coding classification systems or code sets are groups of codes that identify procedures and diagnoses. They are used to record information about health conditions, diseases and treatments in patient medical records and they are used by providers for medical billing. Code sets are used by both public and commercial payers for claims processing and reimbursement.

Revenue Code: A 4-digit number that is used on hospital bills to tell an insurance company either where the patient was when he or she received treatment, or what type of item a patient might have received as a patient. These codes are maintained by the National Uniform Billing Committee (NUBC).

International Classification of Disease (ICD): The ICD code set is maintained by the World Health Organization (WHO). ICD codes identify symptoms, diseases, diagnoses and procedures. As of this writing, the latest version of the ICD code set is ICD-11 (version 11); however, the version currently used in the United States is ICD-10-CM (which means version 10, clinical modification). ICD-10-CM codes, which replaced the ICD-9 coding system in the U.S. in 2015, are more detailed and allow for additional clarification about the severity of diseases and conditions. ICD coding is the primary system that is used to report worldwide statistics on health and disease across all provider types and settings. The code set is also used in claims processing systems.[41]

40 The HCPCS system of coding incorporates all of the Current Procedure Terminology (CPT) codes that are published by the American Medical Association. CPT codes are considered "Level 1" HCPCS codes.

41 "International Classification of Diseases, (ICD-10-CM/PCS) Transition—Background," Centers for Disease Control and Prevention, www.cdc.gov/nchs/icd/icd10cm_pcs_background.htm.

Healthcare Common Procedure Coding System (HCPCS): The HCPCS code set is divided into Level I and Level II. Level I HCPCS are the codes contained in the Current Procedural Terminology (CPT) code set (see below). Level II HCPCS are alpha-numeric codes that are used to identify products, supplies and services not found in the CPT code set, such as ambulance services, drugs and Durable Medical Equipment. Because Medicare and other insurers cover services, supplies and equipment that are not identified by CPT codes, the level II HCPCS codes were established for submitting claims for these items.[42]

Current Procedural Terminology (CPT): CPT is a numeric coding system maintained by the American Medical Association (AMA). The codes identify medical services and procedures performed by physicians and other healthcare professionals that are submitted on claims for reimbursement by public and private payers.[43]

The federal government, through HCFA, contracted with several organizations to conduct research on different approaches to an outpatient hospital reimbursement system, which was to be called the Outpatient Prospective Payment System (OPPS). HCFA then completed a draft report to Congress that recommended that the OPPS be phased in starting with ambulatory surgical procedures, radiology and other diagnostic tests using a grouping approach similar to another system called Ambulatory Patient Groups (APG). The Balanced Budget Act of 1997 mandated the implementation of the Medicare hospital OPPS and the proposed rule for its implementation was published in the Federal Register in September 1998. The rule provided for grouping procedures (HCPCS codes) into 346 "ambulatory payment classification" (APC) groups of services that were comparable in terms of clinical characteristics and resource use.[44]

The OPPS was officially implemented in July 2000. Since then, the APC classification system has been studied extensively and many changes have been made. As of 2022, there are 824 APCs under which most outpatient hospital services are categorized. Like inpatient MS-DRGs, most APCs are assigned a relative weight, which measures the resource requirements of the APC. The relative weights are calculated based on the geometric mean cost of services in that APC. A fixed dollar amount called a "conversion factor" is then multiplied by the relative weight to determine the reimbursement rate. This is similar to the base rate that is used in the inpatient rate calculation but instead of individual hospital conversion factors, there is a single conversion factor that applies to all hospitals, which is updated annually by CMS.

42 "HCPCS Coding Questions," Centers for Medicare and Medicaid Services, www.cms.gov/Medicare/Coding/MedHCPCSGenInfo/HCPCS_Coding_Questions.

43 "Current Procedural Terminology," American Medical Association, www.ama-assn.org/amaone/cpt-current-procedural-terminology.

44 Barbara O. Winn, "Medicare Payment for Hospital Outpatient Services: A Historical Review of Policy Options," RAND Health (May 2005).

The Medicare payment rates for each APC are established by CMS and are updated at least annually based on the costs incurred to provide the services assigned to an APC. Costs are calculated using data from hospitals' claims and Medicare Cost Reports. See Medicare Cost Reports and Cost-to-Charge Ratios on pages 14 and 15 regarding Medicare Cost Reports. The annual review of APCs and their relative weights considers a variety of factors, including changes in hospital and medical practices, changes in technology, as well as addition of new services and removal of obsolete services.

Services that are reimbursed by Medicare outside of the APC structure are clinical diagnostic laboratory services, outpatient therapy services (physical, occupational, speech) and screening and diagnostic mammography. These services are reimbursed using other Medicare fee schedules.

C. Reimbursement under the Medicare Hospital Outpatient Prospective Payment System (OPPS)

Outpatient hospital services provided to Medicare patients are reimbursed under the OPPS. A patient may receive items and services which may include a surgical procedure, lab tests, X-rays, physician-administered drugs, or a combination of these and other services. Similar to when an individual is admitted to the hospital as an inpatient, physicians, nurses and other practitioners record the items and services the patient receives on an outpatient basis and the hospital's certified coders then identify the appropriate HCPCS codes that correspond to the items and services.

The OPPS applies to all hospitals with a few exceptions such as Critical Access Hospitals, Indian Health Service hospitals, and hospitals located in certain U.S. territories. Certain hospitals in the state of Maryland are also exempt because they are reimbursed by Medicare and other payers under a special waiver from CMS.[45] Hospitals, must bill for their services on the CMS 1450 claim form (UB-04). See the Claim Forms sidebar on page 14.

To determine the APCs that are assigned, as well as other information that Medicare needs for payment, special software must be used called the Integrated Outpatient Code Editor (I/OCE). The I/OCE program processes claims for all outpatient facilities, including hospitals, that are reimbursed by Medicare under the OPPS. The I/OCE takes the data submitted by a hospital (including all the patient's demographic information as well as all of the HCPCS codes that identify the services provided) on a claim form and does the following:

- Assigns an APC number for each item or service
- Assigns status indicators
- Assigns payment indicators
- Determines packaging that applies
- Determines payment adjustments

Let's walk through each of these.

45 Medicare Claims Processing Manual, Chapter 4: Part B Hospital, (Revised July 14, 2021), p. 16.

Status Indicator Assignment: First, I/OCE assigns a "status indicator" to every HCPCS code that appears on an outpatient hospital claim. The status indicator identifies whether the service described by the HCPCS code is paid under the OPPS and if so, whether payment is made separately or "packaged" (see next section). Status indicators may also indicate that a HCPCS code is not paid under the OPPS but instead is reimbursed under another payment system or fee schedule. For example, services with status indicator "A" are paid using a Medicare fee schedule or payment system other than the OPPS. HCPCS codes with Status Indicator A include lab tests and physical therapy. Services with status indicator "T" are paid separately under OPPS but a multiple procedure payment reduction[46] applies when two or more services with this status indicator are billed on the same date of service. There are several other status indicators as well. The status indicator for each HCPCS code is published in a file called "Addendum B" on a quarterly basis. Addendum B also contains the relative weights for each HCPCS code, the APC that corresponds to the HCPCS code (if applicable) and the payment rate (before any geographic adjustments are applied). There is also a file called "Addendum A" which contains the relative weight for each APC. These can be found on the CMS website.

Packaging: Packaging is one of the core components of the OPPS. Packaged services are defined as "those items or services . . . recognized as contributing to the cost of the procedures or services in an APC group, and for which [Medicare] would not make separate payment."[47] Packaged services include things like operating and recovery room time, medical and surgical supplies and certain drugs. For example, services with status indicator "N" are paid under the OPPS, but their payment is "unconditionally" packaged into payment for a separately paid service such as a surgical procedure. Unconditionally packaged means the service is always packaged and never reimbursed separately, regardless of the other services that appear on an outpatient hospital claim. Services that are "conditionally packaged" are assigned other status indicators and may or may not be packaged depending on how many units are billed and/or the other services that appear on a claim.[48] There are also many items and services that are not packaged and are reimbursed separately, including expensive drugs and medical devices such as pacemakers. CMS continues to monitor and update the packaging rules and logic under the OPPS.

APC Assignment: Each HCPCS code for which separate payment is made under the OPPS is assigned to an ambulatory payment classification (APC) group.

46 Typically, the first procedure is paid 100 percent of the reimbursement rate and subsequent procedures are paid 50 percent of the reimbursement rate.

47 Office of Inspector General; Medicare Program; Prospective Payment System for Hospital Outpatient Services, 65 Fed. Reg. 18447 (April 7, 2000), www.govinfo.gov/content/pkg/FR-2000-04-07/pdf/FR-2000-04-07.pdf.

48 Medicare Claims Processing Manual, Chapter 4: Part B Hospital (Revised July 14, 2021): 24–25.

All of this information is then used to calculate a reimbursement rate. Similar to inpatient hospital services, Medicare payments for outpatient services are adjusted for geographic wage variations using the same wage index that is used to adjust the base rates under the Medicare IPPS. Under the OPPS, 60 percent of the APC rate for procedures is considered labor-related and is multiplied by the wage index, which is then added to the remaining 40 percent of the rate. Rates for drugs and devices are not adjusted for geographic location. There is also an outlier formula for outpatient hospital services that is similar to the inpatient outlier formula.

There are several key characteristics of the OPPS and APCs that are important to understand. Like the IPPS, the OPPS was designed to be prospective, in the sense that a predetermined fixed rate is paid for a particular item or service. However, it is a somewhat of a hybrid system in that, on the one hand, the system groups procedures and services into categories for payment (APCs) the way the IPPS does using MS-DRGs, but the OPPS also reimburses for many services individually in the way that services would be reimbursed under a simple fee schedule. Here are some key factors:

Key Summary Points About Medicare Reimbursement for Outpatient Hospital Services:

- Most hospitals are reimbursed primarily using the Outpatient Prospective Payment System, which uses the APC reimbursement methodology;
- A HCPCS code can only be assigned to one APC but not every HCPCS code is assigned to an APC because the code may not be paid under the OPPS and is instead paid under another Medicare payment system or fee schedule (for example, lab tests and physical therapy) or is packaged (for example, the code is assigned Status Indicator N);
- More than one APC can be assigned for a single outpatient hospital date of service. This is different from an inpatient stay in which only one MS-DRG can be assigned;
- There is one conversion factor that applies to all hospitals;
- Reimbursement rates are adjusted for geographic location;
- The conversion factor and APC weights are updated annually.

IV. MEDICARE REIMBURSEMENT FOR OTHER TYPES OF HOSPITALS

While short-term acute care hospitals are paid under the IPPS and OPPS, other types of hospitals are reimbursed by Medicare using other payment methodologies. The approaches used for these types of institutions are described next.

A. Long-Term Acute Care Hospitals

In order to be reimbursed by Medicare as a Long-Term Acute Care Hospital (LTCH), a facility must meet the same Medicare certification requirements as short-term acute care hospitals but must also have an average length of stay greater than 25 days.

Similar to the reimbursement approach for short-term acute care hospitals, the reimbursement approach used for LTCHs involves multiplying a base rate by a relative weight in order to arrive at a payment amount. There are several important differences, however. First, there is a single national base rate that applies to all hospitals and is updated by CMS each year. The base rate is adjusted for geographic location and the wage-adjusted payment rate is then multiplied by a relative weight. CMS uses Medicare-Severity *Long-Term Care* Diagnosis Related Groups (MS-LTC-DRGs) for LTCHs. The MS-LTC-DRGs are the same groups used in the IPPS but the relative weights are determined using LTCH charges (see section II.B on how CMS establishes relative weights). Patients are assigned to MS-LTC-DRGs based on their principal diagnosis, secondary diagnoses, procedures, age, sex and discharge status. There are also special outlier provisions for extraordinarily high-cost cases.[49]

B. Psychiatric Hospitals

When the Medicare program implemented DRG-based rates for inpatient hospital services in 1983, it provided an exemption for psychiatric hospitals and certified psychiatric units (CPUs) because CMS was concerned that DRGs were not appropriate for psychiatric cases. Research showed that the DRG approach (prospective per case reimbursement described in Section II of this chapter) did not properly account for the cost of psychiatric cases, primarily because DRG classification relies heavily on diagnosis codes, which some studies found to be an unreliable predictor of costs for psychiatric cases. In addition, some studies found that the characteristics of psychiatric patients varied, as well as their length of stay and the resources needed to care for them. For these reasons, when CMS developed its prospective payment system for inpatient psychiatric services, the decision was made to implement per diem[50] rates rather than case rates.[51]

Since January 2005, Medicare has paid psychiatric hospitals predetermined per diem rates based primarily on the patient's condition (age, diagnosis, comorbidities), length of stay and the geographic area where the facility is located. The base rate for each patient day is calculated by taking the national average daily routine operating, ancillary and capital costs in all psychiatric hospitals in a specific year, updated for inflation. This rate is then adjusted for differences in labor costs by

---

49 Centers for Medicare and Medicaid Services, "Long-Term Care Hospital Prospective Payment System: High Cost Outliers Fact Sheet," (June 2004), https://bok.ahima.org/PdfView?oid=31474#:~:text=A%20high%20cost%20outlier%20is,Group%20(LTC%2DDRG.

50 A per diem rate is a fixed dollar amount that is reimbursed for each day spent in the hospital.

51 Centers for Medicare and Medicaid Services, "Inpatient Psychiatric Facilities Prospective Payment System (IPF PPS) Updates for Fiscal Year (FY) 2022," (October 5, 2021), www.cms.gov/files/document/mm12417-inpatient-psychiatric-facilities-prospective-payment-system-ipf-pps-updates-fiscal-year-fy.pdf.

multiplying the labor-related portion (77 percent) by an area wage index. The wage-adjusted base rate is then further adjusted for patient characteristics including age, diagnosis, comorbidities and length of stay. There is also a rural location adjustment that allows psychiatric hospitals in rural areas to be paid more than their counterparts in urban areas.[52] The per diem rate is paid for each day that a Medicare patient is hospitalized.

C. Cancer Hospitals

Similar to psychiatric hospitals, cancer hospitals were historically reimbursed based on reported costs and were provided an exemption from the IPPS when it was implemented in 1983.[53] In 1984, CMS established three criteria that hospitals had to meet when applying to be a PPS-exempt cancer hospital (PCH):

1. Recognized as of April 20, 1983, by the National Cancer Institute as a comprehensive cancer center or clinical research center;
2. Demonstrate that the entire facility is organized primarily for treatment of, and research on, cancer; and
3. Have a patient population that is at least 50 percent of the hospital's total discharges with a principal diagnosis of neoplastic disease.[54]

Four hospitals meeting these criteria were initially exempted from the IPPS and others were added in subsequent years, bringing the total to 11.[55] These are shown in Table 1.2.[56]

These hospitals are reimbursed for inpatient services on their actual costs but limited to a "target ceiling rate." They are given the option each year to continue with this approach or be reimbursed under the IPPS that is used for short-term acute care hospitals.[57]

52 Centers for Medicare and Medicaid Services, "CMS Manual System, Pub 100–04 Medicare Claims Processing, Transmittal 11039," (October 5, 2021), www.cms.gov/files/document/r11039cp.pdf.

53 See Pub. L. No. 98–21, § 601(e), 97 Stat. 65, 137 (1983) (codified, as amended, at 42 U.S.C. § 1395ww(d)(1)(B)). Among the hospitals specifically excluded from the PPS were rehabilitation, psychiatric and long-term care hospitals, which continued to be reimbursed based on reported costs until the late 1990s and early 2000s when separate PPSs were established for each type.

54 Commerce Clearing House, "Medicare and Medicaid Guide, United States," (1969): 49.

55 U.S. Government Accountability Office, "Medicare: Payment Methods for Certain Cancer Hospitals Should be Revised to Promote Efficiency," Report to the Chairman, Committee on Ways and Means, House of Representatives, (February 2015), www.gao.gov/assets/gao-15-199.pdf.

56 "PPS-Exempt Cancer Hospitals (PCHs)," Center for Medicare and Medicaid Services, Dec. 21, 2021, www.cms.gov/Medicare/Medicare-Fee-for-Service-Payment/AcuteInpatientPPS/PPS_Exc_Cancer_Hospasp.

57 Centers for Medicare and Medicaid Services, "CMS Manual System, Pub 100–04 Medicare Claims Processing, Transmittal 10210," July 10, 2020, www.cms.gov/files/document/r10210cp.pdf.

Table 1.2 Cancer Hospitals Exempt from Medicare IPPS

Hospital Name	*Location*
City of Hope National Medical Center	Los Angeles, CA
USC Kenneth Norris Jr. Cancer Center	Los Angeles, CA
University of Miami Hospital and Clinics	Miami, FL
H. Lee Moffitt Cancer and Research Institute Hospital, Inc.	Tampa, FL
Dana-Farber Cancer Institute	Boston, MA
Memorial Hospital for Cancer and Allied Disease	New York, NY
Roswell Park Memorial Institute	Buffalo, NY
Arthur G. James Cancer Hospital and Research Institute	Columbus, OH
American Oncologic Hospital (Fox Chase)	Philadelphia, PA
The University of Texas M.D. Anderson Cancer Center	Houston, TX
Fred Hutchinson Cancer Research Center (Seattle Cancer Care Alliance)	Seattle, WA

PCHs have also been able to obtain special treatment from Medicare regarding reimbursement for outpatient services as well. Cancer hospitals are not exempt from the OPPS but under the requirements of the Affordable Care Act (ACA), CMS found that outpatient costs incurred by cancer hospitals were greater than the costs incurred by other OPPS hospitals. Therefore, the Medicare program provides additional outpatient payments to each of the 11 cancer hospitals.[58]

D. Critical Access Hospitals

Critical Access Hospitals (CAH) are limited to 25 beds, and most are located in rural areas. Medicare pays for the same services at CAHs as other hospitals, including inpatient stays, outpatient visits, lab tests and so on; however, Medicare reimbursement is based on the hospital's actual costs. Specifically, Medicare reimburses CAHs 101 percent of their costs based on the information that is filed in their Medicare Cost Reports.

In addition to the CAH designation, Medicare also has special designations for hospitals that operate in less populated areas. The "Sole Community Hospital" (SCH) designation requires that a hospital be located at least 35 miles from the nearest "like hospital" (excluding CAHs). Hospitals with a "Medicare-Dependent Hospital" or "MDH" designation are located in rural areas, have no more than 100 beds, are not classified as an SCH and have at least 60 percent of inpatient days or discharges attributable to Medicare patients. These hospitals also receive

58 Centers for Medicare and Medicaid Services, "CMS Manual System, Pub 100–04 Medicare Claims Processing, Transmittal 2453," April 26, 2012, www.cms.gov/Regulations-and-Guidance/Guidance/Transmittals/downloads/R2453CP.pdf.

cost-based reimbursement from Medicare but SCHs and MDHs only receive cost-based payments for inpatient care while CAHs receive cost-based payments for nearly all services.[59]

To help ensure that people who live in rural areas have access to emergency services, some small hospitals that have insufficient inpatient volume to be considered traditional hospitals are now allowed to convert to a "rural emergency hospital." These facilities do not provide inpatient care but instead provide emergency care and other services, and Medicare pays them a fixed monthly fee plus additional payments for providing certain services.[60]

V. CONCLUSION

In this chapter, we have covered a brief history of government health programs and explained how Medicare reimburses for services provided in hospitals. In the next chapter, we turn to physician and other professional services and the various approaches used by the Medicare program to reimburse for these services.

59 Medicare Payment Advisory Commission (MedPAC), "Critical Access Hospital Payment System," November 2021, www.medpac.gov/wp-content/uploads/2021/11/medpac_payment_basics_21_cah_final_sec.pdf.

60 Medicare Payment Advisory Commission (MedPAC), "Critical Access Hospital Payment System," November 2021, www.medpac.gov/wp-content/uploads/2021/11/medpac_payment_basics_21_cah_final_sec.pdf.

CHAPTER 2

Medicare Reimbursement of Physicians and Other Types of Providers

JoAnna Younts

I. MEDICARE PHYSICIAN REIMBURSEMENT

A. Introduction and Historical Background

Until implementation of the Medicare program in 1965, physician reimbursement was primarily based on fee schedules. Physicians in the American colonies began using fee schedules to charge for their services in the 1700s; there were fee schedules specific to individual colonies such as Virginia. New York had a city-specific fee schedule and there were also "rural" fee schedules. By the middle of the 20th century, health insurance had become more widespread and insurance companies began publishing fee schedules that physicians were expected to accept as payment in full. Doctors in some geographic areas complained that the fee schedule amounts were too low for them to earn a living so some insurance plans developed fee schedules that took into account the cost of living in different communities. In 1954, a Blue Shield plan in Wisconsin began reimbursing physicians according to "usual, customary, or reasonable" charges,[1] an approach that was eventually adopted in many other areas of the U.S. Providers and payers continue to debate the definition of usual, customary and reasonable or UCR (see Chapters 7, 8 and 9, describing payer and provider disputes).[2]

1 Blue Cross plans and Blue Shield plans were originally separate entities, with Blue Cross providing insurance coverage for hospital services and Blue Shield plans providing coverage for physician services. The history of Blue Cross and Blue Shield plans is discussed further in Chapter 5. "Blue Cross and Blue Shield: A Historical Compilation," *Consumer Reports* (December 30, 2007), https://advocacy.consumerreports.org/wp-content/uploads/2013/03/yourhealthdollar.org_blue-cross-history-compilation.pdf.

2 Lawrence D. Brown, "Politics as Usual and Customary? Physician Payment in Transition," *Reforming Physician Payment: Report of a Conference*, Institute of Medicine, Division of Health Care Services (1984): 11 to 29.

Physician fee schedules became an important topic when Congress began debating the implementation of Medicare in the early 1960s, and physicians became concerned about what the federal government's fee schedules might look like. Blue Shield plans had mostly adopted the "usual and customary" reimbursement approach and physicians, in particular, the American Medical Association (AMA), lobbied Congress to adopt this approach for the Medicare program as well. The argument at the time was that the approach was superior to fee schedules because it would reflect variations in the services provided and allow for adjustments for changes in the technology and the practice of medicine.[3] The UCR payment approach incentivized physicians to simply raise their usual charges. If all physicians then raised their charges, thus raising the customary amounts in a certain geographic area, the UCR payment approach assured that prices would rise continuously. But Medicare adopted the approach anyway,[4] and similar to the hospital reimbursement increases experienced prior to the implementation of DRGs, the Medicare program also experienced explosive growth in expenditures for physician services in the 1970s and 1980s. Medicare reimbursement for physician services increased 15 percent annually between 1975 and 1987, which was nearly double the gross national product at the time. This increase set the stage for tighter regulation of Medicare costs and the development of a new system for reimbursing physicians.[5]

B. Creation of the Resource Based Relative Value Scale (RBRVS)

The new Medicare physician reimbursement approach began with William Hsaio. Hsaio was a professor of economics at Harvard University and had been studying the costs and relative work of physician services since 1979.[6] By 1985, he had developed a framework for measuring physician costs, called the Resource Based Relative Value Scale (RBRVS). From 1986 to 1988, Hsaio and colleagues developed and tested methods to measure the resources used to provide medical services, as well as the amount of physician work time required to provide them for over 400 different types of services across 18 physician specialties. The RBRVS is built on the concept that reimbursement amounts for physician services should vary depending on the "resource costs" associated with providing those services. Resource costs include equipment and supplies, as well as physician time.

3 Lawrence D. Brown, "Politics as Usual and Customary? Physician Payment in Transition," *Reforming Physician Payment: Report of a Conference*, Institute of Medicine, Division of Health Care Services (1984): 11 to 29.

4 Rick Mayes, "The Resource-Based Relative-Value Scale Reforms for Physician Payment," *Medicare Prospective Payment and the Shaping of U.S. Health Care*, Baltimore, Maryland, The Johns Hopkins University Press (2006): 81–92. https://facultystaff.richmond.edu/~bmayes/Chapter%205_Physician_Payment_RBRVS.pdf.

5 Gregory J. Przybylski, "Understanding and applying a resource-based relative value system to your neurosurgical practice." *Neurosurgical Focus* Volume 12, Edition 3:1 (April 2002).

6 Today, Hsaio is Professor Emeritus at Harvard.

Hsaio's work underwent extensive review by the federal government, the American Medical Association (AMA), the Physician Payment Review Commission (PPRC) and other organizations. Together, they recommended expansion of the methodology to encompass the full range of physician services. In the Omnibus Budget Reconciliation Act of 1989 (OBRA 1989), Congress mandated that Medicare transition reimbursement for physician services under the Medicare program to a fee schedule approach based on the RBRVS.[7]

C. Medicare Reimbursement Under RBRVS

In 1992, the Medicare program implemented the Medicare Physician Fee Schedule (MPFS) using the RBRVS, which replaced the usual and customary charges reimbursement approach. Using the new system, the reimbursement amount for each service was determined by the underlying resource costs needed to provide the service, and a service (identified by a CPT code—See Chapter 1) would be defined by the sum of its relative value units or RVUs. RVUs are the core components of the RBRVS and are divided into three components:

- Physician work
- Practice expense
- Malpractice expense or professional liability insurance (PLI)

Similar to DRG and APC weights discussed in Chapter 1, each of these three components is assigned a numeric value, which is adjusted for geographic cost differences. Then, to calculate the overall value, Medicare adds the numeric values of all the components. The individual components of the RVUs are described, and example RVUs are shown in Table 2.1.

Physician work component: The work component of physicians' services or work RVU is defined as the portion of a medical service that reflects physician time and intensity.[8] Specifically, the physician work RVUs account for the "time, skill, effort, judgment, and stress" associated with providing one service relative to other services.[9] While Hsaio's work provided the basis for the development of the initial RVUs for many medical and surgical services (again, identified by CPT codes), CMS continues to revise the RVUs for existing services and publish RVUs for new services based on review of data and input from the AMA, as well as a group called the "Relative Value Scale Update Committee" (RUC), the Medicare

7 Public Law 101–239, December 19, 1989, at 66, www.govinfo.gov/content/pkg/STATUTE-103/pdf/STATUTE-103-Pg2106.pdf.

8 "Payment for Physicians' Services," Social Security Administration, www.ssa.gov/OP_Home/ssact/title18/1848.htm.

9 "Geographic Practice Cost Indexes," National Center for Biotechnology, www.ncbi.nlm.nih.gov/books/NBK190061/.

Payment Advisory Commission (MedPAC) and others. A variety of methodologies are used to develop and update the physician work RVUs.[10] Currently, the physician work component accounts for about 51 percent of the total relative value of physician services.[11]

Practice expense component: The practice expense (PE) component of the RBRVS or PE RVUs are designed to measure direct costs of providing a service (such as supplies and equipment) and the indirect costs of operating a medical practice (such as administrative and clinical staff salaries, benefits and rent). In the original version of the RBRVS implemented in 1992, only the physician work RVUs were based on the measurement of resources used to provide a particular medical or surgical service, while the PE component was based on average charges.[12] This changed in 1998, when CMS began calculating the PE RVUs based on the actual costs of operating a physician practice. An important aspect of PE RVUs is that separate PE RVUs are established for services provided in facility settings, such as a hospital outpatient department or Ambulatory Surgery Center (ASC), versus non-facility settings, such as a physician's office. As such, PE RVUs for non-facility settings generally have higher values than the PE RVUs for facility settings to account for the facility incurring most of the resource costs. The Medicare payment to the facility would account for the facility's costs. The practice expense component accounts for an average of 45 percent of the total relative value for each service.[13]

Malpractice expense/Professional liability insurance (PLI): Similar to PE RVUs, the malpractice (MP) RVUs were initially based on average charges but became cost-based or resource-based in 2000. The MP RVUs are based on malpractice insurance premium data from all 50 states, the District of Columbia and Puerto Rico. The MP RVUs, also called PLI RVUs, currently account for about four percent of the total relative value for each service.

Since the introduction of the RBRVS, the AMA has worked with national medical specialty societies to provide recommendations to CMS regarding updates to the MPFS. In addition, the RBRVS is updated annually to reflect new and revised CPT codes.

---

10 "Payment for Physicians' Services," Social Security Administration, www.ssa.gov/OP_Home/ssact/title18/1848.htm.

11 "RVS Update Committee: RBRVS Overview," American Medical Association, www.ama-assn.org/about/rvs-update-committee-ruc/rbrvs-overview#:~:text=The%20resource%2Dbased%20relative%20value,CMS)%20and%20most%20other%20payers.&text=Instead%20of%20basing%20payments%20on,payment%20schedule%20based%20on%20RBRVS.

12 Allowable charge includes the amount health insurer (including Medicare) pays as well as the amount the patient pays in the form of coinsurance, copayments and deductibles. It may be less than the provider's billed charge, and in some cases the patient is responsible for the difference. This is discussed further in Chapter 3.

13 "RVS Update Committee: RBRVS Overview." American Medical Association, www.ama-assn.org/about/rvs-update-committee-ruc/rbrvs-overview#:~:text=The%20resource%2Dbased%20relative%20value,CMS)%20and%20most%20other%20payers.&text=Instead%20of%20basing%20payments%20on,payment%20schedule%20based%20on%20RBRVS.

Table 2.1 Example RVUs (2021)

CPT Code	*Description*	*Work RVU*	*Facility Practice Expense RVU*	*Non-Facility Practice Expense RVU*	*Malpractice Expense RVU*	*Facility Total RVUs*	*Non-Facility Total RVUs*
99214	Outpatient or office visit, established patient	1.92	.82	1.70	.14	2.88	3.76
45378	Diagnostic colonoscopy	3.26	1.73	6.56	.41	5.40	10.23
33512	Coronary Artery Bypass Graft 3 veins	43.98	16.72	16.72	10.03	70.73	70.73
71550*	Magnetic Resonance Image (MRI) Chest	1.46	.53	.53	.06	2.05	2.05
88358*	Tumor analysis	.95	.47	.47	.02	1.44	1.44

*Professional component

CMS publishes RVUs for most physician and other professional services. This includes services such as office visits, physical therapy, surgical procedures and imaging. CMS also publishes RVUs for certain services even if Medicare does not cover them. This includes office visits for individuals under the age of 65, contact lens and glasses fittings, certain types of physician consultations and other services.

Each of the three components of the RBRVS—physician work, practice expense (PE) and malpractice (MP) insurance—is adjusted for differences in prices across geographic areas in the U.S. The adjustment factor is called the Geographic Practice Cost Index (GPCI) and GPCIs exist for different geographic areas known as payment localities. Some payment localities are defined according to metropolitan statistical areas, but statewide payment areas that include both metropolitan and nonmetropolitan areas also exist. A GPCI measures the cost of a geographic area relative to the average, and the GPCI schedule is updated every three years. Areas with GPCIs greater than 1, such as those in California, are more expensive, and those with GPCIs less than 1 are less expensive. Table 2.2 shows some example GPCIs.[14]

RVUs are used to establish the relative value of physician services in terms of resource use. However, CMS uses a final step to convert the RVUs to a

14 National Center for Biotechnology. "Geographic Practice Cost Indexes." www.ncbi.nlm.nih.gov/books/NBK190061/.

Table 2.2 GPCIs for Selected Geographic Areas

Locality Name	*Physician Work GPCI*	*Practice Expense GPCI*	*Malpractice GPCI*
Alabama	1.000	0.888	0.921
Los Angeles-Long Beach-Anaheim (Orange Cnty)	1.048	1.175	0.757
San Francisco-Oakland-Berkeley (Marin Cnty)	1.071	1.311	0.504
Miami	1.000	1.023	2.629
Chicago	1.011	1.044	1.871
Kansas	1.000	0.908	0.458
Minnesota	1.000	1.013	0.353
Mississippi	1.000	0.842	0.671
NYC Suburbs-Long Island	1.046	1.223	2.702
South Carolina	1.000	0.903	0.695
West Virginia	1.000	0.858	1.198

reimbursement rate. Similar to hospital reimbursement approaches, which apply base rates or conversion factors to relative weights, CMS calculates the MPFS reimbursement amount by multiplying the total geographically adjusted RVUs for a specific CPT code by a "conversion factor," which is a fixed dollar value. CMS establishes the conversion factor, which it updates annually. Table 2.3 below shows an example calculation.

Medical coders who prepare provider bills that are submitted to insurers such as Medicare and commercial health plans use what are called "modifiers" along with CPT or HCPCS codes. A modifier is two characters, which can be either letters or numbers that are included on a bill with a CPT or HCPCS code. The modifier provides additional information about the service that was provided without changing the underlying CPT or HCPCS code. Some examples of the use of modifiers can be found in Table 2.4.

Using the correct modifiers is important so that the full picture of the service is captured on the bill and because some modifiers determine the amount of reimbursement for the provider.[15]

Key Summary Points about Medicare Reimbursement for Physicians:

- Services are primarily identified by CPT codes;

15 "What Are Medical Coding Modifiers?" American Academy of Professional Codes, www.aapc.com/modifiers/.

Table 2.3 Calculation of Medicare Rate

CPT 99214–Office or other outpatient visit for the evaluation and management of an established patient (Non-Facility)

Geographic area: Chicago, Illinois

Physician Work RVU * Physician GPCI	1.92 * 1.011 = 1.94112
Non-Facility Practice Expense RVU * Practice Expense GPCI	1.70 * 1.044 = 1.7748
Malpractice Expense RVU * Malpractice GPCI	0.14 * 1.871 = .26194
Total Adjusted RVUs	3.97786
Conversion Factor	$34.8931
Medicare Rate = Total Adjusted RVUs * Conversion Factor	$138.80

Table 2.4 Modifier Examples

Modifiers are two-digit codes that provide additional information about a medical procedure. Some modifiers affect the reimbursement amount to the provider.

26, TC	Used to indicate the professional and technical components of a service. *Modifiers affect reimbursement.*
25, 59	Used to indicate distinct evaluation and management (E&M) or other services provided on the same date of service as other procedures. *Modifiers do not affect reimbursement.*
50	Used to indicate a bilateral procedure. *Modifier affects reimbursement.*
LT, RT	Used to indicate left- or right-side procedures. *Modifiers do not affect reimbursement.*
AS, 80, 81, 82	Used to indicate an assistant physician's role during a surgical procedure. *Modifiers affect reimbursement.*

- Most services are reimbursed based on the Resource Based Relative Value Scale (RBRVS);
- Rates are calculated by multiplying a single conversion factor (fixed dollar amount) by a certain number of RVUs;
- RVUs are comprised of physician work, practice and malpractice components;
- Rates are adjusted for geographic location.

It is important to note that ambulance services have also been assigned RVUs but are found in a separate Medicare ambulance fee schedule.

Ambulance services are classified into two categories: ground ambulance and air ambulance. The specific services are identified by HCPCS codes. Ground ambulance codes delineate the level of services provided, such as basic versus advanced life support and emergency versus non-emergency transportation. Air ambulance services are divided into fixed wing (plane) versus rotary wing (helicopter) transportation. Some commonly used codes are as follows:

A0427: Ambulance service Advanced Life Support (ALS), emergency transport, Level 1
A0428: Ambulance service, Basic Life Support (BLS) non-emergency transport
A0431: Ambulance service, conventional air services, transport, one-way, rotary wing

In addition to the transportation codes, there are separate codes that are used to reimburse for mileage.

Physicians or other medical professionals may also provide other services not based on the RBRVS that Medicare covers. Medicare reimburses these services using other methods described in the next section.

II. MEDICARE PHYSICIAN REIMBURSEMENT FOR NON-RBRVS SERVICES

Some healthcare products and services do not have RVUs associated with them and hence Medicare does not reimburse for them under the MPFS. These include timed anesthesia services, physician-administered drugs, certain laboratory tests and Durable Medical Equipment (DME).

A. Timed Anesthesia

Most anesthesia services are reimbursed by Medicare based on the type of anesthesia, as well as the length of time that anesthesia services are provided during a surgical procedure. Specifically, Medicare reimbursement is based on the number of surgical time units as well as the number of anesthesia base units that apply to a surgical procedure. These units are aggregated and then multiplied by a conversion factor. CMS publishes the time units for each surgical CPT code, as well as the base units for each anesthesia CPT code and the conversion factor on an annual basis.[16] One time unit is equal to 15 minutes and CMS establishes anesthesia conversion factors for each state. To calculate the anesthesia fee, the conversion factor is multiplied by the sum of the time and base units for the surgical procedure as in the example below.

16 Revisions to Payment Policies under the Physician Fee Schedule and Other Revisions to Part B. www.cms.gov/Medicare/Medicare-Fee-for-Service-Payment/PhysicianFeeSched/PFS-Federal-Regulation-Notices-Items/CMS-1676-F.html.

Anesthesia Calculation

Year: 2022
Geographic Area: New Orleans

Surgical procedure: CPT 44950 (Removal of appendix [appendectomy] by abdominal incision)
Surgical time: 135 minutes
Anesthesia procedure: CPT 00840 (Anesthesia for intraperitoneal procedures in lower abdomen including laparoscopy; not otherwise specified)
Anesthesia base units: 6
Conversion factor: $22.03
Medicare rate = (6 + (135/15)) * $22.03 = $330.45

Key Summary Points About Medicare Reimbursement for Anesthesia:

- Identified primarily by CPT codes and most begin with "0";
- Most services are reimbursed based on the Resource Based Relative Value Scale (RBRVS);
- Rates are calculated by multiplying a geography-specific conversion factor by base units plus time units;
- Time units are equal to time in minutes divided by 15.

B. Physician-Administered Drugs

While Medicare only began providing coverage for self-administered prescription drugs (pills, tablets and liquids obtained at a pharmacy) in 2003, Medicare has always covered prescription drugs dispensed in a physician's office (which are usually injectable). While self-administered drugs are generally covered under Medicare Part D, "physician-administered drugs" are generally covered under Medicare Part B. For this reason, physician-administered drugs are often called "Part B" drugs.[17] The Medicare program's original intention in providing coverage of physician-administered drugs was to prevent physicians from having to hospitalize patients just to administer a drug (and hence pay for a hospital stay). The expansion of Medicare coverage to patients with end-stage renal disease (ESRD) in 1972 led to reimbursement of erythropoietin, a physician-administered drug used to treat anemia, which is commonly used in ESRD patients. Other drugs that could be administered in a physician office, such as drugs to treat cancer, were also added to Medicare coverage.[18]

17 Self-administered prescription drugs are often called "Part D" drugs because they are covered under Medicare Part D, which was implemented in 2003.

18 Thomas R Oliver, Philip R Lee, and Helene L Lipton, "A Political History of Medicare and Prescription Drug Coverage," Milbank Quarterly 82(2) (June 2004): 283–354, www.ncbi.nlm.nih.gov/pmc/articles/PMC2690175/.

Medicare also covered physician-administered drugs provided on an outpatient basis in a hospital. Like other services provided in hospitals, Medicare historically reimbursed for physician-administered drugs based on actual costs, as described in Chapter 1. When DRGs were implemented in 1983, CMS began including physician-administered drugs provided during an inpatient stay in the DRG payment.[19]

Medicare has used different methods over the past few decades to reimburse providers for outpatient physician-administered drugs. Before 1992, Medicare generally reimbursed for physician-administered drugs based on estimated costs as measured by the Average Wholesale Price (AWP). See Table 2.5 for definitions of common drug pricing terms, including AWP. In 1992, Medicare established a formal policy of reimbursing for physician-administered drugs at 100 percent of AWP, but the Balanced Budget Act of 1997 reduced this amount to 95 percent of AWP.[20] Interestingly, neither law nor regulation defines AWP, and it has been found that AWP does not necessarily reflect discounts or rebates that pharmaceutical manufacturers and wholesalers give to providers. As a result, according to a government study, the Medicare program paid providers for Part B drugs about $1 billion more than acquisition costs each year in the late 1990s and early 2000s.[21] This, in part, led to the Medicare Prescription Drug, Improvement, and Modernization Act (MMA) of 2003, which required the Medicare program to move away from the AWP methodology and establish Medicare rates for Part B drugs at Average Sales Price (ASP) plus 6 percent.[22] ASP is meant to be a more accurate representation of drug manufacturers' final sales prices, and CMS calculates the ASP quarterly from data submitted by these manufacturers.[23]

HCPCS codes identify Part B drugs and usually begin with the letter J or Q. Medicare establishes these rates at the unit level (such as ml, mg), so providers must bill the number of units of the drug used when submitting a claim. Medicare reimburses physicians that bill for physician-administered drugs at the rates contained in the Medicare ASP Drug Pricing File for the quarter and year that apply

19 When the OPPS was implemented in 2000, drugs administered by a physician in an outpatient hospital setting were paid based on APCs, with some being packaged and others reimbursed separately.

20 Medicare Payment Advisory Commission (MedPAC), "Report to the Congress: Variation and Innovation, Chapter 9," (June, 2003), www.medpac.gov/wp-content/uploads/import_data/scrape_files/docs/default-source/reports/June03_Ch9.pdf.

21 Kevin Haninger and Sherry Glied, "Medicare Part B Reimbursement of Prescription Drugs," Office of the Assistant Secretary for Planning and Evaluation (May 31, 2014), https://aspe.hhs.gov/reports/medicare-part-b-reimbursement-prescription-drugs-0.

22 Although Medicare reimburses hospitals for physician-administered drugs based on ASP+6% in many cases, the specific rates are identified by APC and are paid through the OPPS and not the Medicare ASP Drug Pricing Files.

23 "Medicare Reimbursement of Physician-Administered Drugs" Hearing before the Subcommittee on Health of the Committee on Ways and Means, U.S. House of Representatives, Second Session. Serial Number 109–83 (June 13, 2006), www.govinfo.gov/content/pkg/CHRG-109hhrg30451/pdf/CHRG-109hhrg30451.pdf.

to the date of service. Medicare does not use geographic adjustment or modifiers for the reimbursement amount of Part B drugs. In addition to the drug itself, physicians and other professionals may also bill and Medicare may also reimburse for administering the drug. CPT codes, typically beginning with the number "9," identify these services.

Key Summary Points about Medicare Reimbursement for Physician-Administered Drugs:

- Identified by HCPCS codes, most of which begin with "J" or "Q."
- Most are reimbursed at ASP plus 6 percent.
- Rates are national rates, with no geographic adjustment.
- Rates are updated quarterly and are available on the CMS website in the "ASP Drug Pricing Files."
- These provisions do not apply to hospital reimbursement of physician-administered drugs, which are paid using the OPPS.

C. Clinical Laboratory Services

Medicare reimburses physicians, hospitals, independent laboratories and other providers for clinical laboratory services they provide to patients. This includes common lab tests such complete blood count (CBC) and urinalysis, as well as complex genetic tests and pathology exams to identify cancer and other diseases.

Table 2.5 Common Drug Pricing Terms[24]

Average Wholesale Price	AWP	Described as the "sticker price," the AWP is a benchmark used for the pricing and reimbursement of prescription drugs for public and private payers. The publicly available price does not include discounts or rebates and rarely reflects the actual price paid for a drug.
Wholesale Average Cost	WAC	A publicly available list price posted by manufacturers. The price does not include discounts or rebates from manufacturers to wholesalers or pharmacies.
Average Sales Price	ASP	Used to determine the publicly available price for drugs reimbursed by Medicare Part B. Represents the quarterly average of the manufacturer's sales, net of rebates, discounts and other price concessions of a drug to all purchasers included in best price, divided by the total number of units of the drug sold to those purchasers in that same quarter.

24 "Drug Spending Glossary," PEW Trusts, September 20, 2017, www.pewtrusts.org/en/research-and-analysis/fact-sheets/2017/09/drug-spending-glossary.

Laboratory tests are identified by HCPCS codes, most of which begin with the number "8" or the letter "G." The primary modifiers (see Table 2.4 for an explanation of modifiers) used with lab test codes are "26," and "TC."

- Modifier "26" indicates that only the "professional component" of the service is billed. The professional component represents the supervision and interpretation of a procedure provided by the physician or other healthcare professional.
- Modifier "TC" indicates that only the "technical component" of the service is billed. The technical component (TC) represents the cost of the equipment, supplies and personnel needed to perform the procedure.
- A "global" service includes both professional and technical components and is billed without a modifier. The global fee is equal to the fee for the service with a 26 modifier plus the fee for the service with a TC modifier.

Laboratory services that require physician supervision or interpretation are assigned RVUs and are reimbursed under the MPFS. Most laboratory tests, however, are run using automated processing and reporting mechanisms that do not require direct physician interpretation. As such, Medicare limits the laboratory services for which physicians can bill and receive reimbursement. These include commonly ordered tests such as complete blood count (CBC), chemistry panels and drug tests. Medicare reimbursement rates for these tests are found in the Medicare Clinical Laboratory Fee Schedule (CLFS). A physician can bill for surgical pathology services and other services for which they performed a specific task, such as viewing a tissue sample and providing an interpretation of what it contains. For example, a physician can bill Medicare for CPT 88302 (Surgical pathology, gross and microscopic examination), in one of two ways:

1. With no modifier, indicating that the physician performed the service in their office, including the technical and professional components.
2. With modifier 26, indicating that the physician performed the professional component of the service only. A facility such as a hospital would bill for the technical component using modifier TC.

When the Medicare program began, physicians billed Medicare for laboratory services they performed in their offices and for laboratory services they purchased at a discount from hospital-based and independent laboratories. Many physicians routinely "marked up" the cost of purchased laboratory services when billing Medicare and other insurers. New regulations in 1980 prohibited physicians from marking up purchased laboratory services and required them to disclose the actual cost of the laboratory services they purchased from other laboratories, yet CMS had difficulty enforcing these regulations, thus some physicians continued to bill Medicare for marked-up lab tests.[25] The Omnibus Deficit Reduction Act of 1984 explicitly

25 George F. Grob, "Medicare Payments for Clinical Laboratory Services," Department of Health and Human Services (January 2000), https://oig.hhs.gov/oei/reports/oei-05-00-00070.pdf.

prohibited physicians from billing Medicare for laboratory tests they did not perform. Today, most laboratory HCPCS codes reside in the CLFS and are billed by independent laboratories, hospitals or physician-owned laboratories (but not by independent physicians). In addition, most of these codes have no professional and technical component delineation and can only be billed as a global service, that is, with no modifier.

This Omnibus legislation in 1984 also changed how Medicare reimbursed for laboratory tests from charge-based payments to regional fee schedules. Although the Act also required that Medicare establish a national fee schedule for laboratory tests, the requirement was repealed in the Omnibus Budget Reconciliation Act of 1989 and state-specific lab fee schedules remained until 2018.[26] Medicare reimbursement of laboratory services was not addressed again until the Protecting Access to Medicare Act (PAMA) of 2014, which required that a national Medicare fee schedule be established with fees based on rates paid by private insurers.[27] The new payment system resulted in the CLFS that exists today. Medicare reimburses physicians and freestanding laboratories for laboratory services based on this fee schedule. Hospitals may also bill Medicare and receive reimbursement for laboratory services. However, when hospitals bill for separate laboratory tests for patients admitted as inpatients, reimbursement for these tests is included in the MS-DRG payment. If a hospital bills for laboratory services for a patient treated on an outpatient basis, Medicare processes these bills such that the hospital is either reimbursed the rate from the CLFS or the tests may be packaged based on the OPPS reimbursement logic (see Chapter 1).

Key Summary Points about Medicare Reimbursement for Clinical Laboratory Services:

- Identified by CPT codes that begin with "8" and alpha-numeric HCPCS codes, most of which begin with "G."
- Medicare commonly uses Modifiers 26 and TC to identify the professional and technical components of a laboratory procedures. When summed, the rates for the professional component and technical component equal the global rate for the procedure.
- Lab services that require direct physician supervision and/or interpretation are typically found in the MPFS while most other lab tests are found in the CLFS.
- Rates are national rates, with no geographic adjustment.
- Medicare generally updates rates annually and makes them available on the CMS website in the "Clinical Laboratory Fee Schedule" files.

26 George F. Grob, "Medicare Payments for Clinical Laboratory Services," Department of Health and Human Services (January 2000), https://oig.hhs.gov/oei/reports/oei-05-00-00070.pdf.

27 "PAMA Regulations," Centers for Medicare and Medicaid Services, October 26,2022, www.cms.gov/Medicare/Medicare-Fee-for-Service-Payment/ClinicalLabFeeSched/PAMA-Regulations.

- Hospital reimbursement for laboratory tests is included in the inpatient MS-DRG rate for inpatients.
- Medicare processes hospital claims for outpatient laboratory services using the OPPS.

D. Durable Medical Equipment

The healthcare industry defines Durable Medical Equipment (DME) as "[e]quipment and supplies ordered by a health care provider for everyday or extended use."[28] In order to be covered by Medicare, DME must serve a medical purpose, be able to withstand repeated use, and is typically appropriate for home use. DME includes things like wheelchairs, walkers, and oxygen equipment.

The Medicare program uses a fee schedule to reimburse for DME as well as prosthetics, orthotics and supplies (POS) and Parenteral and Enteral Nutrition (PEN).[29] CMS implemented the DMEPOS fee schedule in 1989, which includes rates for diabetic supplies, wheelchairs, oxygen, home infusion pumps, hospital beds, suction equipment and a variety of other medical equipment and supplies. In 2002, CMS implemented the DMEPEN fee schedule, which includes things like infusion pumps, tubing and feeding supplies.[30]

A physician or other health care provider typically orders DME, POS and PEN items for a Medicare beneficiary and a vendor or supplier provides the items and submits a claim to Medicare. Collectively, DME, POS and PEN are often referred to as "DME." Historically, Medicare paid for these items using a fee schedule based on what suppliers charged for the items and services, and annually updated these amounts. However, the U.S. General Accountability Office (GAO), as well as the Office of Inspector General (OIG) in the U.S. Department of Health and Human Services, found that Medicare and its beneficiaries sometimes paid higher than market rates for various DME items. In addition, federal lawmakers had concerns about potential improper DME payments. The Medicare Modernization Act of 2003 addressed these concerns (along with issues related to Part B drugs as described previously) by directing CMS to change the way it paid for DME by implementing a competitive bidding program (CBP). Congress intended for the CBP to improve the Medicare approach to setting DMEPOS payment amounts, reduce the potential for overpayments and ultimately save money for both the federal government and Medicare beneficiaries.

---

28 "Durable medical equipment (DME)," Healthcare.gov, www.healthcare.gov/glossary/durable-medical-quipment-dme/.

29 Prosthetic devices (other than dental) are defined as devices needed to replace body parts or functions. Orthotic devices are defined as providing rigid or semi-rigid support for weak or deformed body parts or restricting or eliminating motion in a diseased or injured part of the body.

30 Centers for Medicare and Medicaid Services, "Durable Medical Equipment, Prosthetics/Orthotics, and Supplies (DMEPOS) Fee Schedules," (Dec. 28, 2021), www.cms.gov/Medicare/Medicare-Fee-for-Service-Payment/DMEPOSFeeSched/downloads/DME11_C_SUMMARY.pdf.

The CBP, which began in 2010, established nine product categories of DME and other products. Suppliers who met CMS's eligibility requirements submitted bids to supply products at the bid price in a certain competitive bidding area (CBA), which was typically a Metropolitan Statistical Area (MSA). CMS then aggregates the bids for each product in a category and adjusts the DME fee schedule rates accordingly. The CBAs have been consolidated since the first round of bidding in 2010. As of 2021, CMS only includes certain MSAs in the CBP, and, in some areas, only subjects certain types of equipment or supplies to competitive bidding. There were 127 CBAs included in the CBP in 2021. These included, for example, four CBAs in the state of North Carolina:

- Asheville, NC
- Charlotte-Concord-Gastonia, NC
- Greensboro-High Point, NC
- Raleigh, NC

The remainder of North Carolina is not subject to competitive bidding.[31]

The Medicare DMEPOS fee schedule contains a "rural" and "non-rural" rate for each piece equipment or supply (identified by a HCPCS code) for each state. The HCPCS codes for DME, POS and PEN typically begin with the letters A, B, E, K and L. CMS generally classifies DME, POS and PEN into the following categories:

- Inexpensive and Other Routinely Purchased Items
- Frequently Serviced Items
- Oxygen and Oxygen Equipment
- Other Covered Items
- Capped Rental Items

Medicare beneficiaries can purchase or rent many of the items on the fee schedule depending on which category they fall into, and the fee schedule includes both purchase and rental rates. Capped rental items, however, include expensive items that beneficiaries have historically rented, and Medicare typically pays the rental rate for up to 13 months, at which point the Medicare beneficiary owns the equipment.[32] This would include things like hospital beds that are used at home.

In general, for DME items subject to the CBP, CMS adjusts fee schedule rates based on information from the competitive bidding program. For items not

31 "Competitive Bidding Areas," DMEPOS Competitive Bidding Program, 2021, https://dmecompetitivebid.com/cbic/cbicr2021.nsf/DocsCat/H5O2KFK4HO.

32 Centers for Medicare and Medicaid Services, "Durable Medical Equipment, Prosthetics/Orthotics, and Supplies (DMEPOS) Fee Schedules," (Dec. 28, 2021), www.cms.gov/Medicare/Medicare-Fee-for-Service-Payment/DMEPOSFeeSched/downloads/DME11_C_SUMMARY.pdf.

subject to CBP, CMS bases the fee schedule amounts on the historical charges for those items.

Key Points about Durable Medical Equipment:

- DME, POS and PEN are identified by HCPCS codes, most of which begin with A, B, E, K and L.
- Rates are state-specific and are split into rural and non-rural.
- There are purchase rates and rental rates for many items (identified by modifiers).
- The fee schedule amounts are adjusted based on the competitive bidding program.
- Facilities such as hospitals can also bill Medicare for DME and be reimbursed based on the same DME fee schedule.

III. MEDICARE REIMBURSEMENT FOR OTHER TYPES OF PROVIDERS

Chapter 1 provided a summary of the ways Medicare reimburses for inpatient and outpatient services provided in short-term acute care hospitals, as well as other types of hospitals. In addition, the first part of this chapter provided an overview of Medicare's approach to reimbursing for most physician services, including those paid through the Medicare Physician Fee Schedule, the Medicare Part B ASP Drug Pricing Files, the Medicare Clinical Laboratory Fee Schedule and the Medicare DMEPOS and DMEPEN fee schedules. In this section, we will look at other types of providers and services and the approaches that Medicare uses to reimburse for them. In each case, CMS has transitioned from cost-based reimbursement to a prospective payment system (PPS).

A. Skilled Nursing Facilities

Medicare covers services in a skilled nursing facility (SNF) when a beneficiary needs short-term skilled nursing or rehabilitation services following an inpatient hospital stay of at least three days. SNFs can be freestanding facilities or hospital-based units.[33]

Medicare began using a PPS to reimburse SNFs in 1998. Like other PPS approaches, the SNF PPS results in a predetermined rate—in this case a daily or per diem rate—for each day a patient spends in a SNF. In 2019, Medicare changed the PPS to better account for the range of services received by SNF patients. As a result, Medicare has base rates for six components of care—nursing, physical

33 Certain hospitals such as rural and critical access hospitals can receive approval to provide skilled nursing services in the hospital beds that are typically used to provide acute care services. These are called "swing beds."

therapy (PT), occupational therapy (OT), speech-language pathology services, nontherapy ancillary services (NTA) and supplies and room and board. The base rate for each component of care is then adjusted for geographic differences in labor costs by multiplying the labor-related portion of the per diem rate (70.8 percent for fiscal year 2023) by a wage index and then adding it to the nonlabor portion.[34] Next, the wage-adjusted base rates for five of the six components are adjusted for case mix, with each component having its own set of factors that are used in the calculation. In addition, payments for three components (PT, OT and NTA) are adjusted for the day of the stay, with higher payments made for services provided earlier in a stay. Medicare also adjusts SNF payments based on quality measures as well.[35]

B. Home Health Providers

Medicare covers and reimburses for home health services, which are typically provided by home health agencies (HHA) and may include skilled nursing care; physical, occupational and speech therapy; medical social work; and home health aide services. Medicare originally had strict requirements for coverage of home health similar to those for coverage of SNF services, such as requiring a prior hospital stay, but these restrictions have been removed. CMS implemented a PPS for Medicare reimbursement of home health facilities in 2000.

The home health PPS also begins with a base payment rate that is adjusted for geographic differences in labor costs, but in this case, the final reimbursement rate covers all home health visits that occur within a 30-day period. The base payment amount for 2023 is $2,010.69.[36] The labor portion of the base rate (76.1 percent) is adjusted by a wage index and added to the nonlabor portion. Unlike most other Medicare payment systems, the beneficiary's residence rather than the provider's location determines the wage adjustment for home health services.[37] Next, the base payment is adjusted for case mix using

34 Medicare Program; Prospective Payment System and Consolidated Billing for Skilled Nursing Facilities; Updates to the Quality Reporting Program and Value-Based Purchasing Program for Federal Fiscal Year 2023; Changes to the Requirements for the Director of Food and Nutrition Services and Physical Environment Requirements in Long-Term Care Facilities, 87 Fed. Reg. 47515 (August 3, 2022), www.govinfo.gov/content/pkg/FR-2022-08-03/pdf/2022-16457.pdf.

35 Medicare Payment Advisory Commission (MedPAC), "Skilled Nursing Facility Services Payment System," (November 2021), www.medpac.gov/wp-content/uploads/2021/11/medpac_payment_basics_21_snf_final_sec.pdf.

36 Department of Health & Human Services, Centers for Medicare & Medicaid Services, "Pub 100–04 Medicare Claims Processing, Transmittal 11802," (January 20, 2023), www.cms.gov/files/document/r11802cp.pdf.

37 Medicare Program; Calendar Year (CY) 2023 Home Health Prospective Payment System Rate Update; Home Health Quality Reporting Program Requirements; Home Health Value Based Purchasing Expanded Model Requirements; and Home Infusion Therapy Services Requirements, 87 Fed. Reg. 66853 (Nov. 4, 2022), www.govinfo.gov/content/pkg/FR-2022-11-04/pdf/2022-23722.pdf.

a grouping system called the Patient Driven Groupings Model (PDGM), to account for differences in patient characteristics. The PDGM categorizes each service period into 432 home health resource groups (HHRGs) based on service period timing, clinical category, functional impairment and comorbidities. Each HHRG is assigned a national relative weight reflecting the average relative costs of patients in that group compared to the costs of the average Medicare home health patient.

What are referred to as "low-use periods," which are periods where a patient has relatively few visits, are reimbursed on a per visit basis using what is called the low-use payment adjustment (LUPA) rate. In addition, when a patient's care requires an unusually high number of visits or a more expensive mix of services, the provider may qualify for an outlier payment.[38]

C. Inpatient Rehabilitation Facilities

Some people require intensive inpatient rehabilitation services, such as physical, occupational or speech therapy following an injury, surgery or hospital stay. SNFs frequently provide these services, but inpatient rehabilitation facilities (IRFs) often provide them as well. IRFs may be freestanding facilities or specialized units in short-term acute care hospitals. To qualify as an IRF, a facility must show that 60 percent of its inpatient population requires intensive rehabilitative services for the treatment of one or more of the following conditions: stroke, spinal cord injury, congenital deformity, amputation, major multiple trauma, fracture of femur (hip fracture), brain injury, polyarthritis (including rheumatoid arthritis), neurological disorders (including multiple sclerosis, motor neuron diseases, polyneuropathy, muscular dystrophy and Parkinson's disease) and burns.[39] There are also other requirements, such as having a medical director of rehabilitation who provides services in the facility.[40] Relatively few Medicare beneficiaries use IRFs, in part because there are fewer IRFs than SNFs across the U.S., but also because, to be eligible for treatment in an IRF, a patient generally must be able to tolerate and benefit from three hours of therapy per day.[41]

---

38 Medicare Payment Advisory Commission, "Home Health Care Services Payment System," (November 2021), www.medpac.gov/wp-content/uploads/2021/11/medpac_payment_basics_21_hha_final_sec.pdf.

39 Centers for Medicare and Medicaid Services, "Medicare Claims Processing Manual, Chapter 3: Inpatient Hospital Billing," (Oct. 29, 2022), www.cms.gov/Regulations-and-Guidance/Guidance/Manuals/Downloads/clm104c03aug_inpatient_hospital_09-3-3.pdf.

40 Medicare Payment Advisory Commission, "Inpatient Rehabilitation Facilities Payment Systems," (November 2021), www.medpac.gov/wp-content/uploads/2021/11/medpac_payment_basics_21_irf_final_sec.pdf.

41 Medicare Payment Advisory Commission, "Inpatient Rehabilitation Facilities Payment Systems," (November 2021), www.medpac.gov/wp-content/uploads/2021/11/medpac_payment_basics_21_irf_final_sec.pdf.

Medicare historically reimbursed IRFs based on a percentage of their costs.[42] However, on January 1, 2002, CMS implemented a per-discharge or per-"case" PPS for IRFs and inpatient rehabilitation units of hospitals. Similar to PPS rates for other provider types, the final reimbursement rate for a case is equal to a base payment rate that is adjusted for geographic differences in labor costs as well as case mix. The IRF base payment rate is $17,912 for fiscal year 2023.[43] Medicare adjusts the base payment rate for differences in labor costs by multiplying the labor-related portion of the base payment (73 percent) by a wage index. Next, the wage-adjusted base rate is adjusted for case mix using what are called case mix groups or "CMGs." CMGs are based on the primary reason for a patient's admission to an IRF (for example, a stroke or hip fracture) as well as age and level of motor and cognitive function. Finally, patients are further categorized into one of four tiers in each CMG based on the presence of specific comorbidities.

Each CMG tier has a specific weight that is used to adjust the payment rate up or down, which reflects the costs of patients in that CMG tier relative to the costs of the average Medicare IRF patient. Payment rates are also adjusted to account for certain facility characteristics.[44,45]

D. Freestanding Dialysis Centers

People with end-stage renal disease (ESRD) typically require either dialysis or a kidney transplant to survive. In 1972, as we learned in Chapter 1, Congress extended Medicare coverage to people with ESRD, including coverage and reimbursement of outpatient dialysis services. In 1983, Medicare began paying freestanding dialysis facilities using a "composite rate," which was a predetermined rate for a specific "bundle" or group of services. The bundle typically included an individual dialysis treatment or visit, as well as certain drugs and lab tests. In an effort to incentivize provider efficiency, Medicare phased in a prospective payment system (PPS) for outpatient dialysis in 2011. The PPS expanded the bundle of services paid under the composite rate to include additional drugs, lab tests and other services that had previously been separately paid.

42 U.S. Congress. United States Code: Social Security Act, 42 U.S.C. §§ 1886, "Payment to Hospitals for Inpatient Hospital Services," www.ssa.gov/OP_Home/ssact/title18/1886.htm.

43 Medicare Program; Inpatient Rehabilitation Facility Prospective Payment System for Federal Fiscal Year 2023 and Updates to the IRF Quality Reporting Program, 87 Fed. Reg. 47056 (Aug. 1, 2022), www.govinfo.gov/content/pkg/FR-2022-08-01/pdf/2022-16225.pdf.

44 For example, rural facilities' payment rates are adjusted higher because they tend to have fewer cases, longer lengths of stay and higher average costs per case. Payments to IRFs that are teaching institutions are also adjusted higher based on the number of residents. Payments to IRFs are also adjusted for the share of low-income patients treated.

45 Medicare Payment Advisory Commission, "Inpatient Rehabilitation Facilities Payment Systems," (November 2021), www.medpac.gov/wp-content/uploads/2021/11/medpac_payment_basics_21_irf_final_sec.pdf.

Medicare covers two types of dialysis—hemodialysis and peritoneal dialysis. In hemodialysis, a patient's blood is cycled through a dialysis machine, which filters out body waste. People undergoing hemodialysis, which is the vast majority of ESRD patients, typically visit a dialysis facility three times a week for their treatments. Peritoneal dialysis uses the lining of the peritoneal cavity for the filtering process, so patients can complete the treatments at home under the direction of a physician and dialysis facility team. The Medicare dialysis PPS reimburses for both modalities the same way but at different rates. In either case, dialysis facilities are paid a bundled rate for a dialysis visit that includes physician-administered drugs (such as erythropoietin, injectable iron and vitamin D) but also ESRD-related oral drugs. The bundled rate also includes nearly all lab tests, medical equipment and supplies.

For 2023, the base payment rate is $265.57 for both freestanding and hospital-based dialysis facilities.[46] Similar to rates for other provider types, CMS adjusts the dialysis base rate for geographic differences in labor costs by multiplying the labor-related portion of the base payment amount (52.3 percent) by a wage index. In addition, CMS adjusts the base rate for case mix using patient age, body measurement variables, specific acute and chronic comorbidities and date of onset of dialysis. For children under the age of 18, case mix is only adjusted by age and dialysis modality.

Finally, the base rate includes facility-level adjustments—one for low-volume facilities (defined as fewer than 4,000 treatments in each of the three years before the payment year) and one for proximity to other commonly owned facilities within five miles of the facility where treatment occurs. There is also an outlier methodology that is applied when treatment costs exceed a certain threshold, and there are certain add-on payments that also may apply to new technologies.[47]

IV. CONCLUSION

Chapters 1 and 2 have provided detailed descriptions of the reimbursement methodologies used by the Medicare program to reimburse hospitals, physicians and many other provider types. Chapter 3 turns to the operations of the commercial or private insurance market.

46 Centers for Medicare and Medicaid Services, "CY 2023 End Stage Renal Disease Prospective Payment System Final Rule—CMS-1768-F," October 31, 2022, www.cms.gov/newsroom/fact-sheets/calendar-year-2023-end-stage-renal-disease-esrd-prospective-payment-system-pps-final-rule-cms-1768-f#:~:text=Updates%20to%20the%20ESRD%20PPS%20for%20CY%202023,current%20base%20rate%20of%20%24257.90.

47 Medicare Payment Advisory Commission (MedPAC), "Outpatient Dialysis Services Payment System," November 2021, www.medpac.gov/wp-content/uploads/2021/11/medpac_payment_basics_21_dialysis_final_sec.pdf.

CHAPTER 3

Commercial Health Insurance Plans and Networks

JoAnna Younts

I. OVERVIEW OF COMMERCIAL HEALTH INSURANCE

As of 2021, over 90 percent of the U.S. population had some type of health insurance coverage while about 9 percent remained uninsured. About one-third (35 percent) of the U.S. population has coverage through Medicare and/or Medicaid, while another nearly 55 percent are covered by commercial or private health insurance. The vast majority of people who have commercial coverage obtain that coverage through their employer or some type of group. This is a unique feature of the U.S. health insurance market that has a complicated history. Another smaller proportion of the population (6.1 percent) has non-group or individual coverage,[1] most of whom are covered by individual plans. While individual plans were historically purchased through insurance brokers, the development of the internet has allowed consumers to purchase insurance coverage directly from health insurance companies via their websites. Since 2014, as a result of the Affordable Care Act (ACA), individual and small group plans can also be purchased on the federal health insurance "marketplace" known as healthcare.gov or on state-administered "exchanges."

II. TYPES OF HEALTH INSURANCE MARKETS

The large group market is the largest portion of the health insurance market in the U.S. It encompasses about one-third of the group insurance market.[2] As of

1 "Health insurance coverage of the total population," Kaiser Family Foundation, www.kff.org/other/state-indicator/total-population/?currentTimeframe=0&sortModel=%7B%22colId%22%3A%22Location%22%2C%22sort%22%3A%22asc%22%7D.

2 Approximately 42 million people in 2019. "Market share and enrollment of largest three insurers—large group market," Kaiser Family Foundation, www.kff.org/other/state-indicator/market-share-and

2016, states must define large groups as having 101 or more employees while small groups are defined as 1 to 100 employees.[3] Large groups are typically composed of the employees of a particular organization, or sometimes people who are joined together in a group through a union or association. The employer-based insurance model is unique to the U.S. In a detailed account of the origins of employer-based health insurance, the Committee on Employment-Based Health Benefits at the Institute of Medicine, stated that

> [t]he current U.S. system of voluntary employment-based health benefits is not the consequence of an overarching and deliberate plan or policy. Rather, it reflects a gradual accumulation of factors: innovations in health care finance and organization, conflicting political and social principles, coincidences of timing, market dynamics, programs stimulated by the findings of health services research, and spillover effects of tax and other policies aimed at different targets.

In particular, the passage of the Employment Retirement Income Security Act (ERISA) in 1974 and other federal regulations have given employers wide latitude and discretion with the regard to the provision and administration of health insurance for their employees.[4]

While it is commonly thought that members of large group plans pay lower premiums for their coverage than members of small groups or individuals, this is not always the case. Premiums are established based on the level of "risk" in a group or "risk pool" and risk is central to pricing across all types of insurance, including health insurance. A health insurance risk pool is a group of individuals whose medical costs are combined to calculate premiums. Pooling risk allows the higher costs of less healthy people to be offset by the relatively lower costs of healthy people, either in a plan overall or within certain categories or lines of business. In general, the larger the risk pool, the more predictable and stable the premiums. Health insurance premiums are set at levels so that insurers have enough money to pay claims to healthcare providers, as well as their administrative costs and taxes, and realize a profit.

The largest component of health insurance premiums is the medical spending paid on behalf of the health insurer's members, that is, the reimbursement to healthcare providers. As a result, the amount of the premiums is intended to reflect

-enrollment-of-largest-three-insurers-large-group-market/?currentTimeframe=0&sortModel=%7B%22colId%22%3A%22Location%22%2C%22sort%22%3A%22asc%22%7D.

3 "Market share and enrollment of largest three insurers—large group market," Kaiser Family Foundation, www.kff.org/other/state-indicator/market-share-and-enrollment-of-largest-three-insurers-large-group-market/?currentTimeframe=0&sortModel=%7B%22colId%22%3A%22Location%22%2C%22sort%22%3A%22asc%22%7D.

4 M. J. Field and H.T. Shapiro *Employment and Health Benefits: A Connection at Risk*, Institute of Medicine (US) Committee on Employment-Based Health Benefits (2006), www.ncbi.nlm.nih.gov/books/NBK235989/.

the expected healthcare costs of those members, that is, the risk pool. However, it is usually a small percentage of (presumably unhealthy) members who account for a large share or even the majority of costs in a health plan, so if a risk pool has a disproportionate share of unhealthy people, premiums will be higher than they would be if the risk pool had more healthy people in it. Thus, even though larger risk pools are typically more stable, a large risk pool does not necessarily mean lower premiums. In other words, premium levels are driven by the healthcare costs incurred by the people in the risk pool—so it's possible that a small group or risk pool with a lot of healthy individuals can result in lower-than-average premiums, while a large group or risk pool with a lot of unhealthy people might have higher-than-average premiums.[5]

Large groups are often what is called "self-insured" or "self-funded," meaning that the "plan sponsor" (usually an employer) collects premiums from employees who are enrolled in the employer's group health insurance plans and then pays employees' (and their dependents') medical claims out of the organization's revenue (or a trust fund for this purpose). Self-funded plans are also sometimes called ERISA plans because they are governed by the federal Employee Retirement and Income Security Act of 1974 which set minimum standards for self-funded health plans and other retirement plans.[6] State insurance laws generally do not apply to self-funded health plans.

Self-funded employers typically contract with a health insurance company for services such as enrollment and claims processing. These arrangements are called Administrative Services Only (ASO) contracts where a health insurance company provides services to a group of employees, but their employer actually pays their claims expenses. For example, "Company A" is self-funded and contracts with an insurer such as Blue Cross Blue Shield to provide certain services, such as access to a network of healthcare providers and claims processing for its employees. The Blue Cross Blue Shield plan provides these services and Company A pays a fee per employee to Blue Cross Blue Shield. Company A also pays for the healthcare services used by its employees.[7] In order to protect themselves when an employee has extraordinarily high healthcare costs, employers may also contract with the insurer for "stop loss" coverage.[8] Stop loss coverage or "reinsurance" requires the insurer instead of the employer to pay medical costs beyond a certain dollar

5 American Academy of Actuaries, "Risk Pooling: How Health Insurance in the Individual Market Works," July 2017, www.actuary.org/sites/default/files/files/publications/RiskPoolingFAQ071417.pdf.

6 "Employee Retirement Income Security Act (ERISA)," U.S. Department of Labor, www.dol.gov/general/topic/retirement/erisa.

7 "Definitions of Health Insurance Terms," U.S. Bureau of Labor Statistics, October 2002, www.bls.gov/ncs/ebs/sp/healthterms.pdf.

8 Reinsurance is "the acceptance by one or more insurers, called reinsurers or assuming companies, of a portion of the risk underwritten by another insurer that has contracted with an employer for the entire coverage." "Definitions of Health Insurance Terms," U.S. Bureau of Labor Statistics, October 2002, www.bls.gov/ncs/ebs/sp/healthterms.pdf.

amount. The stop loss limits can either be established at the individual employee level, that is, an amount at which the insurance begins paying for an employee's healthcare (called an individual limit), or they can be established at the aggregate level, encompassing total expenses for all of the employer's employees (called a group limit).[9]

Unlike self-funded health plans, in a "fully insured" plan, an insurance company is responsible for the employee's healthcare costs that are covered by the employer's health plan, and the insurer charges the employer premiums in exchange for accepting the risk of the group of employees. State insurance departments regulate fully insured health plans; therefore, the plans must follow state rather than federal insurance laws.[10]

The small group market comprises about 3 percent of the U.S. population. A small group ranges from 1 to 100 members. Small employer groups typically purchase insurance either through an insurance broker or through the Small Business Health Options Program (SHOP) that was implemented as a result of the ACA in 2014.

Some experts thought that certain provisions in the ACA such as expanded Medicaid eligibility and premium tax credits for individual coverage might outweigh the benefits of the newly created SHOP program, resulting in fewer small employers offering employee health insurance. They reasoned that these alternatives to employer-sponsored insurance might be more attractive to potential small group members, and unlike large employers who faced tax penalties for dropping insurance coverage for their employees, small employers weren't penalized in this way. But these predictions did not come to pass, and many small employers have continued to offer health insurance coverage to their employees.[11]

Small group plans can also be self-funded or fully funded but are more often fully funded because of the risk of paying potentially catastrophic medical expenses for their employees. In 2020, only about 16 percent of employers with less than 50 employees offered a self-funded plan compared to 75 percent of employers with 500 or more employees.[12]

About six percent of Americans have individual insurance coverage. This percentage has increased since the implementation of the ACA for a variety of reasons, including requiring coverage of essential health benefits (Figure 3.1),

9 "Definitions of Health Insurance Terms," U.S. Bureau of Labor Statistics, October 2002, www.bls.gov/ncs/ebs/sp/healthterms.pdf.

10 "Using Your Health Plan," National Association of Insurance Commissions, https://content.naic.org/sites/default/files/pio-using-your-health-plan.pdf.

11 Jessica Banthin and Elizabeth Grazevich, "Trends in Small-Group Market Insurance Coverage, 2013–20," Urban Institute, January 2022, www.urban.org/sites/default/files/publication/105316/trends-in-small-group-market-insurance-coverage-2013-20_1.pdf.

12 Jessica Banthin and Elizabeth Grazevich, "Trends in Small-Group Market Insurance Coverage, 2013–20," Urban Institute, January 2022, www.urban.org/sites/default/files/publication/105316/trends-in-small-group-market-insurance-coverage-2013-20_1.pdf.

banning medical underwriting, setting minimum medical loss ratios and subsidizing premiums.[13] Consumers may purchase health insurance coverage through the individual market for a variety of reasons, including that they are not employed or that their employer does not provide health insurance. Those who need to purchase health insurance through the individual market can do so by contacting a health insurance company directly via its website or call center, contacting a health insurance agent in the local area or using the health insurance marketplaces or exchanges, which were created under the ACA. The ACA exchanges allow consumers to search for different plan options and purchase a plan that meets their financial and coverage requirements. Consumers who meet certain income and other requirements can receive subsidies in the form of tax credits to reduce their premium costs. As of November 1, 2021, there are 22 state-based exchanges, including California, Minnesota and Pennsylvania.[14] People who live in the other 28 states must use the federal exchange called "Healthcare.gov" to purchase an ACA plan.

Collectively, health insurance companies that administer fully funded plans and employers that are self-insured are called "payors" or "payers." This book will use "payer." The term payer may also be interchanged with "health plan" and "health insurer" throughout this book as well depending on the context.

Essential Health Benefits[15]

1. Ambulatory patient services
2. Emergency services
3. Hospitalizations
4. Pregnancy, maternity and newborn care
5. Mental health and substance use disorder services
6. Prescription drugs
7. Rehabilitative and habilitative services and devices
8. Laboratory services
9. Preventative and wellness services and chronic disease management
10. Pediatric services, including oral and vision care

13 Medical underwriting is a process used by insurance companies to evaluate a person's health status in deciding whether or not to provide coverage and at what price. The ACA banned this practice. A medical loss ratio (MLR) represents the proportion of premiums that are used to pay medical claims. The ACA requires that insurers have at least an 80 percent MLR, www.healthcare.gov.

14 Three of these SBEs are on the "federal platform," meaning that they rely on the federal government to perform certain functions, such as eligibility and enrollment, but still retain responsibility for other functions such as plan certification and consumer outreach.

15 "Health benefits & coverage," HealthCare.gov, www.healthcare.gov/coverage/what-marketplace-plans-cover/.

III. TYPES OF HEALTH INSURANCE PLANS

We learned in Chapter 1 that prior to the Medicare program, older Americans who did not have access to or could not afford commercial health insurance coverage often went without medical services. But younger Americans pre- and post-Medicare also needed healthcare as well as health insurance, so the private health insurance industry emerged in the early 20th century to serve (mostly) younger, working people.

Workers' compensation was the earliest form of reimbursement for bodily injury. Artifacts from ancient Sumeria describe monetary compensation for certain injuries to workers' body parts, including fractures. The code of Hammurabi from 1750 B.C. also cites rewards for injuries to compensate for permanent disability, and other ancient laws around the world included compensation schedules and payment amounts for the loss of a body part. English common law in the late Middle Ages and Renaissance eventually provided a legal framework for this type of compensation that continued through the Industrial Revolution in Europe, but the U.S. was one of the last countries to adopt workers' compensation laws. These laws evolved alongside other labor reforms in the early 1900s, and individual states started passing their own workers' compensation laws beginning with Wisconsin in 1911. Mississippi was the last state to pass such laws in 1948.[16]

Commercial or private health insurance plans as we know them generally trace their roots back to arrangements between employers and employees that allowed employees to prepay for healthcare services. One of the first arrangements occurred in the early 1900s between loggers in the Pacific Northwest and the companies that employed them. Because of the occupational hazards of logging, employees required frequent medical care, so the companies organized plans where physicians would provide medical services for a monthly fee. A more detailed timeline of the development of private health insurance and managed care can be found in Chapter 5.[17]

Generally, health insurance plan models fall into five distinct categories:

1. Health Maintenance Organization (HMO)
2. Exclusive Provider Organization (EPO)
3. Preferred Provider Organization (PPO)
4. Point of Service (POS) and
5. Indemnity

An HMO is typically the most restrictive type of health insurance model because the member must use a specific group of "in-network" providers. If the member is

16 Gregory P Guyton, "A Brief History of Workers' Compensation," *Iowa Orthopedic Journal* (1999), www.ncbi.nlm.nih.gov/pmc/articles/PMC1888620/#:~:text=WORKERS'%20COMPENSATION%20IN%20ANTIQUITY&text=It%20dates%20to%20approximately%202050,and%20their%20implied%20permanent%20impairments.

17 "Blue Cross and Blue Shield: A Historical Compilation," *Consumer Reports* (2013), https://advocacy.consumerreports.org/wp-content/uploads/2013/03/yourhealthdollar.org_blue-cross-history-compilation.pdf.

treated by a provider that is not part of this group, that is, "out-of-network," the services are not covered, except in emergency situations. There will be more discussion of the concept of "in-network" and "out-of-network" later in this chapter. An EPO is a form of HMO, where the member must use in-network providers in order for services to be covered (again, except in emergencies); however, EPO networks are typically larger, which allows the member to have more choices of providers.

A PPO model is less restrictive than an HMO or EPO model. While the member is still encouraged to use in-network providers and will pay less out-of-pocket for doing so, this type of plan does provide coverage when the member chooses to go to an out-of-network provider. The member's share of the cost is typically higher when an out-of-network provider is used. POS plans are a form of PPO. Typically, POS plan members must obtain a referral from their primary care physician in order to see a specialist.[18]

Indemnity plans were the most prevalent form of health insurance until the late 20th century. Under an indemnity plan, the member can choose any almost provider and there is no in-network or out-of-network distinction. Traditional indemnity plans are rarely offered in today's insurance market; however, a relatively new indemnity model called "fixed indemnity" has gained traction in recent years. In some cases, a fixed indemnity plan pays a certain dollar amount per day of illness or hospitalization, or they pay a certain amount for a specific type of health care service. For example, a plan may pay $100 for a physician visit or $1000 for an appendectomy. Although these plans mimic a health insurance plan in many ways, they are not insurance and may not be subject to regulation like traditional health insurance plans. Critics of these types of products say that consumers should not purchase such products as a substitute for traditional health insurance because they place the consumer at financial risk. This is because the companies that offer these products set a payment amount associated with a specific type of service, and consumers are responsible for any difference between this set payment amount and the actual cost of care. If the fixed amount is low, the consumer could be responsible for paying very high medical bills from providers.[19]

All of the above health insurance models rely on the concept of provider networks, and health insurers enter into contracts with providers to participate in their networks. This concept is described in the next section.

IV. PROVIDER NETWORKS AND CONTRACTING OVERVIEW

Health insurers, including those that provide employer-based plans as well as individual plans, must rely on healthcare providers such as physicians and hospitals to

18 "Health insurance plan & network types: HMOs, PPOs, and more," HealthCare.gov, www.healthcare.gov/choose-a-plan/plan-types/.

19 Christen Linke Young and Kathleen Hannick, "Fixed indemnity health coverage is a problematic form of 'junk insurance,'" Brookings, August 4, 2020, www.brookings.edu/blog/usc-brookings-schaeffer-on-health-policy/2020/08/04/fixed-indemnity-health-coverage-is-a-problematic-form-of-junk-insurance/.

deliver medical services to their members. In turn, health insurers pay providers for these services on behalf of their members. Payments for the services are typically shared or split between the health insurer and the member, which is called "cost sharing." Cost sharing usually involves the health insurer paying the majority of the cost for medical services and the member paying a smaller portion in the form of deductibles, copayments and coinsurance. The member's cost-sharing amount typically depends on the type of benefit plan the member has purchased, such as an HMO, PPO or other type of plan. See Figure 3.2 for descriptions of the different types of cost sharing.

Cost Sharing Definitions

Deductible: The amount a member pays for medical services[20] before their insurance plan starts to pay. For example, if a member has a $1,000 deductible, and they have a surgical procedure that costs $5,000, they must pay the first $1,000 of the $5,000. Alternatively, the member may have 10 physician office visits and the rate their plan has negotiated with their plan ("allowed amount"–See Section C.1) is $200 per visit. In this case, the member will pay for five of those visits out-of-pocket until the $1,000 deductible is reached. Once the deductible is paid, the member may also have other cost-sharing obligations such as copayments or coinsurance (see below); however, many plans pay for preventive services without requiring that the deductible be met first. Plans purchased on healthcare.gov or state exchanges, also called "ACA plans," are required by statute to pay for preventive services before the deductible is met. Family plans typically have individual deductibles for each member of the family as well as a family deductible that applies to all family members. Some plans also have different deductible amounts for different types of services such as hospital care versus prescription drugs. Plans with lower monthly premiums typically have higher deductibles while plans with higher monthly premiums often have lower deductibles.

Copayment: A fixed dollar amount (also called a "copay") that a member pays for a medical service once their deductible is met. For example, the copayment for any physician visit (other than preventive services) might be $35, and the physician practice will collect this amount at the time of the visit. The remainder of the cost of the visit is paid by the health plan. If the member has not met their deductible, however, they will be required

20 Cost sharing amounts only apply to "covered" services, that is, services that are included in the member's benefit package. Certain services may not be covered. Some of the most common services not covered by health insurance plans are cosmetic surgery and alternative therapies such as acupuncture. FAIR Health, www.fairhealthconsumer.org/insurance-basics/healthcare/healthcare-services-not-covered-by-health-insurance.

to pay the full cost of the visit. Copayments can vary for different services within the same plan, like drugs, lab tests and visits to specialists. Similar to deductibles, plans with lower monthly premiums typically have higher copayments, while plans with higher monthly premiums usually have lower copayments.

Coinsurance: Rather than a fixed dollar amount like a copayment, coinsurance is a percentage of the costs of a medical service that the member must pay once the deductible is met. A common coinsurance percentage is 20 percent. For example, if the rate negotiated with the health plan for an MRI is $400 and the member has a 20 percent coinsurance obligation, the member would pay $80, as long as the deductible has been met, and the health plan would pay the remaining $320. If the deductible has not been met, the member may be responsible for up to the full $400 for the MRI depending on the deductible amount. Plans with low monthly premiums typically have higher coinsurance and plans with higher monthly premiums often have lower coinsurance.

Health plans may also establish maximum dollar amounts that members are responsible for in each calendar year. This is called an annual "out-of-pocket maximum." Once the member reaches this amount by paying the deductible, copayments and coinsurance, the health plan pays 100 percent of the costs for the member's covered services for the remainder of the year. Some plans also have lifetime out-of-pocket maximums.

Example: The member has an inpatient hospital stay and the reimbursement amount the plan has negotiated with the hospital is $20,000. The member's deductible is $2,000, they have 20 percent coinsurance, and their out-of-pocket maximum is $8,000.

- The member would pay the first $2,000 of the reimbursement amount (the deductible).
- The member would pay 20 percent of the remaining $18,000, or $3,600 (the coinsurance).
- Out-of-pocket costs would be $5,600 and the health plan would pay the remaining $14,400.

However, if the out-of-pocket maximum were $5,000, the member would pay $5,000 rather than $5,600 and the health plan would pay $15,000. In addition, the health plan would pay all remaining costs of services for the remainder of the year.

In administering their various health insurance plans, health insurers enter into contracts with healthcare providers. Under these contracts, providers agree to furnish services to the health insurer's members in exchange for a certain level of payment for the services. Providers who enter into such contracts with a health insurer are considered to be part of the health insurer's network and are often referred to as "in-network" providers. Providers who do not have contracts with the health insurer are considered to be "out-of-network." In some cases, providers may only enter into contracts to participate in certain networks, such as the insurer's PPO network, and therefore would be considered out-of-network for other networks that serve the insurer's members in HMO or EPO plans. Some plans, particularly large national payers such as UnitedHealthcare and some Blue Cross Blue Shield plans have multiple networks that providers may participate in. Most plans have some sort of "broad" network which includes a large percentage of the providers in the plan's geographic service area as well as smaller or "narrow" networks that are designed to cover only a certain type of product or a limited geographic area, or even a specific patient population (see Section C at the end of this chapter on narrow networks and network adequacy). Generally, a broader network means more choices of providers for the plan's members and access to such a network requires the member to pay a higher premium. Conversely, limited or narrow networks generally have fewer choices of providers and members pay lower premiums as a trade-off for these limitations.

Health insurers contract with specific networks of providers to deliver services to members who are enrolled in certain plans. Members enrolled in HMO and EPO plans, which typically have lower premiums, are usually restricted to a limited network of providers. Members enrolled in HMO and EPO plans may have relatively low cost-sharing amounts as long as they use in-network providers, that is, providers specially assigned to the network that provides services to HMO or EPO members. However, other aspects of the benefit structure affect the premium amounts that members pay. For example, a member may choose a plan with a high deductible or a higher coinsurance percentage in order to pay a lower monthly premium. This is important because member out-of-pocket costs can be impacted by the reimbursement rates paid to providers for their services. Specifically, a member may pay more out-of-pocket for the same service if the reimbursement rate is higher at one hospital versus another, particularly if the member has a high deductible or high coinsurance percentage.

As described previously, HMO and EPO plans typically do not provide for out-of-network benefits, meaning that if a member receives services from a provider that does not participate in the network for their HMO or EPO plan, the member is responsible for paying the full cost for the services they receive. An exception is made for emergency services, such as hospital emergency room services and ambulance services.

In contrast, members enrolled in PPO plans, which typically have higher premiums, may have a much larger network of providers from which they can choose. In addition, PPO members typically have out-of-network benefits, meaning that they may use providers who do not participate in the PPO network and the health insurer will pay some portion of the cost. However, members of PPO plans generally have higher cost-sharing amounts for out-of-network services than in-network services, with some exceptions.

Health plan members are provided detailed information regarding the type of plan they have purchased, the benefits that are covered and not covered, as well as cost-sharing requirements when they enroll. This information is typically provided in the form of a hardcopy and/or online benefit booklet. Members are also provided access to the plan's provider directory, which gives members information about the providers that participate in the plan's network. In this way, it is clear to members which providers are in-network and which are out-of-network. For elective services, such as physician office visits, diagnostic procedures and surgeries, members can choose providers that are in-network to ensure that the services are covered by their plan and that they are only responsible for cost-sharing amounts.

In emergency situations, it is understood that out-of-network providers must sometimes be used because the member is not able to select an in-network provider. Members who have HMO or EPO plans may be treated in emergency or urgent situations at an out-of-network hospital and in some cases, a member must be admitted to the hospital as an inpatient. In these situations, the hospital and the member's health plan typically work together to either arrange a transfer to an in-network hospital for the member's hospital stay or the plan may authorize treatment for the member at the out-of-network hospital. In these situations, the health insurer reimburses the out-of-network hospital for the services provided according to the insurer's out-of-network reimbursement policy or the member's benefit policy, and the member is typically only responsible for the cost-sharing amounts that are specified in their benefit plan. Importantly, under the ACA, if a health plan or insurer provides coverage for hospital emergency services, the plan is required to cover the services regardless of whether a provider is in-network or out-of-network. In addition, the member's cost sharing cannot be higher than it would be if the provider were in-network.[21]

Payers (health insurers or health plans) and healthcare providers enter into contracts in which providers agree to provide services to members and the payer agrees to reimburse the provider a certain fee for each type of service rendered, which is called the "contract rate" or may also be called an "allowable," "allowed amount," or "allowed charge." These amounts may be drawn from fee schedules or payment formulas developed by the payer and can apply to multiple providers in the payer's network or may be individually negotiated. Different types of contract rates will be discussed in Chapter 4. Providers also maintain their own list prices or charges (see Chapter 6) and may submit bills to payers that contain these amounts. However, the agreed-upon contract rates may be different from the provider's charges. Contract rates are typically lower than the charges. In addition to the agreed-upon contract rates, other key components of the contract include provisions for timely filing of claims, prompt payment requirements and notification requirements regarding changes to rates or other policies. These will be discussed

21 "Affordable Care Act Implementation FAQs—Set," Centers for Medicare and Medicaid Services, www.cms.gov/CCIIO/Resources/Fact-Sheets-and-FAQs/aca_implementation_faqs#Out-Of-Network%20Emergency%20Services.

through the remainder of this book, including how these contract provisions may give rise to disputes between payers and providers.

A key provision of a contract between a payer and provider is that the provider must agree to accept the contract rate or allowable as payment in full, regardless of the provider's billed charges, and may not collect the difference from the patient. This is called "balance billing" and will be discussed in the next section on out-of-network providers.

A. Out-of-Network and Nonparticipating Providers

There are many reasons for providers to be out-of-network or to not participate in a payer's network. Some providers prefer not to enter into contracts with payers, which may be driven by a desire to minimize administrative complexity, or it may be based on a belief that the provider can collect higher fees from payers and patients by remaining out-of-network. On the other hand, payers may also exclude providers from their networks as well. A payer may feel that the network is robust, not only meeting network adequacy requirements, but also providing a wide range of choice to its members, and, therefore, does not wish to enter into contracts with additional providers. This may be the case for certain types of services but not others. For example, a payer may have an adequate number of hospitals in a certain geographic area and therefore may choose not to contract with some hospitals and include them in its network. On the other hand, the payer may need to add certain types of specialists to its network and may actively pursue contracts with these specialists in order to provide adequate access for members so that they do not have to travel long distances to see an in-network provider or use an out-of-network provider that is closer to home. Payers may exclude providers for other reasons as well. Some payers have "any willing provider" networks in which any provider can participate in the network as long as it agrees to accept the payer's reimbursement rates as payment in full.

When there is no contract with a payer and members need or want to be treated by a certain provider, there are several options that can be employed. These include single case agreements (SCA), letters of agreement (LOA) and rental or wrap networks.

Types of Out-of-Network Agreements

Single Case Agreement: A written agreement between a payer and an out-of-network provider to deliver services to the health plan's member in exchange for a certain reimbursement rate or fee. SCAs are entered into on a case-by-case basis. For example, a member may need a service that cannot be provided by one of the payer's in-network providers. Thus, the payer will enter into an SCA with an out-of-network provider that can provide the service.

Letter of Agreement: An LOA is similar to an SCA in that there is a written agreement between a payer and an out-of-network provider. Rather than applying to one member, however, LOAs may be used to address a certain type of service for any member who needs it. For example, a payer may enter into an LOA with a hospital to pay certain reimbursement rates if any of its members receives emergency services at the hospital.

Rental or Wrap Network: A rental or wrap network is a network of providers that health plans purchase access to in order to supplement their existing network of providers to ensure access to services for their members. Providers sign contracts with rental networks to participate in these networks at mutually agreed-upon rates. Rental networks are not health plans and do not operate like health plans in the sense that they do not collect premiums, they do not have members and they do not accept risk.

B. Out-of-Network Services and Balance Billing

Balance billing is an important issue related to out-of-network providers and services. If an agreement such as those described above is not entered into and a member uses an out-of-network provider, the member is typically responsible for their cost sharing such as copayments and deductibles under their out-of-network benefit provisions.[22] In addition to their cost sharing, however, the member may also be responsible for the difference between the provider's billed charge and the amount paid by the member's plan. Health plans typically try to direct their members to use in-network providers in order to avoid the potential for balance billing. Not all providers balance bill, but some may pursue balance bills, particularly if the amounts are large. Balance bills can be the subject of payer-provider disputes, which are discussed in more detail in Chapters 7 and 9.

In an effort to mitigate the risk of high out-of-pocket expenses for patients receiving services from out-of-network providers, the Patient Protection Final Rule published by the U.S. Department of Health and Human Services (HHS) in November 2015 imposed additional regulations regarding payments for emergency services, which became known as the "Greatest of Three" rule. Under these regulations, health plans were required to reimburse providers for out-of-network emergency services at an amount at least equal to the greatest of the following three amounts (adjusted for in-network cost sharing):

1. The median reimbursement amount negotiated with in-network providers for the emergency service;

22 An exception required by the ACA is emergency hospital services, in which members are only responsible for the amount equivalent to their in-network cost sharing.

2. The reimbursement amount for the emergency service calculated using the method the plan generally uses to determine payments for out-of-network services; or
3. The amount that would be paid by Medicare for the emergency service.

But these provisions still did not address balance billing, nor did they address other situations in which balance bills occur, such as non-emergency services provided by out-of-network professionals at in-network facilities. In addition, the Greatest of Three rule did not provide for a dispute resolution process.

Federal legislation passed in 2020, called the "No Surprises Act," protects members from balance billing when specific conditions are met (see the sidebar below for a summary of the key provisions of the No Surprises Act). Some states also have balance billing protections, and these may supersede the federal protections in certain circumstances.[23]

A variation of a balance bill is a "surprise bill," which can refer to various situations in which a patient is "surprised" when they receive a bill that they were not expecting for healthcare services received from an out-of-network provider. The term "balance bill" is sometimes used interchangeably with a surprise bill, but they are slightly different. Balance bills can occur in almost any out-of-network situation including when a member chooses to use an out-of-network provider. Surprise bills most often occur in two situations. In the first, a health plan member receives emergency care either at an out-of-network facility or from an out-of-network provider, and the second occurs when a member receives non-emergency services at an in-network facility but is treated by an out-of-network professional provider such as a surgeon or anesthesiologist. As described previously, health plans do not have contracts with out-of-network providers, which means there are no pre-negotiated rates for services. Thus, an out-of-network provider may send a bill for their charges, but if the health plan does not pay the full amount (which they are not required to do), the provider may turn to the patient for the remainder. The patient may not know that the provider was out-of-network and is therefore surprised when they receive the bill. A surprise bill from an out-of-network provider can include the amount that is balance billed but can also include deductible and coinsurance amounts as well, and these amounts may be higher than what they would have been if the provider had been in-network.

The ACA required that group and individual health insurance plans cover emergency services without prior authorization[24] regardless of whether the healthcare provider furnishing the emergency services is an in-network or out-of-network provider. However, balance billing was not prohibited by the ACA.

---

23 "Surprise and Balance Billing State Policy Options," National Conference of State Legislatures, October 6, 2021, www.ncsl.org/research/health/surprise-and-balance-billing-state-policy-options.aspx.

24 Prior authorization means that the health plan must approve the service before it is rendered in order for it to be covered.

The No Surprises Act and State Balance Billing Laws

Background

The No Surprises Act (NSA) was signed into law in December 2020 as part of the Consolidated Appropriations Act of 2021 (CAA). The law, which took effect on January 1, 2022, provides federal protection against surprise billing and limits out-of-network cost sharing under many of the circumstances in which surprise bills arise most frequently. While some individual states have statutes related to surprise billing, they vary in the types of services applicable and specific provisions regarding reimbursement rates, cost sharing and dispute resolution. The NSA provides a uniform set of standards, including specific provisions regarding how cost-sharing amounts are calculated and initial payments made by health plans to providers.

Currently, 33 states have surprise billing regulations, but they vary dramatically. State regulations may address some or all of the following issues but may not do so in the same manner.

- Emergency services provided by out-of-network facilities
- Emergency services provided by out-of-network providers at in-network facilities
- Types of health plans to which surprise bill provisions apply
- Hold harmless provisions for members
- Provider prohibition of balance billing
- Payment standard or dispute resolution process

The result has been a patchwork of regulations across the U.S. The NSA was intended to address gaps where no state laws exist, but some state regulations supersede federal regulations in certain circumstances.

Key Provisions of the NSA

The NSA encompasses both emergent and nonemergent services in certain out-of-network circumstances. Importantly, payers must treat out-of-network patients as though they are in-network for purposes of prior authorization, coverage limits, cost-sharing obligations and out-of-pocket maximums. In addition, the NSA provides for an independent dispute resolution (IDR) process for out-of-network reimbursement disputes that sets forth requirements regarding the arbitration process, criteria to be considered by arbitrators and other requirements.

The following *emergency* services are addressed by the NSA:

- Services received at an out-of-network facility;

- Services rendered by an out-of-network individual provider (e.g., emergency physician), whether the facility rendering services is in- or out-of-network; and
- Services provided by out-of-network air ambulances.

The following *non-emergency* services are addressed by the NSA:

- An out-of-network individual provider at an in-network facility; and
- Out-of-network air ambulance services.

In the context of the above services, there are five key elements of the NSA:

1. Limitations on cost sharing for health plan members;
2. Requirements for "initial" payments for emergency services, non-emergency services provided by nonparticipating providers at certain participating health care facilities and nonparticipating providers of air ambulance services;
3. Establishment of an IDR process that allows health plans and non-participating providers to resolve disputes over out-of-network rates;
4. Prohibitions on balance billing for certain items and services;
5. Requirements related to disclosures about balance billing protections.

Qualifying Payment Amount

Central to the cost-sharing provisions are the "recognized amount" and the "qualifying payment amount" (QPA). A member's cost-sharing obligation is based on the recognized amount, which is defined as the amount required under any applicable state law, the amount established through an all-payer rate setting model (which applies in the State of Maryland) or the QPA. In other words, the QPA is used for determining patient cost-sharing unless another state law or policy applies.

The QPA is defined as the median of a health plan's contracted rates on January 31, 2019, "for the same or similar item or service that is provided by a provider in the same or similar specialty and provided in a geographic region in which the item or service is furnished, increased for inflation." Health plans must calculate QPAs for each "market," which is defined as individual, small group, or large group, and each contract rate is treated as a separate amount regardless of the service volume billed by each contracted provider.[25]

25 Requirements Related to Surprise Billing: A Rule by the Internal Revenue Service, the Employee Benefits Security Administration, and the Health and Human Services Department, 87 Fed.

C. Network Adequacy

This chapter has described how payers enter into contracts with providers to participate in their networks and provide services to their members. Some types of plans are required to ensure that their networks meet regulatory requirements. Specifically, "network adequacy" is defined as "a health plan's ability to deliver the benefits promised by providing reasonable access to enough in-network primary care and specialty physicians, and all health care services included under the terms of the contract."[26] The ACA specifically requires that health plans purchased on either the federal healthcare.gov exchange or state exchanges meet certain network adequacy requirements. CMS regulates network adequacy for these plans.[27]

Network adequacy regulation can involve different types of quantitative standards as well as other oversight activities. Examples of quantitative standards include:

1. Time/distance standards, which are used to assess whether participating or in-network providers are geographically accessible to plan members.
2. Minimum provider-to-member ratios, which vary across different types of plans and states. For example, Medicare Advantage networks in metropolitan areas must maintain certain ratios, while exchange plans do not currently have ratio requirements.
3. Appointment wait-times, which sets a maximum wait time for certain types of services. Although CMS has proposed to use this standard for certain types of outpatient appointments for exchange plans, as of this writing, they are not in effect.
4. "Essential community providers," which means that exchange plans are required to contract with a minimum number of available essential community providers (ECP) in their service area. These include community health centers and other providers that serve mostly low-income and medically underserved individuals.
5. Other standards that have yet to be implemented include telehealth availability, as well as standards related to cultural and linguistic competency of network providers.[28]

Exchange plans must also conduct an annual survey of member experiences and report the data to CMS. The survey includes questions about timely access to

---

Reg. 52619 (August 26, 2022), www.federalregister.gov/documents/2022/08/26/2022-18202/requirements-related-to-surprise-billing.

26 "Network Adequacy," National Association of Insurance Commissioners (NAIC), Center for Insurance Policy and Research, Updated July 6, 2022, https://content.naic.org/cipr-topics/network-adequacy.

27 CMS also regulates network adequacy for Medicare Advantage plans.

28 Karen Pollitz, "Network Adequacy Standards and Enforcement," Kaiser Family Foundation, February 4, 2022, www.kff.org/health-reform/issue-brief/network-adequacy-standards-and-enforcement/.

services, patient/provider communication, and the quality of providers. These results are used to establish the "star ratings" for exchange plans that can be found on the healthcare.gov website.[29]

Regulators evaluate network adequacy using health plans' provider directory data. Studies have shown that these directories often contain errors, however, and new rules for ACA plans have been implemented in recent years requiring them to update directories at least monthly.

The National Association of Insurance Commissioners (NAIC) has also published guidance regarding "narrow networks." Health insurers may offer plan options that use narrow networks, which have smaller numbers of physicians, hospitals and other providers and may be located in a limited geographic area. Providers who participate in narrow networks agree to lower reimbursement rates in exchange for potentially higher patient volume. Savings realized by the health plan from lower reimbursement rates are then typically passed on to the member in the form of lower premiums. The NAIC became concerned that networks could become so narrow that some health plan members could have very limited provider options and published its Health Benefit Plan Network Access and Adequacy Model Act in 2015. The model provides guidance to health plans, as well as federal and state regulators, on creating and maintaining adequate provider networks.[30]

V. CONCLUSION

This chapter has provided an overview of various types of commercial health insurance markets, types of health plans and their use of provider networks, as well as out-of-network arrangements and the implications for members that use out-of-network providers. In Chapter 4, we cover how commercial payers set reimbursement rates and the data sources they may use to do so.

---

29 Karen Pollitz, "Network Adequacy Standards and Enforcement," Kaiser Family Foundation, February 4, 2022, www.kff.org/health-reform/issue-brief/network-adequacy-standards-and-enforcement/.

30 "Network Adequacy," National Association of Insurance Commissioners (NAIC), Center for Insurance Policy and Research, Updated July 6, 2022, https://content.naic.org/cipr-topics/network-adequacy.

CHAPTER 4

Commercial Payer Contracting and Reimbursement

JoAnna Younts

I. OVERVIEW

As described in Chapter 3, payers and providers enter into contracts regarding the services that providers will render to a payer's members and the reimbursement rates that a payer will pay to a provider in return. In some cases, commercial payers use the same or similar reimbursement approaches or methodologies that the Medicare program uses (see Chapters 1 and 2) while in other cases they diverge from Medicare. In this chapter, we will explore the methods that commercial payers use to reimburse providers, and how they may or may not align with Medicare approaches. We also will explore other important aspects of payer-provider contracts, as well as reimbursement approaches that payers use as an alternative to fee-for-service payment. As part this chapter, we have also provided a special reference section that describes selected data sources that commercial payers (and providers) may use for benchmarking, rate setting and in disputes and investigations.

II. COMMERCIAL PAYER ALIGNMENT OR DIVERGENCE FROM MEDICARE REIMBURSEMENT APPROACHES

Some commercial payers align some or all of their reimbursement methodologies with Medicare's. This is known as Medicare "reference pricing." Other plans only base their reimbursement on Medicare approaches for certain types of providers or services, and others may diverge from Medicare approaches entirely.

Some of the reasons commercial insurers use Medicare approaches are:

1. Many of the Medicare program's reimbursement methodologies have undergone rigorous development, testing and refinement by academics and other researchers. Methodologies such as DRGs, which have been in place for nearly 40 years, are evaluated and updated every year. In fact,

the amendment to the Social Security Act, which established the DRG payment system in 1983, requires that CMS adjust the DRG classifications and relative weights at least annually to ensure that treatment patterns, technology and other factors that may change the relative use of hospital resources are accounted for appropriately.[1] Commercial payers that either the components of the DRG system or tie their rates to Medicare rates can be assured that these adjustments are made and, thus, need not establish their own evaluation and review programs, which can be administratively complex and costly.

2. Medicare's reimbursement approaches are designed to reflect the underlying costs or resources required to deliver medical services. In fact, Medicare payments are intended to cover the costs of relatively efficient providers.[2] In the development of the Outpatient Prospective Payment System (OPPS), for example, the Health Care Financing Administration (now CMS) hired contractors to collect data on the costs of outpatient services at a wide variety of institutions across the U.S. in order to establish the relative weights that would be used in the Ambulatory Payment Classifications (APCs). For this reason, commercial payers may consider Medicare rates to be a proxy for provider costs and thus, a useful comparator when evaluating their own reimbursement rates.
3. By adopting Medicare's reimbursement methodologies, commercial payers can save time, effort and costs of developing their own approaches. Although commercial payers often do diverge from Medicare's approaches (as described later in this chapter), doing so may result in additional administrative complexity. For example, some payers may negotiate individual dollar amounts for each type of inpatient hospital service with a contracted hospital, as well as specific requirements regarding how many days will be allowed under that rate and provisions for longer stays. While this type of approach may be best suited for some payer-provider relationships (and some hospitals may demand this level of complexity in order to be willing to contract with a payer), it adds administrative complexity for the payer in terms of maintaining and updating the rates and in processing claims. It also adds administrative complexity for the hospital, which must maintain and update the rates in its billing and accounting systems.
4. In addition to relatively less administrative complexity, adoption of Medicare reimbursement methodologies may also mean fewer technical or claims processing adjustments. Commercial payers typically have "claims

1 "MS-DRG Classifications and Software." Centers for Medicare and Medicaid Services, www.cms.gov/Medicare/Medicare-Fee-for-Service-Payment/AcuteInpatientPPS/MS-DRG-Classifications-and-Software.

2 Medicare Payment Advisory Commission, "Report to the Congress: Medicare Payment Policy" (March 2021): 39. www.medpac.gov/wp-content/uploads/2021/10/mar21_medpac_report_ch2_sec.pdf.

configuration" teams or departments that are responsible for the software and programming that ensures that claims are paid according to the appropriate methodology and at the rates specified in payer-provider contracts. Some Medicare-based approaches may be less complex to program and maintain, as opposed to customized fee schedules or other rate setting formulas. In addition, commercial payers that also have Medicare Advantage lines of business may be able to adopt some or all of their claims configuration capabilities for their commercial lines of business without substantial additional investment in terms of staffing and systems.

5. Finally, some commercial payers may adopt Medicare approaches to reimbursement because most providers are already familiar with them and have their revenue cycle systems configured for them. For example, most hospitals have been reimbursed by Medicare using DRGs for nearly four decades and typically do not require additional education, training or system programming to implement a DRG-based reimbursement contract with a commercial payer.

Despite some advantages of adopting Medicare's approaches, commercial payers also diverge from Medicare's way of doing things. First, commercial payers' member populations are typically different from the Medicare population in terms of their demographics. The Medicare population is older by definition because individuals must be age 65 and older to enroll in Medicare. In contrast, commercial payers enroll members of all ages, including children. Older people tend to need and use more healthcare services, and they use a different mix of services, including more inpatient hospital care and prescription drugs, than younger people. In fact, people age 65 and older account for over one-third of healthcare spending even though they make up less than 20 percent of the population. In 2019, people age 65 and older had average annual healthcare costs of $13,051 compared to $3,834 for people age 18 to 34 and $5,163 for people age 35 to 44.[3] Because of the differences in the utilization of healthcare services between commercial payer member populations and the Medicare population, commercial plans may instead reimburse providers according to their own approaches. Commercial payers may also enter into different types of risk-based arrangements with providers than the Medicare program's Alternative Payment Models (APMs)—see Section III of this chapter which describes these.

There are also differences in service utilization between commercial and Medicare populations, resulting in commercial plans not adopting Medicare's reimbursement approaches. For example, Medicare enrollees tend to utilize home health

3 Jared Ortaliza, Matthew McGough, Emma Wager Twitter, Gary Claxton, and Krutika Amin, "How do health expenditures vary across the population?" *Peterson-KFF Health System Tracker* (November 12, 2021), www.healthsystemtracker.org/chart-collection/health-expenditures-vary-across-population/#Average%20adult%20out-of-pocket%20health%20spending%20based%20on%20diagnosis%20status,%202019%C2%A0.

and skilled nursing facility services at higher rates than commercial enrollees. As described in Chapter 2, Medicare uses relatively complex prospective payment systems for both home health and skilled nursing services. However, commercial payers may see no need to adopt complex payment systems for these services if the volume of the services used by their membership is relatively low.

Even for services for which commercial payers have high utilization, such as outpatient hospital services, commercial payers may opt not to utilize certain Medicare reimbursement approaches because of their complexity and need to invest in specific claims processing software and staff to administer them. This is true of the Medicare outpatient hospital APC reimbursement system, which has not seen widespread adoption among commercial payers.

Finally, Medicare's collection of reimbursement methodologies and payment systems also must adhere to regulatory requirements to implement specific Medicare policies and budget constraints established by Congress and CMS. For example, the federal government provides for reimbursement to hospitals for indigent patients, graduate medical education and other programs and services either directly or indirectly through its reimbursement systems. Commercial payers are not required to adhere to the same requirements and may choose not to adopt Medicare approaches that have these additional payments incorporated into them.

A. Reimbursement Approaches Used by Commercial Payers

There are some Medicare approaches that have been commonly adopted by commercial payers and others that are almost never used. These are described by provider type below.

1. Inpatient Hospital Services

Of all of the Medicare reimbursement approaches available for use by commercial payers, Medicare's inpatient hospital reimbursement methodology, or at least components of it, is among the most commonly adopted by commercial payers. The components and adaptations are described below. For a refresher on Medicare's inpatient hospital reimbursement methodology, see Chapter 1.

Medicare Base Rate and MS-DRG Weights: Some commercial payers use Medicare grouping or pricing algorithms used by CMS to establish the DRG assignments. In some cases, commercial payers apply the MS-DRG weights to an individual hospital's Medicare base rate in the same way that CMS would in paying claims. Plans that do this may apply a multiplier to the Medicare rate, which then becomes the commercial payer's contract rate with a particular hospital.

Adjusted Medicare Base Rate/MS-DRG Weights: In some cases, payers apply a hospital's Medicare base rate to the MS-DRG weights but may exclude certain components of the base rate that the payer considers to be specific to the Medicare program. These components include Indirect Medical Education and Disproportionate Share, as well as readmission and value-based payment adjustments and others. These adjustments are described in Chapter 1.

Custom Base Rate/MS-DRG Weights: In some cases, commercial payers adopt the MS-DRG weights but establish a contracted base rate with a provider that is not tied in any way to the hospital's Medicare base rate. Some commercial payers also develop their own DRG weights in order to reflect the resource use of their populations. For example, commercial plans may develop weights for labor and delivery DRGs because they have claims experience showing different resource consumption for those services than the Medicare population, which, due to the age requirements, has comparatively little claims experience.

In most of the above situations, payers purchase special software that must be incorporated into their claims processing systems. This software, which can be purchased from third party vendors, uses ICD-10 diagnosis and procedure codes, as well as other patient characteristics in order to assign appropriate MS-DRGs to each claim. These algorithms are described in more detail in Chapter 1.

Some commercial payers also use All Patient Refined (APR) DRGs, although this is less common. APR-DRGs are most commonly used by state Medicaid programs, and all payers in the State of Maryland use APR-DRGs as well. See the sidebar below that describes Maryland's unique hospital reimbursement system.

Hospital Reimbursement in Maryland

In the State of Maryland, hospital rates for all payers (including Medicare, Medicaid and commercial payers) are established by the Health Services Cost Review Commission (HSCRC) and are exempt from federal Medicare and Medicaid reimbursement rules. The HSCRC is an independent State agency established in 1971. While New York, New Jersey, Massachusetts, Connecticut, Washington and West Virginia also once had rate setting commissions, Maryland remains the only state to retain its system. HSCRC's rates apply to most hospitals in the state (as of this writing, there are 47 short-term acute care hospitals, three specialty hospitals, and three private psychiatric hospitals in the State) for on-campus inpatient, outpatient and emergency services. Rates established by the HSCRC are hospital-specific and service-specific based on total costs and revenues for each institution. The HSCRC performs extensive data collection and analysis of all hospital operations in order to establish rates for each hospital and service that are the same for Medicare, Medicaid and commercial payers. The HSCRC does not regulate physician fees.

In 2014, Maryland was granted a waiver by CMS to establish an all-payer model based on hospital global budgets. Under the Global Budget Revenue (GBR) methodology, the HSCRC establishes prospective fixed annual revenue caps for each hospital. Annual revenue is determined using historical base period and is adjusted to account for changes in population, inflation, payer mix and other things.[4]

4 "HSCRC Overview," Health Services Cost Review Commission, https://hscrc.maryland.gov/Pages/default.aspx.

Commercial payers may also employ other reimbursement methods for hospital services. Typically, these are:

- Per diem rates
- Case rates
- Percentage of billed charges

Per diem reimbursement rates are rates established for each day that a patient spends in the hospital. Per diem rates are commonly used for maternity cases (vaginal and C-section deliveries), intensive care unit (ICU) services, neonatal intensive care unit (NICU) services and psychiatric cases. Historically, there was concern about the applicability of the MS-DRG weights for certain categories of patients for which the Medicare program had little claims experience, such as newborns. Researchers from a number of organizations conducted studies of resource use in these populations that led to adjustments in the MS-DRG weights.[5] Nevertheless, many commercial payers employ per diem rates or case rates for special populations.

Case rates are similar to DRG-based reimbursement rates in the sense that they are predetermined fixed fees for a specific type of inpatient stay. Sometimes case rates have no length of stay limit and in other cases, the case rate applies to stays of a certain length, and a per diem rate is paid to the hospital for each day beyond the negotiated length of stay if it is deemed to be "medically necessary."[6] Case rates are often negotiated for inpatient admissions for organ transplants, for example.

In some cases, commercial payers agree to reimburse a percentage of a hospital's billed charges for some or all services, although this approach has become less common as payers have sought greater predictability of their medical costs. Hospital contracts with rental or wrap networks may contain percentage of charges reimbursement arrangements. See Chapter 3 for an explanation of rental and wrap networks.

2. *Outpatient Hospital Services*

Although the Medicare program has used Ambulatory Payment Classifications (APC) for outpatient hospital reimbursement since 2000, the approach has not seen widespread adoption among commercial payers. It isn't clear exactly why commercial payers have chosen to diverge from Medicare on outpatient hospital

5 See for example, research sponsored by the National Association of Children's Hospitals and Related Institutions (NACHRI). Rachel M. Schwartz, Thomas Michelman, John Pezzullo, and Ciaran S. Phibbs, "Explaining resource consumption among non-normal neonates," Health Care Financing Review Vol. 13 No. 2 (Winter 1991), www.ncbi.nlm.nih.gov/pmc/articles/PMC4193221/.

6 Medically necessary services are defined as, "[h]ealth care services or supplies needed to diagnose or treat an illness, injury, condition, disease or its symptoms and that meet accepted standards of medicine." Medical necessity must be determined by a physician. www.healthcare.gov.

reimbursement, but some have cited the need for specialized software, while others have pointed to hospital resistance. Nevertheless, commercial plans tend to employ case rates and fee schedules most often when contracting for outpatient services, rather than using the APC approach, particularly for cardiac catheterization and interventions, as well as outpatient emergency room visits. Fee schedules that contain rates for each CPT or HCPCS code that can be billed on an outpatient basis are also widely employed.

3. *Physician Services*

Commercial payers frequently base their reimbursement rates for physician services on the Resource Based Relative Value Scale (RBRVS), which is used in the Medicare Physician Fee Schedule (MPFS). Sometimes a multiple of the Medicare rate contained in the MPFS is applied. Other plans have developed proprietary fee schedules that may not be based on Medicare rates but instead are based on their historical claims experience use the underlying relative value units (RVUs) for each service that are found in the RBRVS schedule (see Chapter 2 for information on RVUs and the RBRVS).

In some cases, commercial payers establish fee schedules based on Medicare rates for a specific year and then update the fees periodically using an inflation factor rather than updating the underlying Medicare rates. This is usually because it can be difficult to keep Medicare rates current in claims processing systems as codes may be added or deleted during the year, and Medicare also makes adjustments to the rates for some codes on a quarterly basis. Commercial payers who choose to establish their fee schedules based on a fixed Medicare year may need to "rebase" the fee schedule at some future point in time. In other words, the fee schedule must be re-aligned with a more current Medicare fee schedule. This rebasing then can incorporate changes to the code sets, as well as the RVUs, which reflect new information about the resources required to deliver each service. If a plan does not rebase its fee schedule on a regular basis, especially changes to code sets, the rates may no longer accurately reflect the underlying costs or resources required to provide the services.

Some physician services may also be reimbursed a percentage of billed charges. In more recent years, some commercial payers have adopted reimbursement approaches for physicians to encourage higher quality care and management of chronically ill or other high-cost populations. These types of arrangements include bonus payments for meeting and/or reporting certain quality metrics, as well as risk-based arrangements. These types of arrangements are described in more detail in Section IV of this chapter.

4. *Laboratory Services*

Laboratory services is an area where commercial payers often pay based on the Medicare Clinical Laboratory Fee Schedule. The Protecting Access to Medicare Act (PAMA) was passed in 2014, which resulted in a complete restructuring of the Medicare Clinical Laboratory Fee Schedule. Under PAMA, designated laboratories must periodically report to CMS certain commercial payer rate information, which is used to update the Medicare Clinical Laboratory Fee Schedule. Prior to PAMA, Medicare often paid significantly more than private payers for many lab tests. The new payment system implemented under PAMA more closely aligns Medicare payment rates with commercial payer rates.[7] This has resulted in substantial reductions in Medicare rates for some laboratory tests since 2018.[8]

5. *Other Provider Types and Services*

As we learned in Chapter 2, skilled nursing facilities (SNF) as well as home health agencies are reimbursed by Medicare using relatively complex prospective payment systems. In addition, long-term care facilities obtain most of their revenue from Medicare and Medicaid. Thirty percent of U.S. expenditures on long-term care facilities are attributable to Medicaid, followed by Medicare (22 percent) and commercial insurance (9 percent). The same pattern holds true for home health providers. Thirty-seven percent of U.S. expenditures on home health services is attributable to Medicare patients, 34 percent from Medicaid patients and only 13 percent from patients with commercial insurance.[9] It is important to understand that Medicare only reimburses for SNF services if certain requirements are met, which include having an inpatient hospital stay beforehand. Medicare also does not cover custodial or nursing home care.[10] Commercial payers also have specific criteria that must be met in order for SNF services to be covered[11] and also do not cover custodial care. Thus, some commercial payers have not adopted the Medicare approaches for these types of providers because the approaches are administratively complex and commercial payers typically do not have a large volume of claims.

7 Medicare and Medicaid Programs: CY 2020 Hospital Outpatient PPS Policy Changes and Payment Rates and Ambulatory Surgical Center Payment System Policy Changes and Payment Rates. Price Transparency Requirements for Hospitals to Make Standard Charges Public, 84 FR 65524 (November 27, 2019), www.federalregister.gov/documents/2016/06/23/2016-14531/medicare-program-medicare-clinical-diagnostic-laboratory-tests-payment-system.

8 U.S. Department of Health and Human Services, Office of Inspector General, "Data Brief: Despite Savings on Many Lab Tests in 2019, Total Medicare Spending Increased Slightly Because of Increased Utilization for Certain High-Priced Tests," OEI-09–20–00450 (December 2020) https://oig.hhs.gov/oei/reports/OEI-09-20-00450.pdf.

9 "National Health Expenditure Data," Centers for Medicare and Medicaid Services, www.cms.gov/research-statistics-data-and-systems/statistics-trends-and-reports/nationalhealthexpenddata/nationalhealthaccountshistorical.

10 Medicare Payment Advisory Commission (MedPAC), "Skilled Nursing Facility Services Payment System," (November 2021), www.medpac.gov/wp-content/uploads/2021/11/medpac_payment_basics_21_snf_final_sec.pdf.

11 See for example, Blue Cross Blue Shield of North Carolina's policy regarding coverage of SNF services. Blue Cross Blue Shield of North Carolina, "Corporate Medical Policy: Skilled Nursing Facility Care," (February 2023), www.bluecrossnc.com/sites/default/files/document/attachment/services/public/pdfs/medicalpolicy/skilled_nursing_facility_care.pdf

Commercial payers may reimburse SNFs based on per diem rates. Historically, commercial payers established rates for specific levels of care based on the revenue codes corresponding to the service requirements of the patient. See Codes Sets on pages 17 and 18 for information about revenue codes. Revenue codes for skilled nursing services are as follows:

- Revenue code 191: Level I skilled nursing care
- Revenue code 192: Level II skilled nursing care
- Revenue code 193: Level III skilled nursing care
- Revenue code 194: Level IV skilled nursing care

Some payers use Medicare's reimbursement algorithms, also called "pricer" software, to reimburse SNFs and home health providers.

A Note about Medicare "Pricers"

CMS maintains web-based tools that can be used as a reference when providers, payers, researchers and others are interested in understanding how much Medicare would reimburse for a certain service. There are pricers for end-stage renal disease (dialysis facilities), home health providers, hospice providers, inpatient short-term acute care hospitals, inpatient psychiatric facilities, inpatient rehabilitation facilities, long-term care hospitals and skilled nursing facilities.[12]

Commercial payers who use the Medicare pricing algorithms may choose to reimburse the Medicare rate or some multiple of the Medicare rate.

Physician-administered drugs is another area where commercial payers sometimes diverge from the way Medicare reimburses. While Medicare (under Part B) reimburses based on Average Sales Price (see Chapter 2), commercial payers tend to use a combination of approaches. Some use ASP, while others may use Average Wholesale Price (AWP) or Wholesale Average Cost (WAC) or some combination of these. See Chapter 2 for an explanation of these drug pricing methodologies.

III. OTHER IMPORTANT COMMERCIAL CONTRACTING AND REIMBURSEMENT ISSUES

Commercial payer contracts also contain other reimbursement provisions in addition to the rate provisions. Some key components are:

- Outliers/Stop Loss
- Chargemaster Provisions and "Lesser of" clauses

12 "Web Pricers," Centers for Medicare and Medicaid Services, www.cms.gov/WebPricer.

A. Outliers/Stop Loss

Chapter 1 described the Medicare approach to reimbursement of extraordinarily high-cost cases (i.e., hospital admissions or outpatient visits) using an outlier formula. Commercial payers historically have not followed Medicare's approach regarding high-cost cases and outlier formula. In addition, while the Medicare program typically refers to high-cost cases "outliers," hospitals and commercial payers typically use the term "stop loss." For purposes of this discussion, we will use the term stop loss. The primary components of a stop loss provision within a hospital-payer contract are the stop loss threshold and the stop loss formula.

1. Stop Loss Threshold

A stop loss threshold is the point at which a case is defined as high cost. Similar to stop loss insurance, which provides protection against catastrophic or unpredictable losses for an employer, a stop loss provision for hospital services provides protection for a hospital against catastrophic or extraordinarily costly cases. Generally, stop loss thresholds are dollar amounts or a certain number of inpatient days. Under a dollar threshold approach, a hospital and payer agree to a specific level of billed charges that will trigger the stop loss formula. In other words, if the billed charges for a case exceed the agreed-upon threshold, the case is flagged as an outlier in the payer's claims adjudication system (see Chapter 7, Section V, for more information on claims adjudication) and reimbursed according to an established stop loss formula (rather than reimbursed according to the approach used when the stop loss formula is not triggered). Some contracts have a single dollar threshold that applies to all types of inpatient cases, while others have different thresholds for different types of cases, such as trauma cases, cardiac cases, ICU and others. Still others may employ a DRG-specific threshold whereby the stop loss threshold varies depending on the DRG to which the patient is assigned. Hospitals and payers may determine thresholds using a variety of methods based on historical cost or charge trends.

As an example, for an inpatient case where the hospital charges are $200,000 and the stop loss threshold is $150,000, the stop loss formula would be triggered, and the case would be reimbursed according to the stop loss formula that has been agreed upon in the contract.

Stop loss thresholds are more commonly used for inpatient services, but some hospital-payer contracts may include stop loss thresholds for outpatient services such as cardiac or orthopedic procedures.

Another type of stop loss threshold approach uses the number of days a patient stays in the hospital to trigger the stop loss formula instead of the amount of the billed charges. The average length of inpatient hospital stays in the U.S. decreased dramatically from 7.3 days in 1980 to 5.4 days in 1995,[13] largely

13 Centers for Disease Control and Prevention, National Center for Health Statistics, "National Hospital Discharge Survey: Annual Summary," Series 13, Number 133 (1995).

as a result of the implementation of DRG-based reimbursement by the Medicare program.[14] The average length of stay for hospital inpatients has leveled off in recent years as more services have shifted to outpatient settings and the average severity of illness among patients who are admitted to hospitals as inpatients has risen. Similar to the establishment of dollar thresholds, length of stay thresholds are typically established using statistical methods or claims experience.

For example, if the claims experience shows an average length of stay of five days, with a standard deviation of four days, the threshold may be set at 13 days, which would be two deviations from the mean. Thus, a case with a length of stay of 15 days would trigger the stop loss formula. Similar to dollar thresholds, some contracts provide for a single length of stay stop loss threshold for all lines of business while others identify separate thresholds. Maternity cases typically have different (and shorter) thresholds than other types of cases because most labor and delivery lengths of stay are only one or two days.

2. *Stop Loss Formula*

Once a case has been identified as an outlier based on the stop loss threshold approach used, the case is flagged for reimbursement under the agreed-upon stop loss formula. Although stop loss formulas can be highly variable, formulas are generally classified as either "first dollar" or "second dollar" approaches. Second dollar can also be called "incremental."[15]

Under a first dollar approach, cases identified as outliers are reimbursed a percentage of billed charges for the entire case. In the following example, the billed charges are $200,000, the stop loss threshold is $150,000, and the stop loss formula is triggered, therefore, the case is reimbursed at an agreed-upon percentage of the billed charges for the entire case.

Example:

Billed charges: $200,000
Stop loss threshold: $150,000
First dollar stop loss percentage: 60%
Payment = Stop loss percentage * Billed charges = .60($200,000) = $120,000

Under a second dollar or incremental approach, the hospital is reimbursed some pre-established base amount plus a percentage of charges above the threshold or a

14 Marian Gornick and Margaret Jean Hall, "Trends in Medicare use of post-hospital care," *Health Care Financing Review* (December 1988): 27–38, www.ncbi.nlm.nih.gov/pmc/articles/PMC4195116/.

15 Ryan Gillis and Paul Yun, "Value-Based Payment and Commercial Healthcare Insurers: Getting Paid for Doing What's Right," Healthcare Financial Management Association (October 2, 2017), www.hfma.org/topics/article/56176.html.

per diem rate. The pre-established amount may be equal to either a DRG payment rate, case rate, or the charge threshold amount.

Example:

Billed charges: $200,000
Stop loss threshold: $150,000
Second dollar stop loss percentage: 60%
DRG rate: $75,000

Second dollar stop loss reimbursement

- Option 1: Payment = DRG rate + Stop loss percentage (Billed charges – Stop loss threshold)
  $75,000+ .60($200,000–$150,000) = $75,000 + $30,000 = $105,000
- Option 2: Payment = Stop loss threshold + Stop loss percentage (Billed charges – Stop loss threshold)
  $150,000 + .60($200,000–$150,000) = $150,000 + $30,000 = $180,000

As shown in these examples, the reimbursement for an outlier or stop loss case can vary dramatically depending upon the stop loss threshold formula that is used.

B. Chargemaster Provisions and Lesser of Clauses

Lesser of clauses are present in many payer-provider contracts to protect payers from paying more than the provider charges for a service. Most claims adjudication systems flag cases in which the billed charges are lower than the contracted amount and reimburse the provider at the amount charged.

An explanation of provider billed charges and how they are established can be found in Chapter 6. Because of the variability in the methods used to establish charges and potential variability in the charges themselves, payers and providers typically agree on provisions to protect the payer from unexpected increases in provider charges. While many services are reimbursed without consideration of the billed charges, some services may be reimbursed based on a percentage of charges, and as we have just learned, stop loss provisions are often based on billed charges.

IV. ALTERNATIVE PAYMENT MODELS

While fee-for-service reimbursement continues to be the dominant form of reimbursement for both public and commercial payers, there has been a movement toward alternative models of reimbursement (meaning alternative to fee-for-service). The models are generally designed to provide incentives for providers to alter their behavior in order to deliver services more efficiently. While fee-for-service reimbursement generally rewards providers for providing more services and more expensive services, alternative payment models are designed to reduce unnecessary utilization of services, reduce hospitalizations and unnecessary readmissions, improve quality of care, improve coordination of services and efficiency and ultimately improve the health of patients. Whether certain models actually accomplish their intended goals continues to be debated, but it is likely that these types of initiatives will continue to be pursued as payers and providers seek solutions to better manage the delivery of healthcare services and curb skyrocketing healthcare costs. An overview of some of these models can be found below but is not an exhaustive list of all alternative payment models currently in use.

A. Accountable Care Organizations

Accountable Care Organizations (ACOs) are groups of physicians, hospitals and other types of healthcare providers who come together and contract with payers to deliver care to a certain group of enrollees, such as people with a certain medical condition or people who live in a certain geographic area. The success of this model depends on providers' ability to coordinate services in a cost-effective way while providing high-quality care, avoiding unnecessary duplication of services and preventing medical errors. ACOs that succeed in achieving cost savings while meeting certain agreed-upon quality measures can share the savings with the payer.[16] The Medicare program administers several ACO models and commercial payers also contract with ACOs.

B. Hospital Value-Based Purchasing

Hospital Value-Based Purchasing is a CMS program where Medicare inpatient hospital payments are adjusted based on quality-of-care measures and/or performance improvement. The highest performing hospitals can receive bonus payments, which are added to each MS-DRG payment. Hospitals that do not perform as well receive minimal or no bonus payments.[17] Some commercial payers have also started to experiment with these types of adjustments.

C. Physician Payment Models

As we learned in Chapter 2, the primary mechanism by which the Medicare program reimburses physicians is the Medicare Physician Fee Schedule (MPFS). In addition, as we have learned in this chapter, commercial payers sometimes use the MPFS as the basis for reimbursement rates paid to physicians as well. But several alternative reimbursement models have emerged in recent years.

---

16 "Accountable Care Organizations," Centers for Medicare and Medicaid Services, www.cms.gov/medicare/medicare-fee-for-service-payment/aco.

17 "The Hospital Value Based Purchasing (VBP) Program," Centers for Medicare and Medicaid Services, www.cms.gov/Medicare/Quality-Initiatives-Patient-Assessment-Instruments/Value-Based-Programs/HVBP/Hospital-Value-Based-Purchasing.

In 2015, Congress passed the Medicare Access and CHIP Reauthorization Act (MACRA), which made sweeping changes regarding the methods used by Medicare to calculate the fees paid under the MPFS and other fee schedules. Under MACRA's system called the Quality Payment Program (QPP), participating providers are reimbursed for Medicare patients based on the quality and effectiveness of the care they provide, and providers are assigned to one of two tracks based on the characteristics of their practice:[18]

- Merit-based Incentive Payment System (MIPS): Under MIPS, physicians submit quality and other data to CMS and CMS calculates a performance score based on four categories: quality; "promoting interoperability," which relates to use of electronic health records; improving patient care; and cost. The final MIPS score at the end of the year determines the payment adjustment applied to a physician's Medicare claims.[19]
- Alternative payment models (APM): Physicians can participate in a variety of models, including ACOs and other models that provide for bonus payments for meeting certain quality targets as well as risk-based and shared-savings arrangements. Commercial payers also employ these types of models. For more information on risk-based models, see Chapters 5 and 6.

D. Hospital-Acquired Condition and Hospital Readmission Reduction Programs

Medicare's Hospital-Acquired Condition Reduction Program ties hospital performance on patient safety issues such as infections, bed sores and post-operative blood clots to reimbursement. Each year, CMS penalizes the lowest performing 25 percent of all hospitals by reducing their inpatient payments by 1 percent. CMS also publishes hospitals' performance on these quality measures on its Hospital Compare website.[20] Under the Hospital Readmissions Reduction Program, CMS penalizes hospitals for "excess" readmissions when compared to "expected" levels of readmissions.[21]

---

18 "MACRA," Centers for Medicare and Medicaid Services, www.cms.gov/Medicare/Quality-Initiatives-Patient-Assessment-Instruments/Value-Based-Programs/MACRA-MIPS-and-APMs/MACRA-MIPS-and-APMs.

19 Traditional MIPS Overview," Centers for Medicare and Medicaid Services, https://qpp.cms.gov/mips/traditional-mips.

20 "Hospital-Acquired Condition Reduction Program," Centers for Medicare and Medicaid Services, www.cms.gov/Medicare/Medicare-Fee-for-Service-Payment/AcuteInpatientPPS/HAC-Reduction-Program#:~:text=The%20Hospital%2DAcquired%20Condition%20(HAC,in%20the%20inpatient%20hospital%20setting.

21 "Hospital Readmissions Reduction Program (HRRP)," Centers for Medicare and Medicaid Services, www.cms.gov/Medicare/Medicare-Fee-for-Service-Payment/AcuteInpatientPPS/Readmissions-Reduction-Program.

E. Bundled Payment

A bundled payment is another form of alternative payment model where a provider and payer agree to a predetermined rate, that is, a bundled rate, for a specific set of services or episode of care.[22] Services may be provided by multiple providers such as hospitals and physicians, as well as long-term care providers such as SNFs. When the provider costs are lower than the bundled rate, the providers can share the savings with the payer. If the provider costs are higher, the providers must absorb the loss. Thus, bundled payments are a form of risk-based reimbursement. Bundled payments can be retrospective or prospective. In a retrospective model, providers are reimbursed fee-for-service rates for the bundled services, the fees are tracked against the bundled rate and there is a reconciliation process at the end of the year or agreed-upon period. In a prospective model, the payer pays the bundled rate up front. In this case, one of the providers (typically a hospital) must then pay the other providers who deliver services. These are typically called "downstream" payments.[23]

Bundled payments are commonly used for orthopedic procedures such as joint replacements. Medicare's Comprehensive Care for Joint Replacement Model (CJR) program is a good example of a bundled payment program.[24]

F. Patient-Centered Medical Homes

The patient-centered medical home model is physician practice model that is designed to provide relationship-based comprehensive care, including preventive care as well acute and chronic care services, in coordinated fashion. Typically, the medical home model incorporates teams of providers, including physicians, advanced practice nurses, physician assistants, nurses, pharmacists, nutritionists, social workers, educators and care coordinators. One of the hallmarks of medical homes is the patient-centered focus, which is designed to serve the unique needs, culture and values of individual patients and their families. Like other alternative payment models, the success of a medical home model depends upon the practice's ability to deliver coordinated care, reduce unnecessary utilization and prevent hospitalization, where possible. This often means providing more accessible office hours, such as evening and weekend time slots, telehealth or virtual options and 24/7 telephone and/or email access to providers.[25]

A comprehensive medical home model administered by CMS called Comprehensive Primary Care Plus (CPC+), which encompassed Medicare, Medicaid and

22 An episode of care refers to the entire span of treatment for a patient's specific condition. Commonly defined episodes of care are joint replacement and labor and delivery. The episode encompasses services provided by various provider types including hospitals, physicians, skilled nursing facilities and other providers.

23 "What Are Bundled Payments?" NEJM Catalyst, February 28, 2018, https://catalyst.nejm.org/doi/full/10.1056/CAT.18.0247.

24 "Comprehensive Care for Joint Replacement Model," Centers for Medicare and Medicaid Services, https://innovation.cms.gov/innovation-models/cjr.

25 "Defining the PCMH," Agency for Healthcare Research and Quality, www.ahrq.gov/ncepcr/research/care-coordination/pcmh/define.html.

commercial payers, began in 2016 and ended in 2022. The program offered varying levels of risk, care management fees, advance payments and financial incentives for meeting quality and utilization benchmarks.[26] Some Blue Cross Blue Shield plans and other commercial payers continue to contract with physician practices and other entities as medical homes in exchange for enhanced reimbursement either through bonus payments or shared savings.

V. CONCLUSION

This chapter has provided a look at the ways commercial payers sometimes adopt Medicare reimbursement methodologies, as well as the reasons why they often do not. In addition, we have scratched the surface of the various alternatives to fee-for-service reimbursement that are being employed by both public and commercial health plans. In the next two chapters, we will explore payer-provider contracting operations from both the payer perspective (Chapter 5) and the provider perspective (Chapter 6).

Reimbursement Data Sources Used by Payers and Providers

Commercial health plans often use various sources of data to either establish reimbursement rates or evaluate and modify rates over time. Providers may also use some of the same data sources to establish their billed charge amounts or fees. Researchers, consultants, attorneys and others also use these data sources in various ways, including providing advisory services, publishing peer-reviewed analyses and as evidence in payer-provider disputes.

I. Government Data Sources

Agencies within the U.S. Department of Health and Human Services have become important sources of healthcare data and information. Data collected and analyzed by these federal agencies are used regularly by researchers, consultants, attorneys, payers, providers and others to better understand service utilization and intensity, provider costs and efficiency and reimbursement levels. Federal agencies that are good sources of information include:

- Centers for Disease Control and Prevention (CDC)
- Healthcare Cost and Utilization Project (HCUP)
- Health Resources and Services Administration (HRSA)
- Centers for Medicare and Medicaid Services (CMS)
- Medicare Payment Advisory Commission (MedPAC)

26 "Comprehensive Primary Care Plus," Centers for Medicare and Medicaid Services, https://innovation.cms.gov/innovation-models/comprehensive-primary-care-plus.

In addition, the U.S. General Accountability Office (GAO) and the Office of Inspector General (OIG) within HHS also regularly publish studies on various topics related to healthcare utilization, costs and reimbursement. Data published as a result of recent Transparency in Pricing laws are also described later in this section. These laws require hospitals and health insurers to publish data on their contracted or negotiated reimbursement rates.

CMS is a particularly useful source of data for commercial payers in evaluating and setting reimbursement rates. While Medicare is the largest payer in the U.S., it is also the largest source of publicly available healthcare data, including provider cost information, claims, quality and data. CMS conducts some of its own studies but also provides grant funding and other research funding to academic research institutions, consulting firms and other organizations to conduct research and report findings. In addition, the 65 million beneficiaries currently enrolled in the Medicare program generate large volumes of data when they are treated by healthcare providers who are in turn reimbursed by the federal government.

Medicare sources of data include:

- Reimbursement grouping algorithms and logic to support payment methodologies such as MS-DRGs, APCs and other prospective payment systems.
- Medicare fee schedules and rates, including the Medicare Physician Fee Lookup application[27] and OPPS[28] and ASC addenda[29] containing national payment rates by HCPCS code.
- Medicare claims data[30] encompassing all Medicare beneficiaries and provider types. Many of these files are publicly available with patient identifying information removed.
- Medicare cost reports, which are available through the Healthcare Cost Report and Information System (HCRIS) for hospitals, SNFs, home health agencies, dialysis facilities and other provider types.[31]
- Quality data–CMS began publishing information on hospital performance and quality measures in 2002 through its interactive website called "Hospital Compare." Since then, CMS has enhanced

27 "Physician Fee Lookup Tool," Centers for Medicare and Medicaid Services, www.cms.gov/Medicare/Medicare-Fee-for-Service-Payment/PFSlookup.

28 "Addendum A and Addendum B Updates," Centers for Medicare and Medicaid Services, www.cms.gov/Medicare/Medicare-Fee-for-Service-Payment/HospitalOutpatientPPS/Addendum-A-and-Addendum-B-Updates.

29 "ASC Payment Rates—Addenda," Centers for Medicare and Medicaid Services, www.cms.gov/medicare/medicare-fee-for-service-payment/ascpayment/11_addenda_updates.

30 "Basic Stand Alone (BSA) Medicare Claims Public Use Files (PUFs)," Centers for Medicare and Medicaid Services," www.cms.gov/Research-Statistics-Data-and-Systems/Downloadable-Public-Use-Files/BSAPUFS.

31 "Cost Reports," Centers for Medicare and Medicaid Services, www.cms.gov/research-statistics-data-and-systems/downloadable-public-use-files/cost-reports.

the data it collects, added other provider types and organized the data into a downloadable database called the Provide Data Catalog. The data includes:

- Process of care measures for hospitals and other providers, which are extracted from medical record data;
- Outcome measures such as mortality rates related to specific conditions;
- Hospital readmission data and infection data; and
- Hospital patient experience data, as measured and collected using standardized surveys.[32]

Some states also collect, analyze and publish similar types of data. These include "all-payer claims databases." All-payer claims databases (APCDs) are state-level databases that include medical, pharmacy and dental claims, as well as eligibility and provider files that are submitted by public and private payers. In states that have these databases, payers are required by state mandate to submit data, and the data may contain commercial payer information that can be difficult to obtain from third party vendors or other sources. In addition to hospital data, these databases may also contain data on other provider types such as physicians. As of this writing, more than 30 states currently maintain a database or are developing one, or have a strong interest in developing a database.[33]

II. NON-GOVERNMENT REFERENCE PRICING AND DATA SOURCES

In addition to federal and state data, healthcare providers, payers and others use a variety of third party and proprietary data sources to inform their decision-making. Some of these sources are described below.

A. FAIR Health

FAIR Health collects and aggregates data from health plans across the U.S. and sells the data to providers, payers, researchers and others. The primary products are charge benchmarks and allowed benchmarks. Charge benchmarks are meant to represent prevailing charges that providers bill for specific types of services in a particular geographic area. Allowed

32 "Hospital Quality Initiative Public Reporting: Hospital Care Compare and Public Data Catalog," Centers for Medicare and Medicaid Services, www.cms.gov/medicare/quality-initiatives-patient-assessment-instruments/hospitalqualityinits/hospitalcompare.

33 "All-Payer Claims Databases," Agency for Healthcare Research and Quality, www.ahrq.gov/data/apcd/index.html.

benchmarks are meant to represent prevailing amounts that insurers pay for specific types of services in a particular geographic area.

To derive its charge benchmarks, FAIR Health uses two different methodologies. In the first, called, the "actual methodology," FAIR Health collects the actual billed charges for specific services and arrays them by "geozip"[34] in percentiles from lowest to highest. When data are insufficient for a geozip, FAIR Health uses a "derived methodology" to estimate the benchmarks by applying published relative values.

To derive its allowed benchmarks, FAIR Health does not collect insurers' contracted payment rates and instead applies an approach whereby the ratios of actual allowed amounts to charges for groups of procedure codes are calculated on a national or regional basis and then applied to the actual charges at the geozip level to calculate an allowed amount for each claim line. These calculated allowed amounts are arrayed and percentiles determined to create benchmarks for each code in each geozip, as described above.[35]

Providers can use the charge benchmarks to help them establish the amounts that they charge payers for their services. They can also use the allowed benchmarks to estimate expected revenue based on historical or projected utilization.

Payers can use the charge benchmarks to evaluate prevailing charge levels for certain types of services across different geographic areas and may use the allowed benchmarks to establish fee schedules or other reimbursement rates.

FAIR Health also has a web-based consumer interface, in which users can enter information about a specific procedure or code as well as geographic area and the application provides in-network and out-of-network reimbursement rate estimates.[36]

B. Optum National Fee Analyzer

The Optum National Fee Analyzer uses provider billed charges collected by FAIR Health. Optum repackages these data into charge benchmarks and allowed benchmarks.[37]

C. Physician's Fee Reference

Physician's Fee Reference software compiles information on physician charges across different services. It uses an algorithm to adjust national 75th percentile charges for individual HCPCS and CPT codes for different geographic areas. Geographic areas are identified by zip codes or geozip.

34 A geozip is a geographic area usually defined by the first three digits of U.S. zip codes.

35 FAIR Health, Methodologies, www.fairhealth.org/methodologies.

36 FAIR Health Consumer, www.fairhealthconsumer.org/.

37 "National Fee Analyzer," Optum360, www.optum360.com.

The software is publicly available and is primarily marketed to physicians to assist them in developing their charge schedules or fees.[38]

D. American Hospital Directory

Hospitals, payers and others use the American Hospital Directory (AHD) to identify the billed charges and costs for hospital services. AHD compiles Medicare Cost Report data (see Chapter 1 regarding Medicare Cost Reports) that must be submitted by hospitals to CMS. Data elements include accounting and financial statement information, as well as total billed charges and costs by department, average billed charges and costs per case and per day across different types of services.[39]

E. IBM Watson MarketScan

IBM® MarketScan is a collection of datasets that can be used by providers, payers and researchers. At the core of the datasets is de-identified medical, drug and dental claims data. Claims data contain billed charges, allowed amounts and paid amounts at the service level (inpatient DRG and outpatient HCPCS). The datasets also contain productivity data (workplace absence, short- and long-term disability and workers' compensation), laboratory results and health risk assessments, as well as data contained in electronic medical records (EMR). Data are contributed by large employers, managed care organizations, hospitals, EMR providers, Medicare and Medicaid. According to marketing materials, the databases currently contain data on nearly 40 million people across the U.S.[40]

F. Price Transparency Data

The price transparency movement began in 2018 with federal requirements that hospitals publish their chargemasters on their websites (see Chapter 6 for more about hospital chargemasters). In an effort to improve transparency regarding actual reimbursement rates, CMS published the Hospital Price Transparency Rule, which went into effect on January 1, 2021, and requires hospitals to post a "machine-readable"[41] file on their websites containing charges, discounted cash prices and payer

---

38 "Physician Fee Reference," Wasserman Medical and Dental, www.wasserman-medical.com.

39 American Hospital Directory, www.ahd.com.

40 "IBM MarketScan Research Databases for life sciences researchers," Watson Health, www.ibm.com/downloads/cas/OWZWJ0QO.

41 "Machine-readable file means a digital representation of data or information in a file that can be imported or read by a computer system for further processing without human intervention, while ensuring no semantic meaning is lost," Transparency in coverage—definitions, 29 CFR § 2590.715–2715A1, www.law.cornell.edu/cfr/text/29/2590.715-2715A1.

negotiated rates/prices for all items and services and a consumer-friendly display of the same information for at least 300 "shoppable" services.[42]

The Transparency in Coverage Rule, within the Consolidated Appropriations Act (CAA) of 2021, requires that most health plans, as of July 1, 2022, publish machine-readable files that are updated monthly and contain in-network rates as well as out-of-network allowed amounts. As of January 1, 2023, plans must provide price comparison information for 500 items and services identified by CMS through an internet-based self-service tool, and as of January 1, 2024, the tool must include prescription drug prices as well.[43]

The biggest advantage of the hospital and payer price transparency data over other third-party datasets is that the data is identifiable as opposed to being de-identified, meaning that it is possible to view the actual reimbursement rates that have been negotiated between a specific provider and a specific payer by name. Theoretically, payers and providers could use the data to gain insight regarding the rates that have been negotiated by competitors. For example, payers could evaluate their negotiated rates with specific hospitals compared to their competitor health plans to gauge alignment with their proposed rates and discounts. Providers, in turn, could also use the data to their advantage in negotiating with payers.

Lawmakers' and regulators' stated intent in promulgating the price transparency rules was to provide consumer education, but so far, the data has proved too unwieldy and complex for consumers to use. Further rulemaking and regulation will be required in order to get the data to a point where consumers can use the data to make healthcare decisions.

42 Medicare and Medicaid Programs: CY 2020 Hospital Outpatient PPS Policy Changes and Payment Rates and Ambulatory Surgical Center Payment System Policy Changes and Payment Rates. Price Transparency Requirements for Hospitals to Make Standard Charges Public. 84 Fed. Reg. 65524 (November 27, 2019).

43 "Consolidated Appropriations Act, 2021 (CAA)," Center for Medicare and Medicaid Services, www.cms.gov/cciio/programs-and-initiatives/other-insurance-protections/caa.

CHAPTER 5

Contracting, Reimbursement, and Compliance

Health Plan Perspective

Frank Stevens

I. INTRODUCTION

Health plan contracting and reimbursement is a means to an end—the end being an insurance product where:

- The network is attractive to patients;
- The premium amount is competitive and acceptable to employers and consumers;
- The benefit structure such as copayments, coinsurance and/or deductibles is reasonable and competitive in the mind of purchasers; and
- The health plan realizes a profit.

In offering insurance products that fulfill these requirements, health plans must be compliant with certain legal and regulatory requirements. "Compliance" as an organizational function focuses on both fulfillment of contractual terms, which reduces the risk of litigation, as well as adherence to regulatory requirements, which limits government actions, including imposition of fines, monitorships and state or federal prosecution.

The primary objective of this chapter is to provide the reader with an understanding of the factors that shape health plans' perspectives relative to their contracting, reimbursement and compliance initiatives. As part of that understanding, we will explore business environment factors, including federal and state laws and regulations and particularly the Medicare program as influencers of commercial (non-governmental) health plan perspectives. We will use the term "health plan" and "payer" to refer to an entity that contracts with healthcare providers, develops reimbursement approaches and rates, and has compliance obligations.

Payers include commercial HMOs; health insurance companies that sell benefit plans incorporating PPO, EPO and POS networks; self-funded employers and union trusts;[1] and third party administrators (TPAs), as well as Medicare Advantage plans and Medicaid managed care plans. In addition, payers can also be hospitals and physicians if they accept capitation or other risk-based reimbursement, perform network management, set reimbursement rates and assume certain compliance responsibilities. These types of provider-based payer organizations and their contracting, reimbursement and compliance perspectives will be discussed later in this chapter.

II. HISTORY OF HEALTH INSURANCE AND KEY MILESTONES

During the last century or so, societal events and cultural changes have influenced the financing and delivery of health care across the U.S., including the creation of public and private health insurance as we know it today. As we learned in Chapter 1, before the creation of health insurance, patients paid physicians, hospitals and other providers out-of-pocket. But the Great Depression in the early 20th century resulted in mass unemployment, which had a significant impact on hospitals and physicians because patients had little money to pay for healthcare.[2]

In Dallas, Texas, for example, Baylor Hospital saw its revenue per patient decrease by 75 percent in just one year from 1929 to 1930. In response, Baylor's administrator devised a program where a patient could pay 50 cents per month and receive 21 days of hospital care,[3] an approach that quickly spread to other hospitals.

In 1932, a similar plan was established in Sacramento, California, where patients could pay a fixed amount for what was termed an "indemnity insurance" product[4] administered by a local hospital. But unlike the Baylor approach, benefits under this plan were paid to a patient and the patient, in turn, could receive healthcare services at *any* hospital in the community.

As these hospital insurance plans expanded, the American Hospital Association (AHA) established a committee to approve them. In order to be approved, plans had to be not-for-profit, be designed to improve public welfare, have dignified

1 Unions bargain for healthcare benefits for their members and in some arrangements with employers assume the responsibility for administering health care benefits by receiving funds from the employer, which the Union holds in a Trust for payment of member claims. Martha Hostetter and Sarah Klein, "In Focus: How Unions Act as a Force for Change in Health care Delivery and Payment," The Commonwealth Fund, March 21, 2019, www.commonwealthfund.org/publications/2019/mar/focus-how-unions-act-force-change-health-care-delivery-and-payment#:~:text=Unionized%20workers%20typically%20bargain%20for,deciding%20on%20their%20health%20benefits.

2 Michael A. Morrisey, Ph.D., *History of Health Insurance* (American College of Healthcare Executives, 2013), 1–8.

3 Michael A. Morrisey, Ph.D., *History of Health Insurance* (American College of Healthcare Executives, 2013), 6.

4 The original indemnity benefit plans covered hospital services or physician services only. There were no contracts with providers and payments were made to the patient.

promotion, cover hospital charges only and allow for free choice of physicians.[5] In 1937, the AHA added the criterion that there could be no competition between plans, giving geographic exclusivity to approved plans. The AHA then created the Blue Cross Service Commission in 1946, which became known as Blue Cross.[6] The geographic exclusivity criterion is the reason why most states have just one Blue Cross plan.

Physicians faced the same dilemma with patients who could not afford care and thus developed a similar solution by creating a health insurance plan that paid benefits for physician services. The first plan was established in 1939 by the California Physicians Service. These plans had two key criteria: patients had to have free choice of physicians and the plans had to be indemnity rather than service plans.[7] Under an indemnity plan, the insurer paid the patient a fixed dollar amount for each covered service and the patient, in turn, was responsible for paying the physician. This physician health insurance program became known as Blue Shield.[8]

Blue Cross and Blue Shield officially joined together in 1982 when the Blue Cross and Blue Shield Association was formed by the merger of the Blue Cross Association and the National Association of Blue Shield Plans.[9] Today, Blue Cross Blue Shield is one of the most recognized names in the healthcare industry and these plans cover an estimated 111 million Americans.[10] While commercial insurance had long existed for life, casualty and maritime lines of business, it was not until the advent of hospital service plans like Blue Cross and physician plans like Blue Shield that other commercial insurance organizations began offering health coverage as well.

"Managed care" can be traced back to at least 1929, when a physician in Oklahoma founded a healthcare cooperative for farmers. The community had no physician specialists or hospital, so the physician raised money to build a hospital by selling membership shares and established a fee schedule for medical services.

Around the same time, two physicians in Los Angeles entered into a prepaid contract to provide comprehensive health services to the employees of a local water company. Several prepaid group practice plans like this were founded between

---

5 D.M. MacIntyre, *Voluntary Health Insurance and Rate Making* (Cornell University Press, 1962).

6 Michael A. Morrisey, Ph.D., *History of Health Insurance* (American College of Healthcare Executives, 2013), 6–7.

7 Service plans as offered by Baylor offered 21 days of services at the hospital. The indemnity plans provided a payment for covered events to the patient who then was responsible for paying the physician. Michael A. Morrisey, Ph.D., *History of Health Insurance* (American College of Healthcare Executives, 2013), 8.

8 Michael A. Morrisey, Ph.D., *History of Health Insurance* (American College of Healthcare Executives, 2013), 8.

9 "BCBSA History Fact Sheet," Communications Division of the Blue Cross and Blue Shield Association, March 1997, https://digitalcommons.unf.edu/cgi/viewcontent.cgi?article=3089&context=flablue_text.

10 "Blue Facts," Blue Cross BlueShield Association, October 2021, www.bcbs.com/sites/default/files/file-attachments/page/Blue_Facts_Sheet-2021.pdf.

1930 and 1960, some of which would eventually become well known—including the Group Health Association in Washington, DC, Kaiser-Permanente in California, Health Cooperative of Puget Sound in Seattle, and the Health Insurance Plan of Greater New York in New York City.

Today, these types of prepaid arrangements are called health maintenance organizations or HMOs, although the term "health maintenance organization" was not officially created until 1970.[11] In fact, it wasn't until 1973, with the passage of the federal Health Maintenance Organization Act, that there was an official government directive, along with funding to develop alternative forms of health care delivery and financing such as HMOs.[12]

In the mid-20th century, the advent of World War II, the growth of the labor movement and changes in the federal tax code all fostered the growth of employer-sponsored health insurance coverage. But the Employee Retirement Income Security Act (ERISA) was perhaps the most important factor in the growth of employer-sponsored "self-funded" plans.

ERISA was passed by Congress in 1974 and created standards designed to protect private employee pension and health plans from fraud and mismanagement. All private employers that provide health plans to employees have to follow ERISA, except churches and government groups, which is why employer-sponsored plans are often called "ERISA plans."

ERISA does not dictate the exact benefits that have to be provided but it does establish rules for managing health plans, most of which have to do with providing and reporting information. The ERISA legislation also provided for tax incentives to encourage employers to prefund their pension plans by requiring them to contribute to a government-affiliated reinsurance fund called the Pension Benefit Guarantee Corporation (PBGC). The PBGC then provided protection against pension plan defaults.[13]

ERISA was largely responsible for larger employers moving to a self-insured health plan model for their employees.[14] As we learned in Chapter 3, employers are "self-insured" or "self-funded" when they collect premiums from employees who are enrolled in the employer's health plan(s) and then pay employees' (and their dependents') medical claims out of the organization's revenue or a trust fund set up for this purpose.[15] The premium amounts are based on the actual healthcare costs of an employers' population of employees and their dependents.

11 "Appendix B. A Brief History of Managed Care," National Council on Disability, Accessed March 21, 2023, www.ncd.gov/policy/appendix-b-brief-history-managed-care.

12 U.S. Government Accountability Officer, "Implementation of the Health Maintenance Organization Act of 1973," March 3, 1978, www.gao.gov/assets/105122.pdf.

13 "Employee Retirement Income Security Act (ERISA)," U.S. Department of Labor, Accessed March 21, 2023, www.dol.gov/general/topic/retirement/erisa.

14 Michael A. Morrisey, Ph.D., *History of Health Insurance* (American College of Healthcare Executives, 2013), 15.

15 Michael A. Morrisey, Ph.D., *History of Health Insurance* (American College of Healthcare Executives, 2013), 15.

The passage of ERISA also provided large employers a mechanism to address healthcare cost inflation and increasing health insurance premiums that they paid to indemnity insurers who historically had no motivation to change how healthcare was financed and delivered. As we will see later in this chapter, ERISA was a large contributor to the growth of the HMO model because it gave employers the freedom to choose this model as a way to rein in healthcare costs.

The 1980s were somewhat of a renaissance period for health insurance as alternative models such as HMOs took hold. By 1987, indemnity insurance companies had begun aggressive implementation of PPO benefit plans in response to the success of HMOs in the market. The 1980s also saw the expansion of Medicaid coverage for children and pregnant woman as well as expansion of managed care plans for Medicare beneficiaries.[16]

The development of new reimbursement methodologies, particularly non-fee-for-service approaches, also influenced healthcare delivery and financing models. As we learned in Chapter 1, the Health Care Finance Administration (HCFA), precursor to the Centers for Medicare and Medicaid Services (CMS), implemented DRG-based reimbursement for inpatient hospital services in 1983, which provided incentives for hospitals to reduce costs and lengths of stay and resulted in a reduction in costs for the Medicare program. The Medicare Outpatient Prospective Payment System (OPPS) also reduced Medicare costs, at least temporarily. As we learned in Chapter 2, CMS also rolled out a new physician fee schedule for the Medicare program in 1992 which was based on the Resource Based Relative Value Scale (RBRVS) and helped to rein in physician costs to a certain extent.

By the mid-1990s, in some parts of U.S., some providers became early adopters of "capitation" reimbursement for primary care, which created incentives to change the way healthcare was delivered. In contrast to fee-for-service reimbursement, in which a provider receives a payment for each visit or procedure, capitation reimbursement requires the provider to accept risk. Under capitation, a provider receives a monthly fixed fee called a "per member per month" or "PMPM" for a certain group of a health plan's members. The PMPM amount is then considered payment in full for any services rendered by that physician during the month—whether the physician sees the patient multiple times or not at all. Capitation reimbursement in certain markets eventually expanded to include both primary and specialty physicians, as well as "risk pools"[17] that included hospitals and health plans. By the early 2000s, payers in some geographic locations found increasing

16 Michael A. Morrisey, Ph.D., *History of Health Insurance* (American College of Healthcare Executives, 2013), 21–22.

17 A risk pool is typically composed of a percentage of the capitation payment that is withheld from providers until the end of the year. Hannah Nelson, "What are Capitation Reimbursement Models, Key Strategies?" Revcycle Intelligence, February 16, 2021, https://revcycleintelligence.com/news/what-are-capitation-reimbursement-models-key-strategies#:~:text=Often%2C%20payers%20establish%20risk%20pools,reward%20for%20reaching%20quality%20measures.

numbers of physicians and hospitals who were willing to accept capitation or other similar risk-based arrangements as a method of reimbursement.

In 2010, the Affordable Care Act (ACA) created health insurance exchanges (see Chapter 3) as well as an expansion of Medicaid coverage. The insurance exchanges provided new challenges for health plans and insurance companies[18] as well as a new sales channel for their products.

Finally, as we learned in Chapter 3, the Federal No Surprises Act (NSA) was implemented in 2022, which provided some protection for consumers from balance billing for certain out-of-network services. However, the NSA, as well as similar state laws, has so far failed to address the broader out-of-network billing issues that continue to result in litigation.

These milestones represent just a few of the business environment and market changes that influence the administration of commercial health plans today and the perspectives of the organizations that sponsor and/or administer these plans. So while the title of this chapter may suggest to some readers that there is a singular perspective held by all health plans relative to contracting, reimbursement and compliance, there is not. Health plans are not islands unto themselves, and although some consumers may believe that health plans are unconcerned about patients and providers, a longitudinal look at health plan behavior over the last nearly 100 years tells a different story. In fact, there are many factors that influence a health plan's perspectives regarding patients, providers, contracting and reimbursement, which include both internal organizational factors and external factors in the business environment.

III. TRANSITION FROM INDEMNITY INSURANCE TO MANAGED CARE

Indemnity insurance payers, whose product offerings began during the Great Depression, enjoyed enormous financial success and customer acceptance that generally went unchallenged by other types of benefit plans until well into the 1970s. There are several key reasons that indemnity insurance payers were able to dominate the market for so long, including:

- Patients could choose any provider.
- No contractual relationship existed between the payer and providers. Therefore, payment was made in one of two ways: (1) the insurer paid the patient directly and the patient in turn paid the provider or (2) the patient "assigned" the payment to the provider and the insurance company paid the provider directly.

18 Unlike commercial group and Medicare Advantage products, ACA products are sold on the federal health insurance exchange (healthcare.gov) and state exchanges. In some states such as California, the exchange monitors the characteristics of patients who enroll in these plans and redistributes premiums from plans with healthier populations to plans with less healthy populations.

- Compared to managed care PPO and HMO operations today, indemnity payers had extremely low overhead costs because they had none of the functions that are required to support these models such as utilization management teams, provider contracting staff and compliance departments. These functions will be discussed later in this chapter. Indemnity payers also had relatively small member services departments because there was no need for providers to verify insurance coverage since the patient was ultimately responsible for payment rather than the payer.
- There were no provider disputes because there were no contracts between payers and providers.
- There were limited complaints by patients. If dispute arose, they were usually between patients and providers rather than patients and payers.
- Reimbursement rates were based on "usual and customary" rates.

Usual and customary (U&C) was the approach that was historically used by indemnity insurers to establish the reimbursement amounts that were paid to patients for hospital and physician services. As we learned in Chapter 1, this methodology originated with Blue Cross or Blue Shield plans.[19] While an indemnity insurance policy created a contractual relationship between the *patient* and the insurer, the *provider* was a third party and not involved in the contractual relationship. Therefore, the beneficiary of the insurance payment was the patient, and the patient was responsible for paying the provider an amount the provider was willing to accept. Patients could also "assign" the benefits rather than receiving the payment from the insurance company and then paying the provider. "Assignment of benefits" is the process where a patient can authorize the payment for services to be sent by the insurance company directly to a provider.[20]

Each payer had their own methodology for calculating the U&C amount, which meant that reimbursement amounts could vary across payers. This made it difficult for providers to establish an expected level of revenue for each service provided. Health plans kept records of the individual charge amounts billed by providers for each service[21] within a specific geographic area. However, payers did not necessarily *pay* these exact billed charge amounts as submitted and instead used different approaches to determine the reimbursement amounts. As there was no contract with providers and patients understood that their insurance plan paid a certain amount for a service, indemnity insurers had little incentive to evaluate or update their reimbursement rates. This made indemnity insurance products relatively simple and straightforward.

19 George B. Moseley, JD, MBA, "History of Medicine: The U.S. Health Care Non-System," *American Medical Association Journal of Ethics*, Volume 10, Number 5 (May 2008): 324–331, https://journalofethics.ama-assn.org/sites/journalofethics.ama-assn.org/files/2018-06/mhst1-0805.pdf.

20 "Assignment of Benefits (Health Care) Law and Legal Definition," USLegal.com, Accessed March 21, 2023.

21 Services were identified using code sets such as CPT, etc. (these were described in Chapters 1 and 2).

What proved to be the singular Achilles heel for indemnity insurance was the absence of processes to manage the volume of services used by patients and/or ordered by physicians. In the late 1980s and early 1990s, health plan executives often quipped that the most expensive equipment in healthcare was the physician's pen because most of the services received by patients were driven by physician orders—and this became very expensive.

A. The Rise of the Health Maintenance Organization

From the 1960s through the 1980s, health insurance premiums increased dramatically. This upward spiral of healthcare insurance costs became a significant concern among employers, especially during the recession that occurred in the mid-1970s. In 1973, the Health Maintenance Organization (HMO) Act created a federal program to develop alternatives to the traditional forms of health care delivery and financing by assisting and encouraging the establishment and expansion of HMOs.[22] As part of the Act, employers were required to include HMOs in their insurance benefit offerings if they were available in their geographic location.[23]

Healthcare cost increases for employers, coupled with certain business environment factors (such as the passage of ERISA), were key to the growth of the HMO industry, and HMO start-ups began to spring up in metropolitan areas in California, Arizona, Texas and Florida as former indemnity health insurance companies developed HMO lines of business. But HMOs faced significant challenges that would ultimately impact their decisions regarding contracting and reimbursement. First, HMO executives knew that in order to successfully sell their product to employers, the premiums would need to be significantly lower than those for indemnity products. One of the ways to accomplish this was to limit the member's freedom of provider choice by requiring that they choose from a limited list of providers (i.e., a network), and where no benefits would be paid if members chose providers outside the network. HMOs also made themselves more attractive to *employees* by using a benefit design that reduced out-of-pocket expenses.

To achieve the lower premiums and reductions in patient out-of-pocket costs, HMOs had to reduce claims expense, also called medical expense, that is, the amount of money paid to healthcare providers for healthcare services. This could be achieved by controlling three things: (1) volume of services, (2) intensity of care provided and (3) the price paid to providers. However, HMOs faced substantial resistance from the physician community who believed patients should have the freedom to choose their providers and that providers should make the decisions regarding the care of their patients, not an insurance company. Physicians were concerned that in the absence of these, the doctor-patient relationship would deteriorate.

22 U.S. Government Accountability Officer, "Implementation of the Health Maintenance Organization Act of 1973," March 3, 1978, www.gao.gov/assets/105122.pdf.

23 H.R. 7974-Health Maintenance Organization Act, Congress.gov, www.congress.gov/bill/93rd-congress/house-bill/7974.

Some HMO executives recognized that they would not be able to develop an adequate provider network if they only contracted with independent physicians, small groups or even large group practices. Therefore, some HMOs developed what is called a "staff model" physician network where the HMO leased or built office space and hired both primary care and specialty physicians as salaried employees. As this model took shape, hospitals began to grant admitting privileges to physicians employed by or contracted with HMOs.[24] At the same time, hospitals began contracting with HMOs at lower reimbursement rates because the HMOs promised to direct their members to them.

But early HMO startup organizations that used a staff model had relatively high overhead costs. These costs included physician salaries, leases or building costs, as well as additional costs for support functions such as utilization management and customer service. In addition, these organizations needed large marketing and sales teams in order to build their business and gain market share as quickly as possible. The indemnity insurers who competed with HMOs had none of these additional overhead costs. This is why HMO success ultimately depended on investment in utilization management (see the sidebar below) in order to manage service volume and intensity and, in turn, costs.

Ultimately, HMOs were able to operate more cost-effectively than indemnity insurance companies even though they had materially higher administrative costs. The key was the HMOs' ability to successfully manage the volume and intensity of care, as well as achieve significant discounts[25] on the prices of healthcare services. Indemnity insurance companies were not able to do these things because they did not have operational functions such as utilization management, and they did not contract directly with providers. The efficiency of HMO operations translated into lower premiums for employers, lower out-of-pocket costs for employees and a more simplistic benefit design.

What Is Utilization Management?

The Institute of Medicine's (IOM) Committee on Utilization Management defines utilization management as "a set of techniques used by or on behalf of purchasers of health care benefits to manage health care costs by influencing patient care decision-making through case-by-case assessments of the appropriateness of care prior to its provision."[26]

24 As part of this process, hospitals complete a review of each physician's credentials, including education, training and malpractice history.

25 A discount refers to the percentage difference between a provider's billed charge for a service and the negotiated rate with a health plans

26 Bradford H. Gray and Marilyn J. Field, Editors, *Controlling Costs and Changing Patient Care? The Role of Utilization Management* (Institute of Medicine,1989), www.ncbi.nlm.nih.gov/books/NBK235000/.

Utilization management programs apply widely accepted diagnostic criteria to manage referrals to specialists, imaging, specialty lab and surgical procedures to ensure that patients receive appropriate services by the appropriate providers (i.e., primary care versus specialist or one specialist versus another specialist) and in the appropriate setting (inpatient versus outpatient).

Example 1: Sprained Ankle

The utilization management process would evaluate whether the injury should be treated by a primary care physician (i.e., internal medicine, family medicine, general medicine) versus a specialist (i.e., orthopedist). Typically, a review of a sprained ankle would result in a health plan deciding that coverage of the treatment would be approved if provided by a primary care physician.

Example 2: Coronary Artery Bypass Graft (CABG) Surgery as Treatment for Acute Myocardial Infarction (AMI) or Heart Attack

The utilization management process would evaluate the course of treatment for the AMI and likely would result in the plan deciding that the patient would need to be seen by a cardiologist prior to approving a cardiac surgeon to complete a bypass procedure.

B. The Self-Funded Employer Movement

At the same time that HMOs were gaining a foothold in different areas of the country, large and medium size employers were turning to the self-funded model to provide healthcare benefits to their employees. Facing pressure to reduce healthcare costs for their employees, employers saw self-funding as an opportunity to save money. First, they could eliminate the indemnity insurance company profits on premiums and second, they could reduce administrative costs either by administering plans themselves or by contracting with a third party to do so.

The process of self-funding was generally as follows:

> First, the employer would hire an actuary[27] to prepare an estimate of the next year's total medical expenses for employees and their dependents based on the prior year expenses. Next, the employer might issue a Request for Proposal (RFP) or otherwise solicit organizations to administer the plan. The employer would then choose a third party administrator (TPA). See the sidebar on page 95.

27 Actuaries use a health plan's historical health care payments, utilization and other data to calculate premium amounts for each member, which then allows the health plan or self-funded employer to establish a budget for their employees' health care costs.

In the mid-1980s, some large employers chose to not only self-fund their health plans but also self-administer[28] their plans. One early example was the Walt Disney Company in Orlando, Florida, which leveraged its large employee volume to negotiate favorable rates with major hospitals and physicians in the Orlando area.[29] The company used its own staff to administer the organization's health plan and pay providers.

The combination of the growth of HMOs and self-funded employer organizations was a dual threat to the historic market position of the indemnity insurance companies. To combat these threats, indemnity insurance companies would ultimately be forced to join the managed care movement.

Third-Party Administrator (TPA)

A third-party administrator (TPA) is an organization that receives and manages health insurance claims on behalf of an employer. Typically, the TPA not only pays claims on the employer's behalf, but also contracts with the network providers used by employees, administers wellness programs and performs other managed care functions. TPAs also issue health plan ID cards for employees.[30]

The TPA industry grew dramatically after the passage of the Employee Retirement and Income Security Act (ERISA) as employers increasingly sought alternatives to indemnity insurance companies to process claims. Today, very few self-funded employers administer their own benefit programs. Many TPAs lease PPO networks, which are in turn offered to a self-funded organization's employees. Sometimes TPAs also contract with PPO network companies to conduct utilization management.

C. Preferred Provider Organizations

By the mid-1980s, indemnity insurance companies were feeling the impact of HMOs and the self-funded employer movement, the combination of which was creating competition in the health insurance market. Ultimately, indemnity payers realized that they would not be able to compete on price (meaning premiums) and that employers and their employees were willing to accept a smaller network of providers to provide services. Indemnity payers also had no history of contracting with

28 An employer that self-administers its health plan creates their own claims administration department rather than hiring a third-party administrator to pay claims.

29 Walt Disney was the author's client.

30 Christopher Brown, "Health Care Self-Funding and Stop-Loss: Small Employers Balancing Risks and Rewards," Society for Human Resource Management, September 2, 2008, www.shrm.org/resourcesandtools/hr-topics/benefits/pages/healthcareself-fundingandstop-losssmallemployersbalancingrisksandrewards.aspx.

providers, no experience in applying utilization management to patient care and no experience developing fee schedules or reimbursement methodologies.

During this time period, some organizations began to create provider networks that could be used for a hybrid indemnity product known today as a Preferred Provider Organization or PPO plan.[31] Under a PPO plan model, as we learned in Chapter 3, members typically have a higher level of benefits, that is, lower cost sharing, if they use a "preferred provider" in the PPO network and a lower level of benefits (higher cost sharing) if they use a provider outside of the PPO network (out-of-network).

This was the perfect solution for indemnity payers because they could offer cost savings to employers and their employees that were similar to HMOs through reduced premium rates while also giving patients at least some freedom of provider choice. In fact, indemnity insurance companies became dependent upon PPO network organizations because the PPOs furnished provider networks, utilization management services and data analytics capabilities that indemnity insurers historically did not have but that they needed in order to compete.

During this PPO expansion, large self-funded employers, including the Walt Disney Company, General Mills, Coors Brewing and many union trusts converted their indemnity plans to PPO plans. Many indemnity insurers had been providing TPA services to self-funded employers up to this point, and those that had established PPO networks across multiple states gained a competitive advantage when marketing to their self-funded employer clients. PPO benefit plans provided an opportunity for self-funded employers to reduce their annual expense for employee health insurance while providing a hybrid benefit plan that gave their employees a choice of providers. This ultimately improved employee morale and retention and addressed the financial impact of insurance premium costs for self-funded employers.

With both indemnity insurers and self-funded employer plans using PPO networks, PPO managed care organizations that contracted with providers on behalf of the indemnity insurance companies and self-funded employers gained significant negotiating leverage as they built networks and renegotiated provider contracts each year. A key PPO strategy was to contract with highly respected hospitals and their associated physician groups or individual physicians and direct plan members to use the contracted hospitals through utilization management programs and by leveraging the hospitals' physicians as the preferred in-network physicians.

As we learned in Chapter 1, the Medicare program implemented DRG-based reimbursement for inpatient hospital services in 1983. This, along with the movement of people into restrictive HMO model health plans, had a profound impact on hospital attitudes toward PPOs and their eventual agreement to participate in these networks.

PPO plans also implemented new reimbursement approaches (some of these were described in Chapter 4) as part of their operational strategies. For example,

31 Preferred provider organizations were independent from insurance companies. PPOs built networks that they leased to indemnity insurers. They also offered "repricing" and utilization management services for a fee.

some moved away from reimbursing hospitals a percentage of their billed charges to paying a fixed amount per day. This payment approach became known as per diem reimbursement and was a radical change from the percentage of charges approach that had been in place historically. During the late 1980s, per diem rates, combined with the increasing market share of HMOs, competition among hospitals and other contractual requirements imposed by health insurers,[32] as well as the consolidation of multiple indemnity payer agreements under a single PPO, ultimately convinced many hospitals to enter into managed care agreements using the PPO model.

Health plan contracting with physicians also changed as Medicare and commercial insurers began to reimburse using fee schedules rather than the usual and customary approach. Early PPOs first adopted the California Relative Value Scale (CRVS) for use across several states in the mid-1980s, which provided both payers and physicians with a clear understanding of the reimbursement amount for most services,[33] and physicians liked the predictability of revenue that fee schedules provided. In addition, the PPO plan contracts also guaranteed payment within 30 days of receipt of a claim.

As the PPO movement continued to grow rapidly, the use of fee schedules became even more widespread, and in 1992, the Medicare program implemented its own physician fee schedule based on the Resource Based Relative Value Scale (RBRVS). Under Medicare's reimbursement approach, physicians' billed charges for most services became irrelevant since Medicare paid a fixed fee for each service. With this reimbursement approach in place for the largest payer in the U.S., many PPO plans quickly converted to the RBRVS reimbursement methodology.

D. Summary of Key Changes in the Healthcare System as a Result of HMOs and PPOs

The rise of HMOs resulted in unprecedented changes in the financing and delivery of healthcare. These changes included:

- The availability of health insurance products that restricted provider choice, which ran contrary to historical norms where patients had the freedom to choose any provider they wished.
- The creation of staff model HMOs, which helped reduce physician resistance to contracting but that also created incremental administrative costs that indemnity insurers historically did not have.
- The creation of contract models where medical decisions were reviewed by a third party, which changed the doctor-patient relationship.
- The addition of administrative functions (such as utilization management) and their associated costs, which reduced healthcare service volume and costs.
- The availability of benefit plans with lower premiums and out-of-pocket costs.

32 For example, contractual terms requiring payers to pay providers within 30 days.

33 Some services (identified by CPT codes) were not a assigned a fee and were instead classified as "BR" meaning "by report." Codes identified as BR required the treating physician to submit a detailed description of the treatment provided, which the health plan reviewed and assigned a payment amount.

As the transition to HMOs occurred, indemnity insurers faced pressure from employers to reduce premiums. However, indemnity insurers had not developed utilization management processes and had historically not negotiated rates with physicians and hospitals, so they were unable to reduce healthcare costs the way HMOs could and had to increase premiums for their products. As a result, they turned to third-party PPO organizations for provider networks and utilization management programs so that they could offer benefits plans to compete with HMOs.

The development of both HMO and PPO plans was the result of both internal and external forces that insurance organizations were forced to address. But perhaps most importantly, *employers* forced changes in the delivery and pricing of healthcare services. This resulted in HMO models that were designed to reduce costs by restricting and controlling utilization and PPO models that were born out of the indemnity industry's need to compete with HMOs. Researchers at Harvard concluded that the growth in managed care plans such as HMOs and PPOs in the 1980s and 1990s contributed to slower growth in healthcare costs.[34] Indeed, HMO expansion in the 1980s and PPO expansion in the 1990s correspond to lower annual percentage changes in the National Health Expenditures as shown in Figure 5.1.[35]

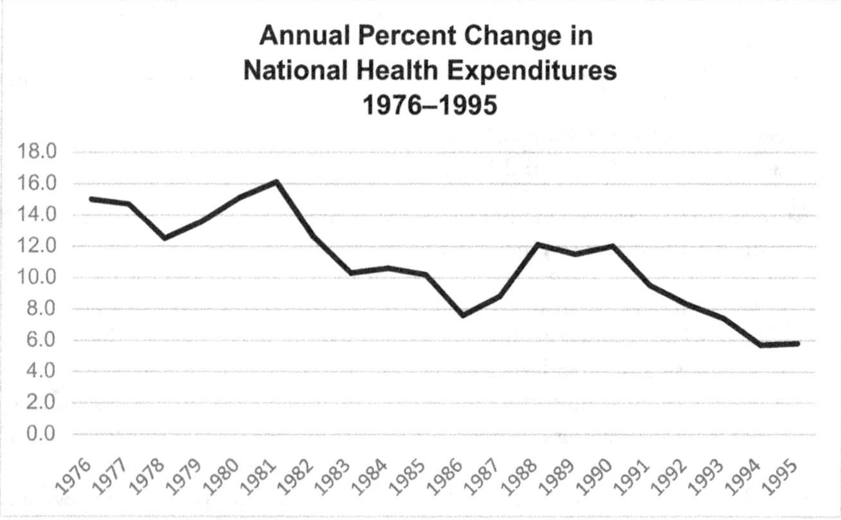

Figure 5.1

34 David M. Cutler and Louise Sheiner, "Managed Care and the Growth of Medical Expenditures," National Bureau of Economic Research, Working Paper 6140, August 1997, www.nber.org/system/files/working_papers/w6140/w6140.pdf.

35 "National Health Expenditure Data: Historical," Centers for Medicare and Medicaid Services, Accessed March 21, 2023, www.cms.gov/research-statistics-data-and-systems/statistics-trends-and-reports/nationalhealthexpenddata/nationalhealthaccountshistorical.

IV. CAPITATION AND RISK-BASED REIMBURSEMENT

At the core of the HMO model was, and continues to be, the concept of capitation. As the HMO model was taking off in the early 1980s, HMOs began to require physicians to accept capitation as the form of reimbursement. Physicians initially resisted this reimbursement methodology, primarily for two reasons:

1. In most geographic markets, HMOs represented a very small portion of commercial health plan membership and therefore had little leverage in negotiating with physicians.
2. Few geographic markets existed where physicians were organized into large groups or independent physician associations (IPA)[36] versus individual or small groups of physicians.

Capitation was a radical change for physicians compared to the fee-for-service reimbursement model that had been used historically. As described earlier in this chapter, instead of receiving a payment based on a visit or treatment, a physician would receive a PMPM payment for all patients assigned to them at the beginning of each month. The physician or physician organization (such as an IPA) would accept the PMPM payment as payment in full regardless of the number of visits or services that a patient incurred during the month. The effect of the capitation approach was a transfer of financial risk from the HMO to the physician or physician organization.

In the mid-1990s, HMOs in Southern California found willing capitation partners in physicians who had organized into large groups or had joined IPAs. These physician groups or IPAs initially only accepted risk for primary care services but eventually expanded their risk-taking to include specialty services and sometimes imaging services as well. This is because physician organizations believed they could manage the specialist and imaging referral process better than the HMOs and thus reap a financial reward for taking on the specialty care risk. This became known as the "gatekeeper model." Under this model, a primary care physician acted as the gatekeeper for referrals for certain services, including imaging, other diagnostic testing and specialist services. Large physician groups often included multiple specialties, which allowed these groups to refer to their own physicians, thus keeping patient revenue in-house rather than contracting with specialists outside the practice.

36 An Independent Physician Association or IPA is defined as a "business entity organized and owned by a network of independent physician practices for the purpose of reducing overhead or pursuing business ventures such as contracts with employers . . . and/or managed care organizations (MCOs)." "Independent Physician Associations," American Academy of Family Physicians, www.aafp.org/about/policies/all/independent-physician-associations.html Historically, IPAs were not affiliated with any hospital, HMO or PPO health plan. IPAs contracted with physicians in the community and then in turn accepted the capitation risk using contracted physicians to deliver care.

Initial forays into risk arrangements between providers and HMOs proved extremely challenging because physicians historically did not have experience managing risk. Under indemnity insurance, which was what they were used to, physicians ordered tests, made referrals to specialists and discharged patients from hospitals, often without regard for costs. Hospitals were also initially reluctant to enter into capitation or risk-based arrangements because they had no control over admissions, discharges or the volume of services ordered by physicians. Instead, they were forced to look to physicians to manage these things for their patients. Hospitals tried to incentivize physicians to help them manage patients by giving them a share of a hospital's risk pool balance at the end of each year. But this was often unsuccessful, and hospitals alleged that physicians gave up on managing the hospital risk pool once the pool was depleted, which resulted in the hospital experiencing a financial loss. As a result, the mid- to late 1990s was a time of significant risk pool settlement litigation between hospitals, physicians and HMOs.

The early negative experiences of hospitals with capitation continues to influence their willingness to accept capitation as a reimbursement methodology today. Hospitals typically limit risk to specific benefit plans and/or specific medical groups or IPAs and demand that capitation rates be adjusted based on the health characteristics of the population. In contrast, physician groups and IPAs are often much more willing to accept risk because they can control the volume of services, and a large portion of their risk is associated with their professional time.

V. INCREASED REGULATION

In the 1990s, large practice management companies formed to manage physician practices and accept capitation as the form of reimbursement. But the subsequent bankruptcy of several of these organizations, such as Coastal Physicians in Durham, North Carolina, FPA in San Diego, California and Med Partners (which affected one million patients), was a wakeup call to regulatory agencies across the U.S. that risk-taking by providers potentially endangered patient access to care.[37] The MedPartners bankruptcy in 1999 and the risk-taking arrangements between health plans and MedPartners that helped precipitate the bankruptcy resulted in changes in regulatory oversight of HMOs in California. The successor company to MedPartners, KPC Medical Management, also filed for bankruptcy in 2000 with significant impact on patients' access to care.[38]

In 1999, the State of California had two regulatory agencies: the Department of Insurance, which regulated all non-HMO insurance companies, and the Department of Corporations which regulated financial institutions, transportation, housing and HMOs. During the course of the MedPartners case, it became

37 "MedPartners collapse leaves a lesson: Keep your hands on the reins," Relias Media, February 1, 1999.

38 Jerry Hirsch, "KPC Medical Files for Chapter 11 Bankruptcy," *Los Angeles Times* (November 28, 2000).

clear to California government executives and the state legislature that the state needed a regulatory agency to focus solely on HMOs and their associated business practices.

The California Department of Managed Health Care (DMHC) was created with the goal of implementing regulations, policies and procedures that would help to avoid the types of insolvencies that disrupted the care of HMO members.[39] In fact, the MedPartners and KPC bankruptcy cases were instrumental in the creation of regulatory oversight in California in terms of the structure of risk-based arrangements between HMOs and their contracting providers. Since the creation of the DMHC, the State of California has continued to revise regulatory requirements regarding risk-based arrangements. Hospitals, physician groups and other organizations that accept risk must submit financial statements to the state, and only those organizations that hold a restricted license[40] may accept full risk (meaning both facility and professional risk) from licensed health plans. The DMHC has also established other regulatory requirements including the following:

- Providers cannot take downside risk. In downside risk arrangements, providers accept the risk if the costs of care exceed agreed-upon thresholds and may be required to refund the payer if they exceed a certain budget for a specific group of services.[41]
- Health plans that delegate utilization management, claims payment or provider credentialing to a provider organization must complete a pre-delegation audit. In addition, a separate delegation agreement must be signed by the HMO and provider organization, and the HMO must conduct a minimum annual audit of the delegated entities.[42] (See Chapter 6 for more discussion of delegated entities.)
- HMOs are required to file reports regarding network adequacy on an annual basis, including a separate report by an external party that validates the accuracy of the HMO report.
- HMOs are responsible for their delegated entities' compliance with regulatory requirements and are accountable for any compliance failures which could include fines, corrective action plans, and/or a requirement to "de-delegate" the organization.

39 Debra Roth and Deborah Reidy Kelch, "Making Sense of Managed Care Regulations in California," California Health Care Foundation, December 6, 2001, www.chcf.org/publication/making-sense-of-managed-care-regulation-in-california/.

40 California Department of Managed Care issues full license and restricted licenses. The restricted license allows the organization to take global risk from fully licensed HMOs but cannot create, sell or market their own product.

41 "Exploring Two-Sided Financial Risk in Alternative Payment Models: Incorporating two-sided financial risk is key to making providers," Revcycle Intelligence, Accessed March 21, 2023, https://revcycleintelligence.com/features/exploring-two-sided-financial-risk-in-alternative-payment-models.

42 California Knox Keene Act, 1371.4 (e)A health care service plan may delegate the responsibilities enumerated in this section to the plan's contracting medical provider.

These regulatory requirements have had a profound impact on HMO perspectives regarding contracting and reimbursement. HMOs' use of capitation and delegation of responsibilities to provider organizations and the resulting complexity of reimbursement and patient access to care have resulted in a higher level of regulatory scrutiny of HMOs. At the same time, the PPO benefit model is perceived by regulators as being less complex; therefore, state and federal regulatory agencies typically apply a lower level of oversight than what is applied to HMOs. The increasing complexity of healthcare financing, administration and delivery is likely to result in increasingly tighter state and Federal regulatory oversight and enforcement activities.

VI. REGULATION OF MEDICARE ADVANTAGE AND MEDICAID MANAGED CARE PLANS

As the Medicare program and some state Medicaid programs transitioned some enrollees from fee-for-service (i.e., Original Medicare—Parts A and B) to managed care programs (Medicare Part C/Medicare Advantage plans and Medicare Part D/Medicare Prescription Drug plans), an opportunity arose for commercial HMOs to leverage their contracting relationships with providers and their experience with capitation reimbursement and apply it in the Medicare and Medicaid spaces.

Today, organizations that want to operate Medicare Advantage plans must submit an application and pricing bid to CMS that includes a detailed list of benefits. Medicare enrollees can then select a Medicare Advantage plan instead of Original Medicare. Individuals who select Medicare Advantage plans typically trade their ability to choose any provider for lower out-of-pocket costs and enriched benefits. Medicaid managed care contracts are awarded by state Medicaid agencies using a bid process as well, and Medicaid enrollees in states with managed care plans can either self-select a plan or the state may auto-enroll Medicaid recipients into a plan in certain cases. CMS regulates organizations that administer Medicare Advantage plans, while both CMS and state Medicaid agencies regulate Medicaid managed care plans. Medicare Part C and D Oversight and Enforcement (MOEG) is the agency within CMS responsible for creating and administering the audit strategy to oversee Medicare Part C and Part D programs. The focus areas of the MOEG include:

- Coverage determinations, grievances and appeals;
- Compliance program effectiveness;
- Formulary and benefit administration;
- Medicare-Medicaid plan service authorization requests, appeals, and grievances;
- Medicare-Medicaid plan care coordination;
- Part C organization determinations, appeals and grievances; and
- Special Needs Plans care coordination.[43]

43 "CMS 2022 Program Audit Process Overview," Centers for Medicare and Medicaid Services, updated December 2021, www.cms.gov/files/document/2022-program-audit-process-overview.pdf.

VII. RECENT BUSINESS ENVIRONMENT AND REGULATORY CHANGES

Commercial payers continue to face an evolving business and regulatory environment that impacts their perspectives on contracting, reimbursement, and compliance. Several issues have been at the forefront in recent years:

- Physician shortages, particularly shortages of specialist physicians across the U.S., have made it difficult for health plans to ensure that their members have timely access to care.
- Health plans' inability to contract with certain hospital-based specialists such as radiologists, pathologists and emergency room physicians have resulted in members facing out-of-network claims from these providers.
- Physicians and midlevel practitioners such as physician assistants organized into IPAs for services such as behavioral health, which have forced health plans to renegotiate higher reimbursement rates.
- Patients with mental health conditions struggle to obtain care due to annual benefit limitations for inpatient and outpatient mental health services.
- Health plans struggling to attract PPO patients as out-of-network cost-sharing obligations have increased.
- Greater numbers of HMO patients are subject to collections by out-of-network providers when their plans do not cover certain out-of-network services.
- Litigation has been initiated by providers who refuse to accept health plan reimbursement rates and seek to collect 100 percent of their billed charges.

Some of these issues have been or are being addressed through legislation, but with unintended consequences. A good example is mental health benefit limitations. In the late 1980s and early 1990s, health plans struggled to apply utilization management oversight for mental health benefits. Because they could not effectively manage the use of mental health services, health plans instead chose to limit their potential financial liability by reducing or limiting inpatient and outpatient benefits, which in turn reduced utilization. This ultimately resulted in the closures of two national psychiatric hospital chains.

In 2014, the Mental Health Parity and Addiction Equity Act was passed in order to address the issue of limitations on mental health services. The Act required that mental health benefits be provided at the same level as physical health benefits.[44] However, the number of mental health providers has not kept pace with population growth, which has limited health plans' ability to arrange for services provided by contracted providers. This has resulted in only a fraction

44 "The Mental Health Parity and Addiction Equity Act," Centers for Medicare and Medicaid Services, www.cms.gov/CCIIO/Programs-and-Initiatives/Other-Insurance-Protections/mhpaea_factsheet.

of mental health needs being met in 2022.[45] In terms of reimbursement, capitation was not a viable option because mental health providers had the upper hand in contracting discussions. And as described above, behavioral health providers in some states organized into groups, which increased their power and leverage, allowing them to reject capitation and accept only fee-for-service reimbursement. Insurers paid increasingly higher rates due to the limited availability of mental health and substance abuse providers and the need to have them in their networks. In fact, some inpatient providers were able to contract at per diem rates that were equal to or higher than medical/surgical or intensive care unit (ICU) per diem rates due to the shortage of available beds and lack of competition. In some states, HMOs faced regulatory actions, including fines and corrective action plans, for not providing an adequate network of providers and appointment availability for mental health and substance abuse services.[46,47]

VIII. COMPLIANCE

Throughout this book, we use the terms, "health plan" and "payer" to encompass HMO, PPO, EPO and POS plans, as well as self-funded employers, union trusts, TPAs and ancillary providers that accept capitation and take on contracting, reimbursement and compliance obligations. In this section, the scope of discussion will be limited to HMO organizations.

In the author's opinion, HMOs have the most comprehensive compliance requirements and regulatory oversight. HMOs are subject to state regulatory compliance requirements, and many states have more regulatory requirements related to HMOs than PPO plans.[48] HMOs also have contractual compliance requirements with self-funded employers and with their network providers. If an HMO also participates in Medicare Advantage and/or Medicaid managed care, it will have Federal and additional state compliance requirements as well.

From a compliance perspective, there are several factors that influence health plan actions, and these can be categorized into *contractual* compliance factors and *regulatory* compliance factors. Contract compliance is influenced by the threat of litigation and potential cancellation of plan-provider contracts. In addition, HMOs also have compliance obligations related to employers and individual members, including those who may purchase ACA plans through federal or state exchanges.

---

45 "Mental Health Care Professional Shortage Areas," Kaiser Family Foundation, September 30,2022. www.kff.org/other/state-indicator/mental-health-care-health-professional-shortage-areas-hpsas/?currentTimeframe=0&sortModel=%7B%22colId%22:%22Location%22,%22sort%22:%22asc%22%7D.

46 "Network Adequacy Standards and Enforcement," Kaiser Family Foundation, Feb 4 2022, www.kff.org/health-reform/issue-brief/network-adequacy-standards-and-enforcement/.

47 U.S. Government Accountability Office, "Private Health Insurance, State and Federal Oversight of Provider Networks Varies," December 2022, www.gao.gov/assets/gao-23-105642.pdf.

48 "AHM Governance and Regulations: State HMO and Other Types of Health Plan Laws," America's Health Insurance Plans, AHM 510—Lesson 7: State Regulation of Health Plans, Accessed March 21, 2023, https://topclass.ahipinsuranceeducation.org/topclass/media/00699915-4290-4c58-ade2-bf720e1b4162/story_content/external_files/Lesson%207%20Transcript.pdf.

Who Are the Regulators?

HMOs are regulated by state departments of insurance or agencies created for regulatory oversight such as the California Department of Managed Health Care (DMHC) or the New York Department of Health's Division of Managed Care. CMS licenses and regulates HMOs that offer Medicare Advantage products. The U.S. Department of Labor also regulates health plans regarding network adequacy. State Medicaid agencies where managed Medicaid HMOs are utilized for Medicaid benefits also have regulatory oversight.

Regulatory compliance by health plans is influenced by the threat of fines, prosecutions, termination of agreements, required corrective action plans and/or the installation of independent monitors to monitor compliance and/or progress in resolving compliance failures. Regulators' compliance initiatives generally focus on two areas: (1) Ensuring patients and providers are not harmed by inappropriate behavior of health plans, and (2) Fraud, waste and abuse detection. Regulators have implemented performance requirements for health plans based on historic patient complaints and audit findings. These performance requirements include:

- Timeliness of claims payments and denials;
- Information required to support denials;
- Notice requirements;
- Accuracy of claims payment;
- Payment of interest when claims are paid late;
- Timely processing of prior authorization for services;
- Notice requirements specific to authorization denials;
- Grievance and appeals procedures for claims and prior authorizations;
- Network adequacy using travel times as a measurement;
- Credentialing requirements for physicians and hospitals; and
- Maximum wait time for appointments.[49]

The State of California, for example, has adopted the following specific timeframe standards for appointment availability:

- Urgent care (prior authorization not required by health plan): 48 hours
- Urgent care (prior authorization required by health plan): 96 hours

49 On January 7, 2022, CMS issued a draft letter to HMOs offering federally facilitated exchange products that proposed standards for appointment availability. "2023 Letter to Issuers in the Federally-facilitated Exchanges," Center for Consumer Information and Insurance Oversight (CCIIO), Centers for Medicare & Medicaid Services, January 7, 2022, www.cms.gov/files/document/2023-draft-letter-issuers-508.pdf.

- Non-urgent doctor appointment (primary care physician): 10 business days
- Non-urgent doctor appointment (specialty physician): 15 business days
- Non-urgent mental health appointment (nonphysician): 10 business days
- Non-urgent appointment (ancillary provider): 15 business days[50]

Regulatory agencies also require HMOs to have in-house compliance programs that include activities designed to prevent fraud, waste and abuse. Humana provides the following definitions of fraud, waste, and abuse in the documentation supporting their compliance program:

- **Fraud** is generally defined as knowingly and willfully executing, or attempting to execute, a scheme or artifice to defraud any healthcare benefit program or to obtain (by means of false or fraudulent pretenses, representations or promises) any of the money or property owned by, or under the custody or control of, any healthcare benefit program (18 U.S.C. § 1347).
- **Waste** is overutilization of services or other practices that, directly or indirectly, result in unnecessary costs to the healthcare system, including the Medicare and Medicaid programs. It is not generally considered to be caused by criminally negligent actions, but by the misuse of resources.
- **Abuse** is payment for items or services when there is no legal entitlement to that payment and the individual or entity has not knowingly and/or intentionally misrepresented facts to obtain payment.[51]

Today, health plans use a variety of tools to address fraud, waste and abuse, including robust analysis of claims and utilization authorization data, enhanced utilization management procedures for items considered high risk for fraud or abuse and processes to identify waste. In some instances, they use third-party vendors who specialize in these areas.

Compliance is also influenced by internal factors within HMOs, particularly attitudes of senior executives regarding the importance of compliance within the organization. HMO leadership determines the level of funding and attention devoted to the compliance function, decides whether the organization is proactive or reactive in evaluating compliance and the level of importance in reacting to compliance failures. All HMOs have policies, procedures and processes that address operational, financial and regulatory compliance. However, if compliance is not prioritized by the organization's leadership, compliance failures often occur.

50 California has established these appointment standards which are used in evaluating network adequacy and timely access to care.

51 "Addressing fraud, waste and abuse," Humana, Accessed March 21, 2023, www.humana.com/legal/fraud-waste-and-abuse.

IX. CONCLUSION

Over the last 40 years, health insurance benefits in the U.S., as well as the financing and delivery of healthcare, have undergone dramatic changes. The business environment, as well as government regulations, legal and societal norms have shaped health insurer perspectives regarding contracting, reimbursement methodologies and compliance. Current and future contracting or delivery system configurations depend upon hospitals' and physicians' willingness to agree to participate and provide acceptable discounts that meet insurer expectations. At the same time, successful benefit plan designs will not be accepted by employers unless they achieve reductions in premiums and cost sharing while also providing access to key providers.

One factor that is likely to impact contracting and reimbursement is the growing shortage of physicians, physician assistants and nurse practitioners across the U.S.[52] As a country, we have been experiencing a shortage of physicians and mid-level providers for decades and the author has found nothing in the literature that indicates this shortage will be resolved anytime soon. The Association of American Medical Colleges (AAMC) has estimated that the U.S. could have an estimated shortage of between 37,800 and 124,000 physicians by 2034, which includes a shortfall in both primary and specialty physicians.[53]

Three key factors that will drive the shortage will be retirement of physicians currently providing care, continued population growth and the cost and timeframe for graduating primary care and specialty physicians. In 2019, there were 935,136 practicing physicians, of which 45 percent were over the age of 55.[54] The shortage of providers will make contracting on a capitated basis very difficult because the balance of power in negotiations will likely tip toward providers. This could limit the growth of this type of reimbursement methodology outside of metropolitan areas as providers demand fee-for-service reimbursement and higher rates. As we will see in Chapter 6, physicians in rural areas or small cities where there is little or no competition are not likely to be willing to take on risk-based reimbursement arrangements when they can receive fee-for-service reimbursement without risk. This physician shortage issue is an external factor that is beyond the control of the health plans.

Increased regulatory oversight is another external factor that will affect health plans and their contracting and reimbursement strategies. As physician shortages

52 Andi Robeznieks, "Doctor shortages are here- and they'll get worse if we don't act fast," American Medical Association, April 13,2022, www.ama-assn.org/practice-management/sustainability/doctor-shortages-are-here-and-they-ll-get-worse-if-we-don-t-act.

53 "AAMC Report Reenforces Mounting Physician Shortage," American Association of Medical Colleges, January 11, 2021, www.aamc.org/news-insights/press-releases/aamc-report-reinforces-mounting-physician-shortage.

54 "Active Physicians by Age and Specialty," Physician Specialty Data Report, American Association of Medical Colleges, www.aamc.org/data-reports/workforce/interactive-data/active-physicians-age-and-specialty-2019.

worsen, regulatory oversight is likely to increase because regulators will become increasingly concerned that patients may be harmed due to lack of access to care. For those states with strong regulatory environments, it is likely that regulatory oversight will continue to expand, creating additional compliance challenges for health plans. In states where regulatory oversight has been more limited in scope, it is likely that negative patient events, which can arise due to things like denial of care and extended delays in approving care, as well as negative financial impacts on providers resulting from capitation, may lead to new regulatory action and enforcement programs.

Last, health plans cannot exist without their physician and hospital partners. While there has been a long history of disputes between health plans and providers and these partnerships appear to be weak and unstable, neither constituency can exist without the other. Chapters 7, 8 and 9 describe how payer-provider disputes arise, and the perspectives of both payer and provider organizations regarding these types of issues and their resolution.

Additional Resources

The Kaiser Family Foundation (www.kff.org) is an excellent source of reliable information. In addition, many state insurance department websites as well websites for HMO oversight agencies are great sources of information regarding regulatory investigations and enforcement actions.

CMS and state Medicaid agencies are also great sources of information regarding existing and new or proposed changes in reimbursement and regulations.

CHAPTER 6

Contracting, Reimbursement, and Compliance

Provider Perspective

Frank Stevens

I. INTRODUCTION

Provider organizations exist with a singular focus of delivering healthcare to patients, regardless of the type of health insurance they have. Ever since the Great Depression, when provider organizations established insurance products as a way of ensuring payment for their services, providers' primary business focus has been patient care.[1] However, as we saw in Chapter 5, the transition from indemnity insurance to PPO health plans and the rise of HMOs changed the relationship between patients and health insurance companies and required providers to make adjustments to the business processes associated with patient care.

The goal of this chapter is to explore the business, government/regulatory and legal environments, as well as the ways the Medicare program influenced provider perspectives regarding contracting (meaning provider network participation), reimbursement and compliance. We also address the issue of market power.

II. HOSPITAL AND PHYSICIAN PERSPECTIVES ON CONTRACTING AND REIMBURSEMENT

Throughout this book, we have used the word "provider" as a collective term for all of the different types of entities that treat or provide care to patients, and we have described the reimbursement approaches used by the Medicare program and commercial payers to reimburse different types of providers. This chapter will focus on two types of providers: hospitals and physicians (or physician organizations).[2]

---

1 There are exceptions such as the Presbyterian Health System in New Mexico, which operates hospitals and physician practices as well as a highly successful HMO.

2 Physician organizations include medical groups and independent physician organizations such as Independent Practice Associations (IPAs), which are community physicians that are members of an organization structured to take capitated risk from health plans for professional services.

Hospitals and physicians/physician organizations together represent the largest share of healthcare costs for the U.S. patient population and are the cornerstone of every managed care network. From 2009 to 2019, hospital and physician services together accounted for well over half of all healthcare costs, with hospital services accounting for 37 percent of healthcare costs and physician services accounting for 24 percent.[3] Hospitals and their affiliated physicians/physician organizations have similar business environment, regulatory and legal factors that influence their management teams' perspectives. However, they sometimes react differently to external forces, resulting in very different contracting and reimbursement perspectives.

A. Hospital Perspectives and Market Power

Individual hospital perspectives regarding contracts, reimbursement and compliance are determined by a diverse set of internal and external factors. These factors also affect a hospital's negotiating power in the market. The management team of a hospital generally considers the following factors with regard to contracting and reimbursement, and these factors also affect the level of power the hospital has when it negotiates with health plans.

- Hospital location (e.g., rural, suburbs, city central)
- Type of hospital from a services perspective (community, full service, tertiary, academic medical center)
- For profit or not-for-profit status
- Religious affiliation
- Whether the hospital is independent or part of a hospital system
- Distance to the nearest competing hospital
- Scope of services offered compared to other hospitals in the area
- Whether hospital is perceived as a "must have" provider in payer networks
- Whether the hospital has its own foundation of physicians or Management Services Organization (MSO)[4]
- Whether physicians with admitting privileges to the hospital are willing to contract with payers
- Whether physicians affiliated with the hospital are part of an organization that can accept capitation as a form of reimbursement
- Patient/community perceptions of the hospital
- Geographic boundaries such as drive time and/or availability of public transportation nearby

3 "National Health Expenditure Data: Historical," Centers for Medicare and Medicaid Services, www.cms.gov/research-statistics-data-and-systems/statistics-trends-and-reports/nationalhealthexpenddata/nationalhealthaccountshistorical.

4 Not-for-profit hospitals often establish foundations to employ physicians while for-profit hospitals typically establish what is called a "Management Services Organization" or MSO to facilitate contracting with health plans on a capitated or risk-based basis.

- The hospital's participation in competitive payer networks as a limiting factor for negotiating with other competing payers
- Age of the hospital facility (i.e., older versus newer facility)
- Experience of individual members of the management team in contracting with specific health plans

Among these factors, there are typically a handful that have the most influence over the power dynamics in contract negotiations with health plans. The ability to provide specialized services or services that are not commonly found in a certain geographic areas may make a hospital a "must have" in a health plan network. Hospitals that are members of a multifacility system that dominates a geographic market can also exert significant market power. Other key factors that allow hospitals to exert power in negotiations are reputation, relationships with physician organizations and ability to negotiate rates that use a variety of reimbursement methodologies.

Regarding reimbursement specifically, hospitals today are generally comfortable accepting fee-for-service payments that apply per diem, case rate or DRG methodologies. When payers propose other reimbursement methodologies such as bundled or package rates or risk-based arrangements (which we will describe later in this chapter), a hospital's willingness to agree to them is often influenced by its experience with the payer's contracted physicians and their ability to efficiently and effectively manage patient care. This is because physicians are the ones who admit patients, order treatments and discharge patients from the hospital. The level of physician engagement in these processes and ability to perform them efficiently impacts a hospital's financial operations and profit margin.

The complexity and diversity of all of these factors can result in a lengthy and challenging negotiation process between hospitals and health plans.

B. Physicians/Physician Organization Perspective and Market Power

Individual physician perspectives are far more diverse than hospitals or physician organizations regarding contracting with health plans, but similar factors also impact their power in negotiating with health plans. The key factor that often influences an individual physician's willingness to contract with a health plan or join a medical group or IPA is their specialty. Specialists that are in short supply in certain geographic areas such as neurologists, neurosurgeons, allergists and dermatologists have historically been difficult for health plans, medical groups and IPAs to contract with and recruit. In recent years, health plans, medical groups, foundations and IPAs have been more successful in contracting and recruiting these types of specialists, but the trade-off has been having to pay materially more in reimbursement than for other specialists due to the regulatory pressures regarding access to care (see Chapters 4 and 5 regarding network adequacy and regulatory requirements).

Another key factor that often influences a physician or physician organization's decision to contract with a health plan is whether the hospital where they have admitting privileges has entered into a contract with that health plan. Because health plan contracts typically require physicians to refer and admit patients to in-network hospitals, a physician has little incentive to enter into contracts with a health plan if the hospital where they have privileges is out-of-network with that plan.

Other factors that influence a physician or physician organization's perspective regarding contracting, as well as the level of power in the market, include:

- Geographic location (rural, suburbs, central city)
- Composition of the practice or organization:
  - Individual practitioners
  - Small group
  - Large group or IPA
  - Hospital affiliation
  - Primary care versus specialist
  - Specialist whose specialty has very limited availability in the geographic market

The following factors also may influence a physician organization's management team regarding contracting with health plans:

- The type(s) of hospital from a services perspective (community, full service, tertiary, academic medical center) with whom the group is affiliated;
- Whether the physician organization is associated via admitting privileges with one hospital or multiple hospitals in the market;
- Distance to the nearest competing hospital and its affiliated physician organization locations;
- Existence of contracts with specialists outside of the organization to ensure full specialty coverage;
- Hospital and its affiliated physician organization are perceived as a "must have" by health plan network(s);
- Hospital has its own physician foundation;[5]
- Physician organization has experience in managing professional services risk[6] and is willing to accept risk-based reimbursement methodologies;
- Patients perceptions of the hospital and affiliated physician organization;
- Geographic boundaries such as drive time and or public transportation;
- Available satellite physician offices that limit or expand a physician organization's service area;
- Existing contractual relationships with competing health plans that may limit the ability to negotiating with other health plans;
- Management teams' past experience in contracting with specific health plans;

5 The physicians are members of a hospital foundation that makes the contracting decisions.

6 Physician organizations that have no experience in accepting and managing capitation may not be willing to accept a capitated contract with a health plan.

- Prior experience as a delegated entity[7] to perform utilization management, credentialing and claims payment for professional services;
- Prior experience managing risk and participating in shared-savings agreements with an affiliated hospital. See Chapter 4 for a summary of alternative payment models.

Like hospitals, many of the same factors that shape a physician organization's perspectives are also the same factors that allow them to create leverage in contracting and reimbursement negotiations with health plans, but three factors generally play prominent roles regarding market power: They are affiliated with a "must have" hospital in a health plan's network, specialty (because highly specialized physicians tend to have more power in negotiating rates with health plans) and ability to accept and manage risk.

Another factor that influences market power for both hospitals and physicians is the size of the health plan they are contracting with. Health plan size is typically defined by the number of members it has. The lines of business offered by the plan (commercial, Medicaid managed care, Medicare Advantage) are also important. Managed care reimbursement rates are often based on volume discounts—the more patients a plan can direct to a provider, the more likely the provider is to accept lower reimbursement rates.

But plans with fewer members are generally at a disadvantage compared to larger plans in their ability to direct large numbers of members to certain providers. In addition, plans that only administer a single line of business, such as a Medicaid managed care plan, may be less appealing to providers than plans that have multiple lines of business such as commercial HMOs and PPOs and/or Medicare Advantage plans. Smaller health plans may also be less able to negotiate risk-based agreements with providers because the relatively low number of members means a smaller population over which to spread risk. For all of these reasons, providers typically have the upper hand when it comes to negotiating with smaller health plans.

III. HISTORICAL HEALTHCARE MILESTONES AND THEIR IMPACT ON HOSPITALS AND PHYSICIANS

While Chapter 5 identified key milestones in the evolution of health insurance, this chapter will focus on other milestones in the U.S. healthcare system and their influence on hospitals and physicians prior to and during the transition from indemnity insurance to managed care products.

A. Hospital and Physician-Developed Health Plans

While hospitals and physicians developed indemnity health insurance beginning in the 1930s as a way to ensure they were paid for their services, their primary

7 Chapter 5 provided a discussion of health plans' delegation of utilization management and claims processing to provider organizations.

mission was still patient care. For that reason, the fundamental principles of these provider-developed insurance plans were not-for-profit status, patients' ability to choose their health care providers and the belief that there should be no contract between health insurance plans and providers.[8] These perspectives held by hospitals and physicians would ultimately become a point of contention when the transition of indemnity insurance to managed care began. It is important to remember, however, that the origins of the Blue Cross Blue Shield indemnity insurance plans as provider-inspired organizations helped smooth the transition from indemnity to managed care products and helped the managed care model gain the dominant market position it has today.

The Blue Cross Blue Shield Association membership is currently composed of 34 independent, community-based and locally operated companies servicing all 50 states, Washington, D.C. and Puerto Rico, with approximately 114 million people enrolled in "Blue" branded plans. While these Blue Cross Blue Shield plans hold a substantial share of the health insurance market, perhaps these plans' greatest asset as direct result of their early provider-based roots is the expansive network of providers that includes 1.7 million doctors and hospitals.[9]

The introduction of Medicare in 1965[10] and passage of the Health Maintenance Organization Act in 1973[11] did not have an immediate impact on hospitals and physicians and the transition to managed care. This is because early on, services provided to Medicare patients and employees of self-funded employers were reimbursed on a fee-for-service basis using some type of usual and customary approach and required no contract with a health plan. These arrangements continued to operate with no contracts and freedom of provider choice for patients until the early to mid-1980s. At the same time, the HMO concept was so radically different compared to providers' historical experience with indemnity insurance that they remained unconcerned about it (and not willing to participate in these types of plan models) initially. As we learned in Chapter 5, it was not until the passage of ERISA,[12] which gave large employers more latitude with regard to the benefits they provided to their employees, that hospitals and physicians were forced to participate in PPO networks and ultimately HMO plans.

8 Michael A. Morrisey, Ph.D., *History of Health Insurance* (American College of Healthcare Executives, 2013), 6–8.

9 "Blue Facts," Blue Cross BlueShield Association, September 2022, www.bcbs.com/sites/default/files/file-attachments/page/Blue_Facts_Sheet-2021.pdf.

10 Michael A. Morrisey, Ph.D., *History of Health Insurance* (American College of Healthcare Executives, 2013), 6–8.

11 U.S. Government Accountability Officer, "Implementation of the Health Maintenance Organization Act of 1973," March 3, 1978, www.gao.gov/assets/105122.pdf.

12 Michael A. Morrisey, Ph.D., *History of Health Insurance* (American College of Healthcare Executives, 2013), 6–8.

B. Influence of Medicare Reimbursement on the Transition to Managed Care

The implementation of Medicare reimbursement methodologies beginning in the 1980s had a profound impact on hospitals and physicians during the transition from indemnity insurance to managed care. First, Medicare implemented the DRG (Diagnostic Related Group) methodology in 1983 for hospital inpatient reimbursement (see Chapter 1).[13] This was the first reimbursement methodology that established a predetermined payment amount for providers (in this case, hospitals). The implementation of DRG reimbursement by the Medicare program did not immediately change provider perspectives regarding reimbursement because commercial health plans at this time still reimbursed hospitals primarily using a percentage of billed charges approach. However, DRGs would become important during the transition to managed care reimbursement because the DRG amounts would initially be used as a reference point for the development of inpatient per diem rates used by commercial health plans, and eventually, many commercial plans would adopt the DRG methodology as well. In fact, the adoption of this Medicare reimbursement approach by commercial plans would set an important precedent as they made use of the vast amounts of Medicare data to help establish their own reimbursement rates (see Chapter 4).

On the physician side of things, the implementation of the Medicare Physician Fee Schedule based on the Resource Based Relative Value Scale (RBRVS) in 1992 (see Chapter 2) also established a new standard for professional services reimbursement. While RBRVS was a national methodology, the rates were established for individual market geographies. Up to this point, the California Relative Value Scale (CRVS—see Chapter 5) had been adopted by many health plans for professional reimbursement in the mid-1980s in over 40 states, but the underlying payment approach was different from RBRVS and was not geographically adjusted.

As a result, physicians argued that the CRVS was not applicable to their specific geographic areas and proposed alternative reimbursement schedules be used instead. When Medicare implemented the RBRVS-based approach, commercial health plans quickly adopted it and found greater acceptance by physicians. This marked the second time that Medicare had established a reimbursement methodology that would become the standard by which commercial health plans would ultimately reimburse provider organizations.[14]

Today, RBRVS-based reimbursement is used by Medicare for physician reimbursement and some outpatient hospital services (see Chapter 2). As we learned

13 Violet B. Latta and Charles Helbing, "Medicare short-stay hospital services by diagnosis-related groups," Health Care Financing Review, 1991, www.cms.gov/Research-Statistics-Data-and-Systems/Research/HealthCareFinancingReview/Downloads/CMS1191173dl.pdf.

14 Medicare implemented DRGs for inpatient hospital reimbursement in 1983.

in Chapter 4, many commercial plans have adopted this payment approach for physicians and some of Medicare's other reimbursement methodologies as well.

IV. CONTRACTING WITH MANAGED CARE PLANS AND NEW REIMBURSEMENT METHODOLOGIES

In Chapter 5, we learned about the pressure that indemnity insurance companies experienced to develop managed care products that could compete with HMOs and address employer and patient concerns about spiraling healthcare premium increases. The HMO model required patients to see in-network providers. PPO benefit plan designs incentivized members to use in-network providers, while at the same time providers and patients were bound by health plan utilization management decisions, which sometimes limited or denied services.

Thus, favorable contract rates for the health plan and utilization management were the two primary factors that would drive cost savings for plans under these models. But the primary obstacle to managed care plans' success was convincing hospitals to participate in their networks and to agree to reimbursement rates that were materially lower than their prior usual and customary amounts or percentage of charges compensation from indemnity insurance companies.

What ultimately convinced hospitals to contract with managed care plans in many cases was competition or the fear of potential competition. The existence of provider networks, by definition, meant that some hospitals would be excluded from certain networks, and this would preclude some patients from using them (except on an emergency basis) or would result in higher out-of-network cost-sharing amounts for other patients. In addition, being excluded from a health plan's network could mean a significant reduction in patient admissions and outpatient services, which, in some cases, could result in a hospital's failure.

Unequivocally linked to a hospital's decision to contract with a health plan was the willingness of affiliated physicians to contract with the plan as well. If affiliated physicians did not contract with the health plan, there would be no reason for the hospital to sign a contract because there would be no physicians in the network to admit patients to the hospital. Fortunately for the health plans, physicians also had concerns about being excluded from networks and losing patient revenue.

A. Contracts, Reimbursement Methodologies and Rates

For physicians, the concept of managed care networks and utilization management oversight was often more of an obstacle to contracting with health plans than the reimbursement methodologies they used. Physicians often viewed managed care fee schedules and benefit plans, which included copayments for office visits, as a welcome change from the usual and customary reimbursement approaches used by indemnity plans.

In addition, under these contracts, the health plan determined the amount the patient was required to pay rather than the physician. All of these things simplified physicians' financial billing and posting of payments. Ultimately, the negotiation of an acceptable fee schedule amount, along with hospital encouragement, resulted in many physicians overcoming their concerns about patient loss of provider choice and utilization management limiting services. Hospitals, however, were faced with more dramatic changes in reimbursement methodologies used by commercial insurers as they transitioned from a percentage of charges approach to per diem rates and DRGs.

1. *Changes in Contractual Relationships and Reimbursement Methodologies*

Per diem reimbursement required hospital management to change the way they evaluated rates proposed by health plans. Historically, hospitals had not directly contracted with health plans, and contracts that did exist typically stipulated a percentage of charges approach with a very small discount (1 to 5 percent).[15] A hospital without a contract with a certain health plan (i.e., out-of-network) was typically based on the plan's usual and customary policy. Until Medicare implemented DRGs, hospitals evaluated their reimbursement from each health plan based solely on a comparison to their total charges, without considering the patient volume or service volume directed to the hospital by that health plan.[16]

Typically, hospitals ranked the health plans they contracted with according to the percentage of total charges they paid for the year. DRG reimbursement changed all of this because the methodology called for a fixed payment amount for a specific set of diagnoses and conditions. This meant that if the attending physician did not efficiently manage the use of resources to treat the patient or allowed the patient to stay longer than the targeted length of stay for the DRG, the hospital could experience a reduced margin, or no margin at all.

Thus, managed care contracting for providers, particularly hospitals, became largely based on volume discounts. In other words, hospitals were often willing to accept a discount off of their published charges with the expectation that health plans would direct their members to use the contracted hospitals. Reimbursement rates under this model were often based on historical or projected patient volume expected from a health plan. Interestingly, some hospitals entered negotiations thinking that they wanted the PPO plans to be more successful and maintain a greater market share than their HMO competitors. This is because hospitals understood that if they were excluded from an HMO network, the plan's members would not be able to use the hospital (because the benefit plan would not allow the use of out-of-network providers except in emergencies). On the other hand,

15 Percent of charges payment was based on the total billed charges minus a few percentage points, i.e., the "discount" off of the hospital's billed charge amount. Thus, a payment rate that was 97 percent of total billed charges had a discount of 3 percent.

16 The practice where a health plan directs its members to use certain providers through benefit design is called "steerage."

PPO plans allowed patients to use out-of-network providers if they paid higher cost-sharing amounts.

As we learned in Chapter 5, for most of their existence, indemnity insurers functioned without contractual relationships with providers, and hospitals invested little time managing relationships with these types of health plans. Hospitals were paid on a usual and customary basis, which was somewhat of a "black box" with little transparency with regard to the derivation of the rates. In the 1980s and early 1990s, most hospitals did not have in-house data analytics capabilities; therefore, they depended on health plans to provide information regarding the members who were treated, including the number of admissions and number of inpatient days. But eventually, hospitals began to evaluate reimbursement rates proposed by health plans by comparing them to their Medicare DRG payments and, in turn, use these comparisons to counter health plan proposed rates.[17]

During the early 1980s, some indemnity insurance companies signed contracts with hospitals that provided for a discount off of billed charges. Some hospitals found this acceptable because they could maintain the same level of revenue by simply increasing their prices through a chargemaster increase (see Section VI.A of this chapter). When reimbursement approaches transitioned to per diem and case rates for inpatient services, however, the rates were established in the contracts and could not be changed until the contract terms were renegotiated.

Contracts were structured such that the reimbursement terms were typically referred to in an exhibit, which contained the specific amounts agreed to by the health plan and hospital. There was typically no defined time frame or term of the contract relationship; therefore, contracts automatically renewed each year until one party or the other gave notice of termination.[18] In turn, the reimbursement schedule (contained in the exhibit) continued in effect until the parties renegotiated and agreed to new reimbursement rates. With these new types of managed care contracts and reimbursement structures in place, hospitals had to devote resources to monitoring and renegotiating agreements in order to achieve increases in reimbursement.

a. Case Rates

As we learned in Chapter 4, case rates are similar in concept to DRGs, where a hospital is reimbursed a fixed amount for a specific treatment or service with an established length of stay. The primary difference between a DRG rate and a case rate is the payment for additional days. While the same DRG rate is paid regardless of the number of days (except for certain outlier cases—see Chapters 1 and 4), a case rate may provide for per diem payments for additional days beyond a certain number. In other words, when additional days are determined by the health plan

17 At this time, health plans typically proposed per diem and case rates for inpatient services.

18 This form of contract was referred to as an "evergreen" contract as it continued in place until terminated or renegotiated.

to be medically necessary, the hospital is paid a per diem rate for each additional day the patient is approved to be in the hospital.

Case rates were first introduced for obstetrics cases such as normal vaginal and C-section deliveries. Historically, managed care contracts had different per diem rates for vaginal delivery versus C-sections because the costs for these services were different. The length of hospital stays decreased significantly during the 1970s and 1980s because health plans began to apply medical necessity requirements versus allowing physicians and patients to decide how long a hospital stay should be. Later, under managed care contracts, health plans determined that they could achieve cost savings by reducing lengths of stay, particularly for obstetrics cases.

In the late 1980s, based on certain clinical standards, health plans typically established two-day case rates for normal vaginal deliveries and three-day case rates for C-section deliveries, with separate per diem rates for additional days, as long as they were approved as medically necessary.[19] Case rates are now commonly used across a variety of service lines.

b. *Packaged or Bundled Rates*

Packaged rates, also called bundled rates, were initially used exclusively for organ transplant services. Organ transplants are provided almost exclusively by academic medical centers and tertiary hospitals and often require relatively extensive pre- and post-operative services. Thus, a package rate for an organ transplant typically includes all facility and professional fees associated with these services, as well as the surgical procedure itself. Historically, the unique relationship between hospitals and transplant surgeons was what made package pricing possible, and, interestingly, package rates for transplants were hospital-driven, not health plan-driven. This is because, unlike other specialty physicians, transplant surgeons are part of a small elite group of individuals who have limited hospitals where they can practice.

Over the last decade, commercial health plans and hospitals have negotiated packaged rates for other types of services, including highly specialized treatments for heart disease, orthopedics and other services. The primary key to a hospital's financial success with package rates is having highly skilled physicians who work in partnership with the institution by effectively managing patient care.

V. RISK-BASED ARRANGEMENTS

When describing risk-based arrangements between health plans and providers, capitation is typically what comes to mind (see Chapter 5), and the terms "upside risk" and "downside risk" are often used to describe the type of risk model

19 "Trends in Length of Stay for Hospital Deliveries—United States 1970–1992," Centers for Disease Control and Prevention (CDC), May 5, 1995, www.cdc.gov/mmwr/preview/mmwrhtml/00036988.htm.

in capitation contracts. In upside-risk models, providers are rewarded for keeping costs to provide services below a certain threshold but not penalized if they exceed the threshold, putting the risk entirely on the payer. In a downside risk model, the risk is either shared between the payer and provider or assumed entirely by the provider. Other risk-based contracting methodologies include shared-savings pools and medical budgets. Because capitation has historically been the most widely used risk-based methodology, this section will focus on the mechanics and perspectives of this reimbursement approach.

Historically, hospitals and physician organizations have had very different perspectives regarding capitation as a reimbursement approach. As we learned in Chapter 5, physician organizations were early adopters of capitation reimbursement and continue to accept this arrangement more often than hospitals. The key differences between hospital and physician organization perspectives regarding capitation are influenced by the following factors:

1. Capital structure of the organization
2. Level of fixed costs
3. Level and control of variable costs
4. Market competition
5. Ability to control volume and intensity of services
6. Amount of "catastrophic" patient expense

These factors are explained for physician organizations and hospitals subsequently.

A. Physician Organizations

In general, physicians and physician organizations have been more willing to accept capitation and other alternative payment models as their form of reimbursement for patient services than hospitals. The reasons for this difference are based largely on differences in fixed costs, variable costs, control over services to be provided and competition. Physician organizations also have much lower capital cost structures than hospitals because their facilities are typically smaller in size, are often leased space and have less expensive equipment.

Fixed costs for physician organizations are typically related to lease expense, physician salaries, utilities, administrative staff, clinical support staff and outsourced cleaning expense. The most common reason for an increase in fixed cost is the addition of physicians to the staff and the support costs associated with adding them.

A typical staffing ratio is one clinical assistant (such as a nurse or certified nursing assistant) to one physician, but depending on the services provided, physician organizations can and do operate with one clinical assistant per two physicians. Variable costs such as exam room supplies are relatively low (compared to hospital variable costs) for both primary care and specialty care practices. Physicians also largely have control over the volume and intensity of healthcare services, both in their own practices and at hospitals. In addition, catastrophic patient expense for a physician organization is limited to the physician's time to treat patients. Even a physician organization's patients who are hospitalized are typically managed by hospital-employed physicians (such as hospitalists), which places the risk of a costly patient with the hospital rather than the physician organization.

Overall, competition is perhaps the most important driver in a physician organization's decision to accept capitated arrangements. If the geographic market where a practice operates has other competing physician organizations who are willing to take capitation, it is more likely that a practice will also decide to accept this type of arrangement as well. The tipping point regarding capitation usually comes when competing physician organizations agree to accept capitation from multiple health plans.

B. Hospitals

Hospitals are influenced by the same key factors (listed above) when it comes to deciding whether to accept capitation reimbursement or other alternative payment models, but in different ways. In contrast to physician organizations, hospitals have capital-intensive structures, primarily due to the size of the buildings, building costs (versus lease expense) and expensive equipment required to provide services (MRI, CT, specialized operating rooms, laboratory etc.).

Hospital fixed costs also typically dwarf those of physician organizations due to relatively large administrative and nursing staffs. In addition, hospital staffs tend to be more heavily weighted toward registered nurses (RNs) and licensed practical nurses (LPNs), who have higher hourly wages, rather than certified nursing assistants (CNAs). Hospitals also typically have large support teams including orderly attendants and individuals working in laundry, housekeeping, medical records and food service, as well as specialized technicians for imaging and laboratory testing. Perhaps most importantly, most hospitals are staffed 24 hours a day compared to eight hours a day for a typical physician's office.

Variable costs related to both inpatient and outpatient services are typically patient or service-driven and can be exceptionally high for patients admitted in trauma cases or other catastrophic situations. For example, an individual who is admitted to the hospital for a medical condition such as pneumonia will likely use a medical or intensive care unit (ICU) bed, receive IV medication and have a chest X-ray, among other things. In contrast, a cardiac bypass patient will use the operating room and operating room support staff and is likely to need blood transfusions and a specialized heart-lung bypass machine, as well as a higher level of nursing staff and monitoring equipment in a coronary care unit (CCU). A trauma patient who has been admitted through the emergency department may require multiple surgeries and possibly a ventilator and may have an extended hospital stay requiring ICU or CCU care for several weeks.

Competition is less of a factor for hospitals in deciding whether to enter into capitation arrangements. This is because most hospitals limit the scope of patient populations covered by capitation payments and typically only agree to capitation agreements with health plans whom they have trust and confidence in as business partners. On the other hand, a hospital's lack of ability to control the volume and intensity of services is a very important factor for hospitals in deciding whether to accept capitation (or any risk-based arrangement) because, as described previously, physicians generally control these things—that is, each patient's admission, treatment and discharge.

In addition, patients with extraordinarily high costs represent a significant financial threat to a hospital in a capitated arrangement. Examples of these types of patients include premature babies that require long-term neonatal intensive care and individuals who contract severe infections and require ICU-level care for long periods of time. These and other types of medical conditions are not predictable when capitation rates are agreed to between a health plan and hospital.

To overcome concerns about accepting risk arrangements, hospitals typically look to partner with physician organizations that have been proven to manage patient admissions efficiently and effectively for specific patient populations over a period of years. In these types of arrangements, a hospital will often create a "bonus pool" out of which the partnering physician organization can receive a bonus payment if cost savings are achieved compared to a pre-established budget. Hospitals also typically purchase what is called "reinsurance" to provide protection against potentially catastrophic costs.[20]

In comparing the decision drivers between physician organizations and hospitals, it is easy to understand why hospital organizations may have less interest in capitation as a reimbursement methodology as well as contractual arrangements where a portion of revenue is at risk based on quality or patient outcomes. Many of the same factors influence a hospital's willingness to be paid case rates or packaged/bundled rates as well.

VI. PROVIDER PRICING

One of the most common sources of patient complaints and confusion is the price of healthcare services, particularly the difference between the charges shown on a provider bill and the actual amount reimbursed by a health plan. Unlike other products and services Americans buy, for which there is generally a single price, healthcare services typically have two prices: the "billed charges" and the actual health plan reimbursement amount, and consumers often struggle to understand the relationship between the two amounts. This section will explore both hospital and physician pricing of services and the interesting history that has played a role in creating the gap between billed charges and reimbursement amounts.

---

20 A reinsurance policy can be purchased by a health plan, hospital or physician organization. The policy limits the liability of a risk agreement setting specific levels for individual patients and an aggregate level for the pooled risk during a contract year.

A. Hospital Rate Setting and the Chargemaster

A charge description master ("CDM" or "chargemaster") is a fancy name for a hospital's list of prices that correspond to all of the items and services that are used to treat patients. Hospitals created chargemasters during the early indemnity phase of health insurance development because patients could see any provider, and hospitals had to establish a price for each service that could then be submitted to health insurers for payment. Indemnity health insurers then established their own usual and customary rates that were used to reimburse patients based on the hospital chargemaster amounts. A hospital chargemaster contains a price for a single unit of an item or service delivered. Each item or service is identified by CPT or HCPCS code, a revenue code or other charge code (see Chapter 1 regarding code sets).

The codes contained in the hospital chargemaster are similar to grocery store barcodes, which are scanned at check-out and matched to the store's price list. At the grocery store, these prices are totaled, and the consumer pays the amount. A similar aggregation process occurs when a patient is discharged from a hospital. Hospital staff, such as nurses, therapists, imaging technicians and others record the items and services provided to a patient during the course of treatment (either an inpatient stay or outpatient procedure or visit) in the electronic medical record (EMR). The data entered into the EMR is integrated with the hospital billing system, which generates bills based on the items and services recorded and attaches the prices to them based on the chargemaster. Unlike the grocery store bill, however, the total charges are not typically what is paid.

As described in Chapter 1, the Medicare program initially reimbursed hospitals based on their billed charges and early commercial plans also reimbursed hospitals this way. This created incentives for hospitals to increase their charges in order to increase the reimbursement they received. Although Medicare implemented reimbursement methodologies such as DRGs that ignored billed charges, commercial plans continued to reimburse for at least some services based on billed charges, which perpetuated incentives for hospitals to increase the charges contained in their chargemasters.

Today, it would be difficult to identify a clear relationship between the actual costs of most items and services and the prices listed on a hospital's chargemaster.[21,22] There are no legal requirements or standard formulas for establishing the prices contained in a chargemaster, and health plans now rarely tie their reimbursement rates to chargemaster amounts except in outlier or stop loss situations. (See Chapter 4.) Many states require hospitals to submit chargemaster information

---

21 Deb Fournier, Trish Riley, and Marilyn Bartlett, "Can We Please Stop Fixating on Hospital Chargemasters?" National Academy for State Health Policy, January 17, 2020, https://nashp.org/can-we-please-stop-fixating-on-hospital-chargemasters/.

22 Heather Tirado Gilligan, "Through the Looking Glass: What's Behind Hospital Prices for Care," California Health Care Foundation, December 20, 2021, www.chcf.org/blog/through-looking-glass-whats-behind-hospital-prices/.

in regulatory filings[23] and in 2019, the federal government began encouraging hospitals to post their chargemasters on their websites. As discussed in Chapter 4, federal price transparency rules now (as of January 1, 2021) also require hospitals to post not only their charges, but also their negotiated reimbursement amounts with health plans on their websites as well. While such requirements were originally intended to benefit consumers by making prices available for comparison across facilities, data have proven to be unwieldy and difficult to understand. It remains to be seen whether these issues can be resolved to allow consumers to truly compare prices across hospitals.

B. Physician Pricing

Similar to hospitals, physicians also developed price lists or chargemasters in order to bill patients and insurance companies for their services. And physicians historically had the same difficulties as hospitals in obtaining reimbursement increases from health plans under the usual and customary reimbursement model because no contract existed between the health plan and physician.

Some physicians, like hospitals, periodically increased the charges contained in their chargemasters. Interestingly, however, physician practice chargemasters historically contained different charges for each individual physician in a group, and the charges could vary across physicians. For example, the charge for an office visit for physician who had been in practice for 20 years could be $80 for an office visit while the charge for the same service for a newly trained physician might be $120. This is because practices often set prices and rarely updated them.

When commercial plans largely migrated to fee schedules (based on CRVS or RBRVS) in the 1980s, there was no longer a need for *individual* physicians to maintain their own fee schedules or chargemasters, but practices continued to maintain practice-wide chargemasters that were used as the basis for bills submitted to payers. When practices began to contract with managed care plans, practices were careful to ensure that chargemaster amounts were greater than the contracted fee amounts because of "lesser of" clauses contained in the contracts (see Chapter 4).

Today, physician billed charges are generally not a core consideration in payer-provider contracting. They may come into play in cases where a physician does not accept insurance and requires the patient to pay the full billed charges.

VII. COMPLIANCE

Hospitals, physicians and other healthcare providers, like health plans, must comply with a wide array of Federal and state regulations. Thus, hospital and physicians'/physician organizations' perspectives regarding the ways they operate have

23 Heather Tirado Gilligan, "Through the Looking Glass: What's Behind Hospital Prices for Care," California Health Care Foundation, December 20, 2021, www.chcf.org/blog/through-looking-glass-whats-behind-hospital-prices/.

been shaped by these regulations, as well as the legal environment and the threat of enforcement actions.

When health insurance transitioned from indemnity coverage to managed care, new areas of compliance were created, including requirements related to contractual terms such as billing, chargemaster increases, utilization management, credentialing,[24] balance billing and delegated entities.[25] With this transition also came organizational compliance requirements such as the creation of policies and procedures and requirements regarding the Health Insurance and Portability and Accountability Act (HIPAA),[26] as well as requirements related to labor and employment and anti-trust.

Health plans and provider organizations have compliance departments typically led by a compliance officer who is a senior member of the management team and reports to the Board of Directors or Trustees. The compliance officer is responsible for overseeing adherence to governmental and regulatory requirements as well as organizational policies and procedures. To address HIPAA compliance specifically, provider organizations may also have a privacy officer who is responsible for the specific compliance requirements related to Protected Health Information (PHI). Three of the most important areas related to compliance are described below.

A. Billing and Coding Compliance

Code sets used by providers to bill for their services were described in Chapters 1 and 2. Providers have been subject to regulatory requirements regarding the accurate use of code sets for billing since the 1970s[27] and coding accuracy is critical to accurate and appropriate reimbursement. Across nearly all types of healthcare, CPT (or DRG) codes identify the services for which a provider is requesting payment from an insurer and ICD-10 codes identify the diagnoses that support the provision of those services. Code sets are also used in other ways as well. For example, ICD-10 codes are used by CMS to calculate the "morbidity" (relative wellness or illness) of each Medicare Advantage Plan's patient population, which directly impacts the premium amount that CMS pays to the plan. A healthier population results in lower premiums paid by CMS to the plan. State Medicaid agencies often use a similar ICD-10 based methodology to determine future premium levels for Medicaid managed care plans. Coding compliance requirements

24 Credentialing is a regulated activity, required by CMS and the Joint Commission (www.jointcommission.org), whereby health plans and hospitals must verify each provider has the education, training and appropriate licenses to deliver services to patients.

25 A delegated entity is a provider organization that takes on certain responsibilities on behalf of a health plan, such as utilization management and claims processing.

26 HIPAA was passed in 1996 and required the creation of national standards to protect sensitive patient health information from being disclosed without the patient's consent or knowledge.

27 Regulatory requirements regarding the ICD-9-CM code set (now ICD-10) were created in the 1970s and CPT requirements followed later in 1983.

also affect provider reimbursement under the Medicare Merit-Based Incentive Program (MIPS) and other Alternative Payment Models (APMs). See Chapter 4 for a brief explanation of these programs.

Failure to submit accurate CPT and/or ICD-10 codes can lead to Federal or state investigations under the False Claims Act (FCA), which provides for both criminal and civil prosecution. Regulatory requirements and enforcement actions have resulted hospitals and physicians investing in infrastructure, software and staffing to ensure that claims that are submitted to government payers have the correct information, and most hospitals and providers also use the capabilities of electronic medical records (EMR) to help ensure coding accuracy. In addition, many providers employ medical coding specialists to evaluate medical records and bills to ensure completeness, accuracy and compliance with coding requirements.

B. HIPAA Compliance

In addition to compliance requirements specific to billing for services, hospitals and physicians/physician organizations also have compliance requirements regarding HIPAA, which was passed by Congress in 1996.[28] Hospitals and physicians/physician organizations are considered "covered entities"[29] and must comply with HIPAA requirements regarding "permitted uses and disclosures" of PHI. In addition to PHI disclosure and use requirements, HIPAA includes a security rule specific to PHI that is created, received, maintained or transmitted in electronic format.

As with billing and coding compliance, hospital and physician behavior are influenced by HIPAA requirements because violations could result in financial penalties, reputational harm and patient dissatisfaction. HIPAA violations can also affect contractual relationships with health plan partners and depending on the state, result in state-imposed regulatory oversight which could take the form of an independent monitor.[30]

C. Delegated Entity Compliance

As an increasing number of physician groups, IPAs, foundations and hospitals agree to accept capitation or other risk-based payments, health plans often contract

28 "Health Insurance Portability and Accountability Act," Centers for Disease Control and Prevention (CDC), 1996, www.cdc.gov/phlp/publications/topic/hipaa.html#:~:text=The%20Health%20Insurance%20Portability%20and,the%20patient's%20consent%20or%20knowledge.

29 "Health Insurance Portability and Accountability Act," Centers for Disease Control and Prevention (CDC), 1996, www.cdc.gov/phlp/publications/topic/hipaa.html#:~:text=The%20Health%20Insurance%20Portability%20and,the%20patient's%20consent%20or%20knowledge.

30 Independent Monitors are responsible for measuring and reporting an organization's compliance with regulatory requirements, corrective action plan initiatives or compliance with agreed upon settlement terms with a regulator or government body.

with a third-party hospital or physician organization to perform the utilization management function, as well as claims adjudication and payment. Organizations that perform these functions are called "delegated entities." When a health plan delegates these responsibilities to a third-party hospital or physician organization, the delegated entity takes on the compliance requirements of the health plan related to utilization management and claims processing.

Typical compliance requirements related to claims processing include:

- Timely payment per contract terms or regulatory requirement
- Timely denial per contract terms or regulatory requirement
- Accurate payment per contract terms
- Payment of interest for late claims payment per contract terms or regulatory requirement
- Specific language requirements for denials of payments, including information regarding filing an appeal

Utilization management compliance requirements can be more burdensome for delegated entities and may include:

- Timely determination of a prior authorization request within contractual or regulatory requirements
- Inclusion of the specific criteria used to deny authorization, which must be communicated to both the attending physician and the patient
- Notification of appeal and grievance processes

In some states, a patient has the right to seek an independent review of denied services by an appointed third-party team of physicians.

Some provider organizations do not have experience in meeting specific health plan compliance requirements and their compliance departments may not have experienced staff who are familiar with the oversight and testing of utilization management and claims payment processes. In addition, some delegated entities also do not have adequate systems in place that are required to perform utilization management and/or claims payment functions. In situations where a delegated entity does not have requisite experience, the entity may hire a third party administrator (TPA, see Chapter 5) for utilization management and claims processing. Some delegated entities are also not experienced in reviewing claims appeals and patient grievances and may rely on a third-party organization to conduct these activities as well. However, compliance responsibilities remain with the delegated entity and cannot be delegated to the TPA, and the delegated entity must develop and implement a compliance testing program for any activities it has contracted out.

Provider organizations that take on delegated health plan responsibilities as part of risk-based arrangements are typically audited annually by each health plan they work with and potentially by a state regulatory agency as well. Health plan audits typically mirror the regulatory agency audits in terms of scope, but the sampling methodologies may vary between regulators and from health plan to health plan.[31]

Health plans are responsible for ensuring that each delegated provider organization is compliant with the regulatory requirements for timeliness, accuracy and appropriateness of determinations and can be held responsible for a delegated entity's failures. Penalties may include substantial financial fines. Some delegation agreements include language requiring delegated entities to be responsible for paying any fines levied against a health plan as a result of delegated entity's failure to comply with regulatory requirements. Thus, hospitals and physician organizations are heavily influenced by the consequences of non-compliance, which may include potential enforcement actions by regulators, potential "de-delegation" by health plans and ultimately termination of contractual agreements.

In this chapter, we have explored provider perspectives relative to the contracting process, including network participation, pricing, reimbursement rates and market power. We have also touched on the issue of compliance and the responsibilities providers have in meeting regulatory requirements. Now that we have provided an overview of reimbursement methodologies and payer-provider contracting from an operational perspective, the next three chapters focus on the issues that can arise in payer-provider disputes.

31 Compliance testing requires either a testing of every transaction during a specific period or using a sampling methodology to look at a subset of the transactions to evaluate compliance. A random sampling approach is typically used, which is sometimes stratified. Sample sizes vary but some organizations limit their sample size to 30, 40 or 50 records processed during a specific time interval (i.e., quarterly, annual). The precision or confidence level of a sample is the key to predictive accuracy of the sample to the entire population.

CHAPTER 7

Setting the Stage for Payer-Provider Disputes

Steven Hamilton

I. INTRODUCTION

Why are there so many payer-provider disputes? The answer is simple: healthcare involves a lot of money. As discussed in Chapter 1, the federal government tracks National Health Expenditures ("NHE") each year dating back to 1960 and in 2021, U.S. healthcare spending was $4.3 trillion. This amounts to $12,914 per person and 18.3 percent of the country's gross domestic product.[1] The primary drivers of healthcare expenditures are hospital services (31 percent), physician and clinical services (20 percent) and retail prescription drugs (9 percent).[2] In 2021, Medicare accounted for $900.8 billion (21 percent) of the NHE, Medicaid accounted for $734.0 billion (17 percent), and private (commercial) health insurance expenditures accounted for $1.2 trillion (28 percent).[3]

Not many industries account for trillions of dollars in expenditures, and when there is that much money at stake, litigation is sure to follow. As a result, disputes between payers and providers are common. At the same time, due to the rapidly evolving business practices and regulatory environment, these disputes can involve complex legal issues. Further complicating disputes is the fact that payers and

---

1 "National Health Expenditures, Historical," Centers for Medicare & Medicaid Services, accessed March 18, 2023, www.cms.gov/research-statistics-data-and-systems/statistics-trends-and-reports/nationalhealthexpenddata/nationalhealthaccountshistorical#:~:text=The%20data%20are%20presented%20by,For%20additional%20information%2C%20see%20below.

2 "National Health Expenditures, NHE Fact Sheet," accessed March 18, 2023, www.cms.gov/research-statistics-data-and-systems/statistics-trends-and-reports/nationalhealthexpenddata/nhe-fact-sheet.

3 "National Health Expenditures, Historical," Centers for Medicare & Medicaid Services, accessed March 18, 2023, www.cms.gov/research-statistics-data-and-systems/statistics-trends-and-reports/nationalhealthexpenddata/nationalhealthaccountshistorical#:~:text=The%20data%20are%20presented%20by,For%20additional%20information%2C%20see%20below.

providers are often in continuing symbiotic business relationships, which impacts the course of the litigation.

Attorneys that represent health plans and providers in payer-provider litigation must have a full understanding of the applicable plan types, laws and contract requirements at the outset of any case as they will form the foundation of a dispute. Due to this vast web of legal requirements—some of which are murky at best—litigation between payers and providers can quickly become complex. To help set the stage for the complex nature of payer-provider litigation, this chapter provides a high-level discussion of certain managed care industry issues that form the foundation for payer-provider disputes, including the various health insurer lines of business, as well as operational aspects of managed care organizations such as utilization management, claims adjudication and special investigation units. While the overview set forth in this chapter is by no means comprehensive, it is intended to give the reader a solid baseline understanding of these issues because they ultimately are important factors in litigation. For instance, a health plan and provider attorney will need to have a full understanding of the applicable business lines because there will be different contracts, regulatory environments and policy considerations for each. After this chapter, readers will have a better understanding of the backdrop for litigation, which will be discussed in greater detail in Chapters 8 and 9.

II. HEALTH INSURER LINES OF BUSINESS AND THEIR IMPACT ON PAYER-PROVIDER LITIGATION

A. Commercial Lines of Business

A "commercial" line of business (LOB) is a relatively loose term used to describe a health plan LOB involving non-government programs. As described in Chapter 3, commercial LOBs or commercial health plans can either be "individual" or "group" health plans. Individual health plans are purchased by individuals (or individuals and their family members) and coverage is limited to the policy holder and approved beneficiaries of the policy, such as a spouse or children. Group health plans, as their name suggests, are health plans that cover a group of people. In the vast majority of cases, these are health plans that are either formed or purchased by an employer or other group such as a union. Group health plans can, in turn, be either small group (i.e., 100 employees or less) or large group health plans.

Some individual health plans can be purchased on the federal or state exchanges created by the Affordable Care Act (ACA). Two key features of "on-exchange" plans are premium subsidies, where the federal government subsidizes premiums for eligible individuals, and cost-sharing subsidies, where the federal government subsidizes cost-sharing obligations for low-income individuals. An "off-exchange plan" is a policy that consumers purchase directly from an insurance company rather than on the federal or state exchanges. In most instances, individual plans are governed by state law. But whether a plan is an on-exchange or off-exchange plan can be important for litigation between payers and providers because most provider contracts will have requirements specific to the plan type, as well as payment rates that may differ by plan type. Likewise, out-of-network requirements and payment rules may be different depending on the plan type. As a result, it is important for lawyers to understand what types of plans are specifically at issue to ensure they fully understand the contractual and regulatory requirements.

The terms "fully insured" and "self-insured" group health plan have also been used throughout this book and these types of plans have been described previously. The differences between these two plan types are also very important in the context of payer-provider litigation. Specifically, when a plan is fully insured and the health insurer is at risk for paying claims, the insurer is usually the defendant in any lawsuit brought by a provider. On the other hand, if the plan is self-funded, the health insurer often acts as the administrator of the plan, but the plan itself is ultimately liable for payment. In addition, the plan may have ultimate decision-making authority. As a result, the plan may be the primary defendant.

B. Government Programs (Medicare Advantage, Medicaid Managed Care, Part D)

In the past two decades, government programs such as Medicare Advantage and Medicaid Managed Care have become more and more popular LOBs for private or commercial health plans in large part because they offer a consistent revenue stream and growth opportunities. At the same time, the federal government and some states have turned to managed care because it can offer substantial cost savings and care management infrastructure that states are often not equipped to handle through their fee-for-service Medicaid programs.

Thus, by contracting with commercial managed care organizations (i.e., commercial health plans) to administer benefits for government program beneficiaries such as Medicare or Medicaid enrollees, governments can reduce program costs, better manage utilization of health services and shift the financial risk onto the commercial health plans.[4] Commercial plans that administer Medicare Advantage plans are called Medicare Advantage Organizations (MAO).

The Medicare Advantage program effectively experienced linear growth between 2007, when 19 percent of Medicare beneficiaries were enrolled in Medicare Advantage plans, and 2022, when 48 percent were enrolled in such plans. It is projected that 61 percent of Medicare beneficiaries will be enrolled in Medicare Advantage plans by 2032.[5] Similarly, with respect to Medicaid managed care, over 70 percent of all Medicaid beneficiaries are enrolled in some form of managed care, and states are increasingly using innovative managed care models to deliver

---

4 *New Jersey Primary Care Ass'n Inc. v. New Jersey Dep't of Human Servs.*, 722 F.3d 527, 530 (3d Cir. 2013); *see also Starko, Inc. v. New Mexico Human Servs. Dep't*, 333 P. 3d 947, 952 (N.M. 2014).

5 Meredith Freed, Jeannie Fuglesten Biniek, Anthony Damico, and Tracia Neuman, "Medicare Advantage in 2022: Enrollment Update and Key Trends," Kaiser Family Foundation, August 25, 2022, www.kff.org/medicare/issue-brief/medicare-advantage-in-2022-enrollment-update-and-key-trends/.

traditional Medicaid and other enhanced benefits to beneficiaries.[6] See Chapter 1 for a description of Medicare Advantage, Medicare Part D and Medicaid managed care plans.

In addition to Medicare and Medicaid managed care plans, there are also the Federal Employee Health Benefits (FEHB) and TRICARE programs. FEHB plans are offered to current and retired government employees and TRICARE plans are offered to active duty and retired military personnel and their families.[7] Similar to the arrangement between the federal government and MAOs, the federal government contracts with commercial plans to offer FEHB plans to eligible federal employees. The FEHB program is considered the largest employer-sponsored group health insurance program in the world. Similar to FEHB, under TRICARE, the federal government contracts with commercial health plans to administer covered benefits.[8]

Why is it important to understand the differences between these plans for litigation purposes? The short answer is because each program has different statutes, regulations and guidance that will dictate covered benefits, procedural requirements such as appeal rights and the applicable law. As a practitioner, whether on the plan side or provider side, it is extremely important to understand the regulatory and legal landscape before engaging in litigation because there are nuances to each program that will frame the litigation.

For instance, the procedural aspects of litigation involving a commercial health plan that is governed by federal law will differ greatly from those involving a Medicaid managed care organization (MCO). Likewise, the substantive claims that can be alleged will vary by plan type. Therefore, if practitioners are not familiar with these differences, they may find themselves unnecessarily spending time and resources on issues that ultimately lead to dead ends.

III. UTILIZATION MANAGEMENT

Utilization management is a cost management approach used in managed care and was described in Chapters 5 and 6. Almost all health plans, including commercial and government-sponsored plans, have some form of utilization management, with health maintenance organizations (HMO) using some of the most rigorous approaches.[9] Indeed, government-sponsored managed care organizations are generally required to have some form of utilization management program.[10]

---

6 *Id.*

7 "Healthcare & Insurance," U.S. Office of Personnel Management, accessed March 18, 2023, www.opm.gov/healthcare-insurance/healthcare/.

8 "About Us," TRICARE, accessed March 18, 2023, www.tricare.mil/About.

9 Angelo Giardino and Roopma Wadhwa, "Utilization Management," StatPearls Publishing, July 11, 2022, www.ncbi.nlm.nih.gov/books/NBK560806/.

10 *See, e.g.*, 42 CFR § 438.210.

Utilization management is widely recognized as being an effective form of cost management in healthcare.[11] There are multiple methods employed under the umbrella term of utilization management, including prior authorization, concurrent review and retrospective review, and federal and/or state laws may exist that delineate when certain functions may be used and under what circumstances. When it comes to litigation between health plans and providers that involve utilization management determinations, it is important to learn what laws, if any, may apply in the jurisdiction.[12] For instance, with respect to MAOs, CMS has explained:

> Coordinated care plans are designed to manage cost, service utilization, and quality by ensuring that only medically necessary care is provided. This is done in part through the use of utilization management tools, including prior authorization, expressly referenced at section 1852(c)(1)(G) and (c)(2)(B) of the Act. These tools are designed to help MA plans determine the medical necessity of services and minimize the furnishing of unnecessary services, thereby helping to contain costs and protect beneficiaries from receiving unnecessary care. Additionally, section 1852(g)(1)(A) of the Act states that MA plans shall have a procedure for making determinations regarding whether an enrollee is entitled to receive a health care service and that such determinations must be made on a timely basis; that provision applies to both prior authorization determinations and to post-service decisions about coverage and payment.[13]

Alternatively, states may have laws that apply to commercial health plans or even Medicaid MCOs that must be followed regarding utilization management.

The following are different types of utilization management tools:

- **Prior authorization** means that approval from the health plan is needed before a person receives a service or item.[14] Prior authorization is also known as precertification, preauthorization, prior approval and predetermination.[15] Prior authorization is designed to ensure that the services are medically appropriate and delivered in an appropriate setting (*e.g.*, inpatient vs. outpatient). In the prior authorization process, providers or enrollees

---

11 *See, e.g.*, *Kondell v. Blue Cross & Blue Shield of Fla., Inc.*, 187 F. Supp. 3d 1348, 1362 (S.D. Fla. 2016) ("the Court notes that such" utilization management and utilization review programs "constitute one type of the cost-containment procedures and provisions *required* under Florida insurance law. *See* Fla. Stat. § 627.4234.").

12 "NAIC Model Law, Utilization Review and Benefit Determination Act," National Association of Insurance Commissioners, accessed March 18, 2023, https://content.naic.org/sites/default/files/model-law-073.pdf.

13 87 FR 79452, 79497–79498 (Dec. 27, 2022).

14 "Prior Authorization," Healthcare.gov., accessed March 18, 2023, www.healthcare.gov/glossary/prior-authorization/.

15 Amanda DeMarzo, "What Is Prior Authorization?" December 15, 2020, www.priorauthtraining.org/prior-authorization/.

generally submit information (usually clinical in nature) to the health plan and the plan usually uses generally accepted clinical criteria to determine the appropriateness of the request. While prior authorization is often criticized because of the procedural requirements associated with it, it is recognized as an important tool, especially in government programs.[16]

- **Concurrent review** occurs when the patient is receiving care, such as when admitted as an inpatient to a hospital.[17] Under the concurrent review process, enrollees or providers submit information to the health plan while the member is receiving care so that the health plan can monitor the care and ensure that the care remains medically necessary.[18] Concurrent review helps ensure the delivery of efficient and effective health care and reduce overutilization of services, as well as overspending on care.[19] Concurrent review is most often used with government-sponsored managed care plans pursuant to the plans' care management obligations and responsibility to ensure government program dollars are being properly utilized.
- **Retrospective review** is the process by which a health plan reviews a claim after services are rendered to determine if the claim is payable. This occurs for many reasons. For instance, a plan may undertake retrospective review to ensure group health plan benefits are being properly provided by confirming member eligibility, for coordination of benefits, or to determine whether claims submitted by the provider are payable under the plan's policies and procedures. In addition, retrospective review may be used to determine if a provider ostensibly engaged in fraud, waste, or abuse.

Over the years, the federal government and many states have passed laws and regulations relating to prior authorization that impact various types of health plans and providers, including delineating the process for prior authorization, when plans can deny payment after granting prior authorization and other requirements.[20] In recent years, federal and state regulators have focused more closely on prior authorization requirements. For instance, in early 2023, the federal government proposed rules impacting prior authorization requirements for MAOs, including how such plans would process prior authorization requests and what information and guidelines they could rely upon in assessing those requests.[21]

16 87 Fed. Reg. 79452, 79498 (Dec. 27, 2022) ("CMS understands that utilization management tools are an important means to coordinate care, reduce inappropriate utilization, and promote cost-efficient care.").

17 Angelo Giardino, Loopma Wadhwa, "Utilization Management," StatPearls Publishing, July 11, 2022, www.ncbi.nlm.nih.gov/books/NBK560806/.

18 *Id.*

19 *Id.*

20 "2021 Prior Authorization State Law Chart," American Medical Association, accessed March 18, 2023, www.ama-assn.org/system/files/2021-04/pa-state-chart.pdf.

21 87 Fed. Reg. 76238 (Dec. 13, 2022); *see also* 87 Fed. Reg. 79452 (Dec. 27, 2022).

Similarly, as many as 16 states have laws that limit or change prior authorization for state-regulated health plans.[22]

Often litigation between payers and providers revolves around utilization management decisions, such as medical necessity decisions where the plan denies certain services as not being medically necessary, or the utilization management process such as when the provider did not obtain authorization prior to rendering services. In addition to the laws identified above, if the provider is contracted with the insurer or plan, the contract will in most instances contain details about utilization management requirements and indicate that the insurer or the health plan (if self-insured) has the authority and discretion to make medical necessity determinations under the plan terms. In these types of disputes, it is very important for both the plan lawyer and the provider lawyer to understand the applicable state and/or federal laws, as well as contractual requirements, that may be implicated with respect to utilization management.

IV. SPECIAL INVESTIGATION UNITS

Special Investigation Units ("SIUs") are used by health plans as part of their program integrity and compliance requirements to prevent, detect and correct putative fraud, waste and abuse. For instance, MAOs are required under federal law and guidance to establish an SIU or generally perform SIU functions through their compliance department by conducting surveillance, interviews and other methods of investigation relating to potential fraud, waste and abuse by providers.[23]

While SIUs generally have been used by government-sponsored managed care plans, in recent years commercial health insurers have also been increasingly utilizing SIUs for their products to ensure appropriate use of resources, especially by insurers acting as administrators to self-funded employers. This is not a law enforcement function; however, SIU staff often includes former law enforcement personnel, certified coders and data analysts, who utilize advanced data analytics and other methods to identify and investigate providers who may be committing fraud. Moreover, SIUs for government-sponsored managed care organizations often work closely with law enforcement and are required in some instances to report potential fraud, waste and abuse to law enforcement.[24] For instance, consider the following August 2022 statement from the Texas Office of the Inspector General ("OIG"):

> One tool managed care organizations (MCOs) use to reduce fraud, waste and abuse (FWA) is a team of in-house investigators known as the special

22 Arielle Dreher, "States Jump into Fight Over Prior Authorization Requirements," January 27, 2023, www.axios.com/2023/01/27/states-target-doctor-authorization.

23 "Medicare Managed Care Manual Chapter 21—Compliance Program Guidelines and Prescription Drug Benefit Manual Chapter 9—Compliance Program Guidelines, Section 50.6.10," Centers for Medicare & Medicaid Services, accessed March 18, 2023, www.cms.gov/regulations-and-guidance/guidance/manuals/downloads/mc86c21.pdf.

24 *Id.*

investigative units (SIUs). This team reviews all services provided under an MCO's contract with Texas Medicaid. A 2019 contract amendment requires these teams to include a full-time SIU manager and credentialed investigator, which examine improper claims by Texas Medicaid clients and service providers. To support these efforts, the OIG has a dedicated coordinator to assist with referrals, investigations and training. MCOs and the OIG also work collaboratively through the Texas Fraud Prevention Partnership, which helps identify, investigate and refer cases. These changes likely contributed to a 33 percent increase in SIU referrals for provider investigation from fiscal year 2020 to 2021.

The OIG uses its access to referrals and encounter data across all MCOs and programs to identify potentially widespread issues. Running analytics on a referral set helps the agency determine if something that looks like a small problem with one MCO is a repeated issue across the Medicaid program. The OIG's data analytics process can uncover systemic trends that might not be visible at the MCO level. For example, a provider may bill multiple MCOs for the same hours worked, establishing an issue where Medicaid pays a single healthcare provider for "impossible hours."[25]

The pending Department of Health and Human Services, Office of the Inspector General (HHS-OIG) work plan items outline what HHS-OIG intends to analyze and potentially investigate, and these show that the agency intends to take a close look at Medicaid fraud referrals in its anticipated report OEI-03–22–00410.[26] As HHS-OIG explained in this report:

> For Medicaid managed care, States contract with private health insurance companies, or managed care plans, that have the primary responsibility for processing, paying, and monitoring the claims of providers in their networks. As such, managed care plans play a critical role in safeguarding Medicaid program integrity. According to Federal regulations, State contracts with managed care plans must require that plans promptly refer any potential fraud, waste, or abuse to State Medicaid agencies or Medicaid Fraud Control Units (MFCUs). However, both OIG and CMS have ongoing concerns about managed care plans' efforts to combat fraud, including concerns about a lack of fraud referrals. This evaluation will determine the number of potential fraud referrals managed care plans made to States, MFCUs, and other entities; determine whether managed care plan processes support the referral of potential fraud;

25 "Special Investigative Units Help Prevent Fraud, Waste and Abuse," Texas Health and Human Services, Inspector General, August 18, 2022, https://oig.hhs.texas.gov/about-us/news/special-investigative-units-help-prevent-fraud-waste-and-abuse.

26 "Medicaid Managed Care Plans' Focus on Fraud Referrals," Department of Health & Human Services, Office of the Inspector General, accessed March 18, 2023, https://oig.hhs.gov/reports-and-publications/workplan/summary/wp-summary-0000727.asp.

and identify the factors that influence whether managed care plans make referrals. This work may identify ways to increase the total number of managed care plan referrals and ensure the quality and timeliness of referrals.

MAOs also generally are required to refer potential fraud, waste and abuse to the applicable oversight agencies. As such, any SIU investigation—especially those involving government-sponsored managed care—has a strong potential to lead to true government enforcement action if there is wrongdoing. Thus, provider attorneys need to be aware of requests from health plan SIUs and take them seriously. If there is no wrongdoing, cooperating with the SIU and demonstrating that fact will be important, because it could prevent a referral to law enforcement. And if there is potential wrongdoing, it is a good idea to get ahead of the issue to determine whether a self-referral is appropriate.

V. CLAIMS ADJUDICATION

Probably the most important relationship and functionality between health plans and providers is the claims adjudication process, as the submission and payment of healthcare claims are the backbone of the healthcare system. Claims adjudication is the process by which healthcare providers submit claims to healthcare insurers for review and payment. Historically, providers would submit claims to insurers on paper forms, but in modern times the vast majority of claims are submitted electronically using HIPAA-compliant transactions (see Chapter 6 for more on HIPAA). The insurer then reviews the claim—through automation and/or manual review—to decide whether it will pay the claim (in whole or part), deny the claim or pend the claim for further review.

In general, a health insurer will only pay claims if the billed services are covered services under the applicable health plan, and the claims are billed according to the insurer's policies and procedures as well as the provider's agreement with the plan, if applicable. The insurer then pays the claim according to any applicable agreement, the plans policies and procedures, and in some cases, external fee schedules.

The federal government, in the case of Medicare Advantage and Medicaid managed care plans, as well as most states, have laws relating to the submission and payment of claims. These are usually referred to as "prompt pay" laws. In most instances, these laws specify what types of claims, providers and health plans to which the laws apply and the requirements for processing those claims. For instance, in North Carolina, N.C.G.S. § 58–3–225 requires a health insurer to either pay a claim or send a notice to the claimant within 30 days of receipt of the claim.[27] The notice must state the good faith reason or reasons for the denial, including benefit limitations, coordination of benefits, lack of eligibility or lack of coverage for the services provided.[28]

27 "Prompt Pay Requirement," North Carolina Department of Insurance, accessed March 18, 2023, www.ncdoi.gov/insurance-industry/form-and-rate-filings/life-and-health/prompt-pay-requirement.
28 *Id.*

VI. CONCLUSION

As is evident, health insurance is complex as it involves multiple lines of business, which are each regulated by different sets of statutes and regulations. In any litigation, it is imperative that the attorneys involved have a comprehensive understanding of the underlying regulatory scheme as it will without doubt impact the litigation. For instance, in cases between contracted providers and insurers/plans, the contract will often be the baseline, but the laws that are generally incorporated into every provider contract may ultimately control the dispute. Likewise, in disputes between non-contracted providers and plans, the laws may provide the baseline for the dispute. The same is true for any operational issue that underlies the dispute. If the issue is utilization management and a medical necessity decision, it is important for the practitioner to understand the functions performed by managed care organizations to make medical necessity determinations and the appeals process associated with those decisions. As we move into the following chapters that discuss payer-provider litigation in more detail, the reader needs to keep this background in mind to provide context and gain a better understanding of the disputes.

CHAPTER 8

Payer-Provider Disputes from the Payer Perspective

Steven Hamilton

As set forth in Chapter 7, disputes between payers and providers can often be complex due to the intersection of varying contracts, statutes, regulations and policies. This chapter delves into greater detail about payer-provider disputes from the payer perspective, including discussing common types of disputes, issues that arise in those disputes and practical pointers for health plan lawyers. This is not intended to be a comprehensive list or analysis of these issues, but rather to provide a solid core understanding so that practitioners can perform their own analysis and research.

I. CONTRACTUAL RELATIONSHIPS AND DISPUTES

At a high level, there are three foundations for disputes between payers and providers: contracts, common law and statutes/regulations. However, each dispute can present a complex, and at times daunting, web of these issues that must be untangled by the practitioners. Let's examine these issues further.

A. The Contractual Framework

The backbone of the healthcare industry is the three-way contractual relationship between healthcare providers, members/patients and payers. This tripartite relationship has been in place for decades but at the same time creates legal issues that often arise during disputes between providers and payers. This is shown in Figure 8.1.

1. The Provider Agreement

Focusing on the contract between the health insurer and the provider, this agreement sets out the parties' relationship usually in great detail, including requirements relating to claims submission, claims adjudication, credentialing, utilization

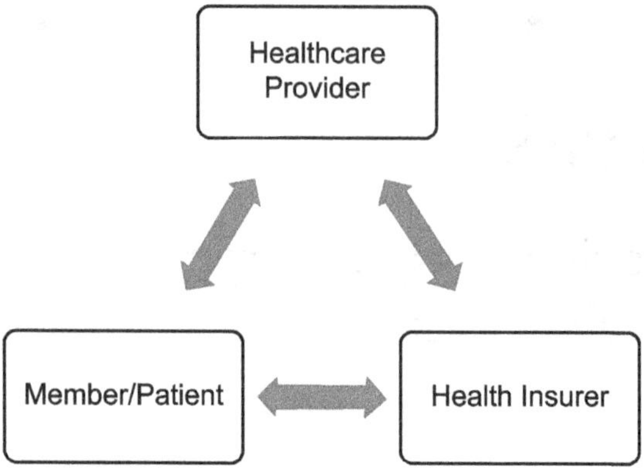

Figure 8.1

management, appeals, dispute resolution and—most important—the payment rates. Provider agreements have evolved over the years and are often very sophisticated and specific to provider specialties.

As an example, a hospital provider will have an agreement specific to hospital services, whereas a home health provider will have an ancillary services agreement specific to home health. In most instances, these provider agreements have been developed over several years, often based upon templates that were approved by state or federal regulators depending on the line of business. Sometimes these agreements are entered into without any meaningful negotiation. Other times, however, providers and health plans can engage in lengthy contract negotiations. Either way, the resulting agreement forms the cornerstone of the parties' relationship and health plans, depending on their size, may have thousands of these agreements.

The provider agreement is usually not composed of a single document. Rather, these contracts will in most circumstances incorporate by reference the health insurers' policies and procedures, including a provider manual, which contain additional detail as to the parties' respective operating obligations. From the plan's perspective, the incorporation of its policies and procedures is extremely important because plans need to be able to adopt certain policies, such as coverage and reimbursement policies, that apply uniformly across providers and members without having to negotiate an amendment to each provider agreement. If health plans could not rely upon their policies and procedures, they would not be able to operate in a consistent manner for all of their members and clients.

Likely the most important aspect of the provider agreement is the payment arrangement, which can take many forms. The fee-for-service methodology is the most traditional and historically common form. Under this methodology, the health plan pays the provider for each service rendered. However, over the years, this methodology has been replaced or augmented by alternative payment models such as bundled payments or capitated payments, which have been described in greater detail throughout this book. As we learned in Chapters 5 and 6, capitated arrangements can involve providers having both upside and downside risk, such that if a provider's capitated payments are sufficient to cover the costs of services provided, the provider gets to keep the remaining profit. However, if the payments are not sufficient to cover the costs of services, the provider is at risk for the shortfall. While the provider agreement will detail the parties' obligations under a risk-sharing arrangement, some states have also enacted laws that delineate regulatory obligations for these contracts.[1]

Provider agreements may also have value-based payments or "pay-for-performance" arrangements, which are intended to reward the provider for patient outcomes. Pay-for-performance arrangements will often be combined with other payment methods and include financial incentives to meet certain clinical outcomes or performance measures.[2] These arrangements became more popular in the past decade or so as concerns about the fee-for-service payment structure increased due to the incentives associated with paying based upon volume instead of quality.[3] Typically, a pay-for-performance program includes a bonus payment to a provider if they meet certain agreed-upon quality or performance measures.[4] Provider agreements can be very dynamic and include multiple payment methodologies, especially agreements involving large provider organizations that have more expansive administrative and clinical capabilities and a higher financial risk-reward tolerance.

2. *The Member's Benefit Agreement*

In addition to the provider agreement in this tripartite relationship, the member benefit agreement (often referred to as an "Evidence of Coverage") is the agreement between the member and the health plan. This document is important because it will, among other things, dictate the coverage available to the member as well as the responsibilities of the member. In addition, it typically identifies exclusions such as experimental and investigational services and lays out the member's payment obligations such as copayments, deductibles and coinsurance. In most instances, the benefit agreement is incorporated into the provider agreement by reference either directly or indirectly.

3. *The Member-Provider Agreement*

Finally, we have the agreement between the member/patient and the provider. This agreement is usually in the form of a consent and authorization signed by the

1 "Overview of Risk Sharing Arrangements," California Department of Managed Health Care, accessed March 19, 2023, www.dmhc.ca.gov/Portals/0/AbouttheDMHC/FSSB/Meetings/a020129_info.pdf.

2 Julia James, "Pay-for-Performance," Health Affairs Health Policy Brief, October 11, 2012, www.healthaffairs.org/do/10.1377/hpb20121011.90233/.

3 *Id.*

4 *Id.*

member/patient at the provider's office and grants consent to receive treatment and obligates the member/patient to pay for the services in the event the health insurer does not. In the past few years, as discussed in further detail below, many states and ultimately the federal government have passed laws relating to notices that providers need to give members/patients regarding their payment obligations and the circumstances in which providers can bill members for services not paid for by insurers (this is called balance billing and was described in Chapter 3).

B. Types of Contractual Disputes

Now let's turn to the different types of common contractual disputes between payers and providers.

1. *Claims Payment and Other Operational Disputes*

Claims adjudication, as discussed previously, is one of the primary operational functions of health insurers. Providers submit claims for payment; health insurers process those claims through the claims payment system; and the insurer issues payment. While simple in concept, it is highly complex in practice as the claims adjudication process involves multiple steps. As a result, disputes between contracted providers and payers routinely arise. In many instances, the issue with respect to claims adjudication is whether the health plan properly processed the claim according to the contract terms. For instance, a provider may contest that an insurer has the ability to adjudicate claims according to a health plan policy or procedure that was recently implemented by the insurer.

In any claims payment dispute, the starting point is the provider agreement—what does it say about the issue, including any of the documents incorporated therein such as the plan's provider manual?[5] Since most cases involve issues that are not clearly addressed in plain contractual terms, often the dispute revolves around what the parties intended, if anything, regarding the disputed issue, which may be gleaned from the parties' course of performance and industry standards.[6]

In addition, because the parties' provider agreement will incorporate the relevant law, the practitioners must assess whether federal or state law imposes a requirement or otherwise addresses the disputed issues. As explained in this book, there are numerous state laws that may apply to claims processing, including how claims are processed and the standards used in processing claims. Furthermore,

5 *See, e.g.*, *Vyera Pharms., LLC v. Walgreen Co.*, No. 19 CV 5652, 2020 U.S. Dist. LEXIS 13656, *14–15 (N.D. Ill. Jan. 28, 2020) ("Under Illinois law, a court looks first to the plain language to interpret the contract. . . . If the contract language is ambiguous, a court can consider extrinsic evidence to determine the parties' intent.").

6 *NanoeXa Corp. v. Univ. of Chi.*, No. 10 C 7177, 2011 U.S. Dist. LEXIS 39973, *7–8 (N.D. Ill. Apr. 13, 2011) ("If, however, the trial court finds that the language of the contract is susceptible to more than one meaning, then an ambiguity is present and the court may look to extrinsic evidence. Appropriate extrinsic evidence includes industry custom.").

with respect to government-sponsored managed care organizations, where these organizations are contracted with and operate on behalf of the federal and/or state government, the applicable Medicare or Medicaid statutes, regulations or program guidance may provide dispositive requirements as to the basis for the adjudication of claims that the plans follow.

In many instances, claims disputes (whether between contracted or non-contracted providers and plans) can involve a significant number of claims and large dollar figures, often reaching into the tens of millions. These cases present unique challenges because they often involve numerous complex legal and factual issues that need to be unpacked by the lawyers. For instance, these disputes often involve claims from various lines of business, such as commercial and government-sponsored, which will have different legal frameworks.

Similarly, the underlying issues may range from medical necessity determinations to coding issues, as well as timely submission and other issues. As a result, each claim often presents individualized facts that need to be analyzed to be resolved. So what do you do with cases with large numbers of claims and a potentially wide range of issues? There is no set rule or formula to resolve these disputes, and each one needs to be evaluated on its own. However, practitioners should consider several things, including: (1) how to present the evidence for each claim in dispute and whether there are common facts and legal issues that apply to multiple claims; (2) the use of experts for both the merits underlying each claim and the presentation of the evidence such as sampling; and (3) how to compartmentalize the claims and whether any can be addressed in a dispositive motion. If these cases end up going to trial or hearing, then they need to be thoroughly vetted so that the evidence is presented in the most efficient and effective manner.

2. *Medical Necessity Disputes*

The concept of "medical necessity" determinations is a broad concept that covers many types of disputes. The most common is when a managed care organization makes a utilization management determination that a certain type of care is not covered because it is not the most efficient, did not comply with the plan terms or is experimental or investigational. Another type of issue that involves medical necessity determinations is when a provider bills a certain level of care, such as inpatient hospitalization, when the plan determines that another, lower level of care such as observation was more appropriate. In these circumstances, the plan is making a determination that the care provided is not a covered service, with the determination being made after a medical review.

Yet another concept that is tied to medical necessity is when a plan reviews an inpatient hospital claim billed using a specific DRG, including the corresponding medical information submitted by the provider, and determines that the DRG billed by the provider was not proper. In that scenario, the plan makes a determination that a different DRG (usually a lower level one) was proper, which is in part often a medical decision.

Medical necessity disputes are often mischaracterized as the plan "second-guessing" the provider, but the reality is that health plans and insurers often have the contractual right to determine what constitutes medically necessary care under the plain terms of the provider's agreement and/or the member's benefit plan. Thus, if medical necessity determinations become the subject of litigation, plans and providers should be fully aware of the contractual and/or statutory rights to make these decisions. Indeed, as explained herein, under the Employee Retirement Income Security Act (ERISA), the plan typically has the discretion to make medical necessity determinations and courts will not second-guess the decisions made except in limited circumstances.

The same concept applies with government-sponsored managed care, where plans are charged with ensuring government dollars are most appropriately spent. The discretion typically granted to plans and insurers to make medical necessity determinations does not mean that the provider is without the authority to determine the medical care needed or services rendered. To the contrary—plans will not interfere with a medical provider's judgment. And if a provider or member still believes the plan's determination is wrong, in almost all circumstances the provider or member can appeal the decision through one or multiple channels. If the plan or insurer does not have the discretion to make medical necessity determinations, then the resulting litigation can be cumbersome and expert-driven, with the results often hinging on the more reasoned and credible expert opinions.

3. *Other Contractual Arrangements*

With the shift to capitated/bundled payment arrangements and the growth of risk-sharing agreements, providers and plans are now becoming more involved in disputes relating to these contractual arrangements. In many instances, the parties work these disagreements out short of litigation because they are involved in an ongoing and mutually beneficial business relationship. However, when litigation does arise, ultimately the dispute is usually one of pure contract interpretation because there are not usually any laws that may regulate the relationship. As such, these disputes can be more straightforward from a strict legal perspective. At the same time, however, they can be more complex due to the evolving nature of these arrangements and the lack of extensive historical implementation in the industry.

4. *Practical Considerations in Contract Disputes: Arbitration vs. Court*

Most payer-provider contracts these days contain arbitration clauses, which are often inserted at the behest of both sides.[7] If the parties do have an arbitration clause, it will

7 In payer-provider disputes that do not have an arbitration clause, both attorneys should consider whether a judicial forum is the best place to obtain resolution, which may hinge on the type of dispute and the amounts at issue. For instance, a dispute over thousands of claims involving medical necessity determinations—which may necessitate individualized expert testimony—may be cost-prohibitive to try before a judge or jury. Therefore, the lawyers from both sides should consider whether it is better to agree to arbitration. This may be particularly useful if the issues would benefit from arbitrators who have experience in these matters and the parties can structure the hearing in a way that is more conducive to these disputes.

usually dictate the arbitral forum—often either the American Arbitration Association ("AAA") or the American Health Law Association ("AHLA")—and the applicable rules. Notably, both the AAA and AHLA have worked to cater to disputes in healthcare, particularly between payers and providers. For instance, the AHLA markets itself as being an expert in the healthcare field and maintains a "fair and balanced roster" because "AHLA recruits neutrals with experience representing both payers and providers, employees and employers, and residents and facilities."[8] Several years ago, the AAA introduced its "Payor Provider Arbitration Rules and Mediation Procedures" as a way to market its services relative to these disputes.[9] As such, the AAA stated that it "collaborated with distinguished members of its Healthcare Advisory Council and Payor Provider experts" to develop these rules.[10] Some of the benefits identified by the AAA with respect to the Payor Provider Arbitration Rules compared to the standard complex rules include the following:

- The number of depositions is limited to one or two;
- The award cannot be disseminated or published except in limited circumstances; and
- The award has no precedential effect on future disputes or rulings.[11]

It is up to the parties and their counsel to determine whether one of these specific forums or sets of rules better fits the needs of their case, taking into account the variations in the rules, the potential arbitrator pool and costs associated with each forum.

II. STATUTORY AND REGULATORY REQUIREMENTS AND THEIR IMPACT ON PAYER-PROVIDER DISPUTES

Beyond the parties' agreement, if one exists, there are numerous state and federal statutes, regulations and agency guidance documents that directly impact the relationship between providers and payers. There are numerous types of laws and regulations that apply, but discussed next are several that are fundamental.

A. State Laws Impacting Disputes

Each state has a complex array of statutes and regulations that apply to healthcare entities, including insurers and providers, and those laws often play an integral

8 "Dispute Resolution Services, Arbitration," American Health Law Association, accessed March 19, 2023, www.americanhealthlaw.org/dispute-resolution-services/arbitration.

9 "Rules, Forms, Fees," American Arbitration Association, accessed March 19, 2023, www.adr.org/active-rules.

10 "The Benefits of the New AAA Healthcare Payor Provider Arbitration Rules," American Arbitration Association, accessed March 19, 2023, www.adr.org/sites/default/files/document_repository/Payor%20Provider%20Rules%20vs%20Commercial%20Rules%20At%20A%20Glance.pdf.

11 *Id.*

role in disputes between payers and providers. In any dispute, practitioners need to familiarize themselves with potentially applicable state laws to determine whether they may apply to the dispute—with some of the most common being state "prompt pay" laws. In addition, there are numerous other laws that may tangentially apply to payer-provider disputes such as network requirements, notice requirements, "any willing provider" laws[12] and others. In this discussion, we will focus on prompt pay laws because they are most commonly involved in disputes.

Many states have enacted "prompt pay" laws that, among other things, dictate the submission of healthcare claims to insurers and the insurers' payment of those claims, such as the timeframe in which the claims must be paid and penalties for late payment.[13] While there are commonalities among the laws, the laws and their applicability may vary from state to state.[14] There are a few key factors that a practitioner must consider with respect to these laws. First, one needs to consider whether the law allows for a private cause of action. Second, a practitioner needs to evaluate whether the law applies to the dispute and the claims at issue in the dispute. That can only be done through an extensive and thorough understanding or analysis of the case law in that jurisdiction.

B. The Employee Retirement Income Security Act of 1974 (ERISA)

As we learned in Chapter 5, ERISA is a federal law that sets minimum standards for most voluntarily established retirement and health plans offered by employers (not including governmental entities or churches). At a high level, ERISA governs both pension plans and welfare benefit plans (*i.e.*, health plans) offered by employers. While ERISA does not mandate healthcare coverage, if an employer chooses to provide such coverage, ERISA contains detailed requirements regarding what the plan can and cannot do. The purpose of ERISA is to provide a comprehensive legislative scheme to govern employee benefit plans.[15] As the U.S. Supreme Court stated in one case:

> Congress enacted ERISA to protect the interests of participants in employee benefit plans and their beneficiaries by setting out substantive regulatory

12 An "any willing provider" law is generally a law that requires a health insurer to contract with a particular provider type (*e.g.*, pharmacist) under the plan's standard terms. *See, e.g.*, 215 Ill. Comp. Stat. 5/370h ("Before entering into any agreement under this Article an insurer or administrator shall establish terms and conditions that must be met by noninstitutional providers wishing to enter into an agreement with the insurer or administrator . . . An insurer or administrator shall not refuse to contract with any noninstitutional provider who meets the terms and conditions established by the insurer or administrator.").

13 "Prompt Pay FAQ," Texas Department of Insurance, accessed March 19, 2023, www.tdi.texas.gov/hprovider/ppsb418faq.html.

14 *See, e.g.*, Ala. Code §§ 27–1 *et seq.*; Fla. Stat. § 627.613 & 627.6131, OCGA § 33–25–59.14. These are just a few statutes.

15 *See Morstein v. National Ins. Servs.*, 93 F.3d 715, 718 (7th Cir. 1996) ("The Supreme Court has described the overall intent of ERISA as follows: 'ERISA is a comprehensive statute designed to promote the interests of employees and their beneficiaries in employee benefit plans.'") (citing *Shaw v. Delta Air Lines, Inc.*, 463 U.S. 85, 90 (1983)).

> requirements for employee benefit plans and to provide for appropriate remedies, sanctions, and ready access to the Federal courts. The purpose of ERISA is to provide a uniform regulatory regime over employee benefit plans [so that] employee benefit plan regulation would be exclusively a federal concern.[16]

Some of the core requirements of ERISA include requiring plans to provide participants with plan information, setting standards for participation and vesting, benefit accrual and funding, establishing fiduciary responsibilities for those who manage and control plan assets, setting grievance and appeal requirements and allowing beneficiaries to sue for benefits and breach of fiduciary duty.[17] Specifically, Section 502 of ERISA provides plan participants with available causes of actions and remedies for violations of ERISA, including denial of benefit claims under Section 501(a)(1)(B), breach of fiduciary duty under Section 501(a)(1)(B) and for injunctive relief under Section 501(a)(3).

An important component of ERISA is that it allows participants and beneficiaries to sue for benefits. Participants generally include any covered employee or former employee, and a beneficiary is defined as any person "designated by a participant, or by the terms of an employee benefit plan, who is or may become entitled to a benefit thereunder."[18] In addition, courts have allowed assignees of participants and beneficiaries to sue for benefits provided they have a valid assignment. As one court explained,

> Under § 502(a), a civil action may be brought by a participant or beneficiary of an ERISA plan to recover benefits due to him under the terms of that plan. ERISA defines a beneficiary as "a person designated by a participant, or by the terms of an employee benefit plan, who is or may become entitled to a benefit thereunder." Although § 502(a) is narrowly construed to permit only the enumerated parties to sue directly for relief, we have carved out a narrow exception to the ERISA standing requirements to grant standing to healthcare providers to whom a beneficiary has assigned his claim in exchange for health care.[19]

Assignments are vital in the context of disputes between health plans and providers that do not have a contract with the plan. Specifically, in order for a non-contracted provider to bring a claim under Section 502 against a health plan for the denial of payment for services rendered to a beneficiary, the provider generally must have a valid assignment of benefits from the beneficiary.[20] Notably, many ERISA plans include anti-assignment provisions within their plan documents

---

16 *Aetna Health Inc. v. Davila*, 542 U.S. 200, 208–209 (2004).

17 "Employee Retirement Income Security Act (ERISA)," U.S. Department of Labor, accessed March 19, 2023, www.dol.gov/general/topic/retirement/erisa.

18 See 29 U.S.C. § 1002(7)&(8).

19 *McCulloch Orthopaedic Surgical Servs., PLLC v. Aetna Inc.*, 857 F.3d 141, 146 (2d Cir. 2017).

20 *Id.*

that prohibit beneficiaries from assigning benefits under the plan, and many courts have enforced these provisions to prevent non-contracted providers from bringing ERISA claims.[21]

1. ERISA Preemption

Preemption can be a confusing topic. As one court put it: "any court forced to enter the ERISA preemption thicket sets out on a treacherous path."[22] The confusion usually stems from the fact that there are different forms of preemption (and those forms are often given different names)—complete and defensive, with defensive having three subsets called express, field and conflict preemption. The terms are often intermixed, or the words used in cases are sloppy such that even courts themselves get turned around and litigants are often left bewildered.[23] However, in ERISA litigation, preemption is extremely important and a powerful tool for health plans.

Before looking at ERISA specifically, it is important to consider the differences between complete and defensive preemption. Stated simply, complete preemption is when Congress intended for a federal law to completely supplant state law and create exclusive federal jurisdiction such that the claims asserted cannot be raised in state court.[24] Thus, the claims are removable to federal court no matter their form. Defensive preemption is different as it is a defense to a claim, and not a basis for federal court jurisdiction including through removal.[25] Defensive preemption can take a few forms, including express, field and

---

21 *Id.*; *see also Physicians Multispeciality Grp. v. Health Care Plan of Horton Homes, Inc.*, 371 F.3d 1291, 1295 (11th Cir. 2004) ("[W]e are persuaded by the reasoning of the majority of federal courts that have concluded that an assignment is ineffectual if the [ERISA benefit] plan contains an unambiguous anti-assignment provision.") (collecting cases); *see also Hishmeh v. Horizon Blue Cross Blue Shield of N.J.*, Case No. 19-cv-4727, 2020 U.S. Dist. LEXIS 185515, at *7 (E.D.N.Y. Sept. 28, 2020) ("For an out-of-network provider to bring a cause of action under ERISA, the assignment of benefits must be valid. If a plan contains an unambiguous anti-assignment provision, any assignment in the face of that clause is invalid.") (collecting cases).

22 *Gonzales v. Prudential Ins. Co. of America*, 901 F.2d 446, 451–52 (5th Cir. 1990).

23 *See, e.g., Greenbrier Hotel Corp. v. Unite Here Health*, 719 Fed. Appx. 168, 179 (4th Cir. 2018) ("The district court thus erred in relying instead on a literal reading of the phrase 'relate to' in ERISA § 514(a) and in confusing case law on preemption for federal removal and preemption as a substantive matter."); *York v. Ramsay Youth Servs.*, 313 F. Supp. 2d 1275, 1280–1281 (M.D. Ala. 2004) ("In a previous case, this court expressed concerns about whether the existing case law contributes to the morass that is ERISA law by confusing defensive preemption, which should not confer jurisdiction over state law claims upon a federal court, with complete preemption, which would provide a federal court with jurisdiction.").

24 *See, e.g., Iskowitz v. Northridge Subtenant, LLC*, Case No. 21-cv-1108, 2021 U.S. Dist. LEXIS 235400, *11 (S.D. Cal. Dec. 8, 2021) ("Complete preemption is a limited doctrine that applies only where a federal statutory scheme is so comprehensive that it entirely supplants state law causes of action.").

25 *See, e.g., Metro. Life Ins. Co. v. Taylor*, 481 U.S. 58, 63 (1987).

conflict, but their result is the same (if any of them apply)—the state law claim must be dismissed.[26]

> Express preemption occurs when congressional intent to preempt state law is made explicit in the language of a federal statute. Conflict preemption takes place when state law imposes a duty that is inconsistent, i.e., in conflict, with federal law. Field preemption comes about when federal law occupies a field of regulation so comprehensively that it has left no room for supplementary state legislation.[27]

Given that ERISA was designed to create a uniform regulatory scheme with respect to employee benefit plans, Section 514 contains a broad preemption provision that states, in relevant part: "[T]he provisions of this title and title IV shall supersede any and all State laws insofar as they may now or hereafter relate to any employee benefit plan described in section 4(a) [29 USCS § 1003(a)] and not exempt under section 4(b) [29 USCS § 1003(b)]."[28] In other words, this section preempts any state law that "relates to" ERISA, and that includes any state law cause of action that duplicates, supplements or supplants the ERISA civil enforcement remedy.[29]

ERISA is just one of a few federal statutes where the U.S. Supreme Court has found complete preemption to exist, as well as defensive preemption.[30] Thus, ERISA completely preempts state laws such that it provides for exclusive federal

---

26 To complicate things further, field and conflict preemption are often referred to as "implied" preemption because the statute does not expressly contain a preemption clause but it is implied given the language and context. *See, e.g., Morgan v. Ford Motor Co.*, 224 W. Va. 62, 69 (2009) ("There are two recognized types of implied preemption: field preemption and conflict preemption. Implied field preemption occurs where the scheme of federal regulation is so pervasive that it is reasonable to infer that Congress left no room for the states to supplement it. Implied conflict preemption occurs where compliance with both federal and state regulations is physically impossible, or where the state regulation is an obstacle to the accomplishment or execution of congressional objectives.").

27 *Consumer Data Indus. Ass'n v. Frey*, 26 F.4th 1, 5 (1st Cir. 2022).

28 29 U.S.C. § 1144(a).

29 *Davila*, 542 U.S. at 209; *see also Quality Infusion Care, Inc. v. Humana Health Plan of Tex., Inc.*, 290 Fed. Appx. 671, 673–674 (5th Cir. 2008).

30 *Prop. Trust v. United Bhd. of Carpenters & Joiners of Am.*, 768 F.3d 938, 947–948 (9th Cir. 2014) ("the Supreme Court has recognized only three instances of complete jurisdiction."). Certain statutory exceptions to preemption may apply. Namely, state laws that regulate state insurance, banking or securities will generally not be preempted—this is known as the "savings clause" of ERISA preemption. 29 U.S.C. § 1144(b)(2). Nevertheless, ERISA further includes what is known as the "deemer clause," which states that no employer health plan "shall be deemed to be an insurance company or other insurer . . . or to be engaged in the business of insurance . . . for purposes of any law of any State purporting to regulate insurance companies [or] insurance contracts." 29 USCS § 1144(b)(2)(B). In other words, a state cannot deem a self-funded employee benefit plan as an insurance company for purposes of regulating it. *See, e.g., FMC Corp. v. Holliday*, 498 U.S. 52 (1990).

jurisdiction (and, thus, removal), as well as a defense to any state law claims within the ambit of the preemption provision. Nevertheless, courts tussled with ERISA preemption for years, resulting in a wide body of case law addressing the differing forms of preemption. Ultimately, the U.S. Supreme Court in *Aetna Health Inc. v. Davila* weighed in to establish a two-part test to determine whether a claim is "within the scope" of ERISA.[31] Specifically, "a state claim is completely preempted by ERISA if (a) the plaintiff could have brought a claim under ERISA based on the same claim; and (b) there is no legal duty implicated by Defendants actions that is independent of ERISA or the ERISA plan's terms."[32] However, since *Davila*, courts have continued to grapple with the two-part test and its application.[33] At this juncture, most knowledgeable provider-side lawyers have come to terms with the preemptive scope of ERISA. However, providers often plead multiple causes of action in an attempt to circumvent ERISA's preemptive force, and health plans need to be sure that they assess the potential for both removal under complete preemption and a defense of preemption in any litigation.

2. *Denial of Benefits*

Because this chapter is focused on payer-provider disputes, we will focus on benefit denials under Section 502(a)(1)(B) as that is the most common method through which out-of-network providers sue under a valid assignment of benefits. Under this section, participants (and valid assignees) can bring claims against a plan for a denial of benefits or rights set forth in the plan. If the plan administrator wrongfully denied benefits under the plan, the beneficiary can typically recover the benefits owed under the plan. As indicated above, ERISA requires certain appeals procedures for benefit denials.[34] Appeals must give a full and fair review of the benefit denial, including permitting beneficiaries to submit information in support of the appeal, requiring the plan to provide access to and copies of all information relevant to the claim, and requiring review of the claim based upon all information provided by the claimant.[35]

Although Section 502 permits a beneficiary or participant to sue for benefits, one must first generally exhaust the plans' available administrative remedies before bringing suit in any forum. This is not a statutory requirement; it is a court-created mandate. As the Fourth Circuit explained:

> ERISA does not contain an explicit exhaustion provision. Nonetheless, an ERISA claimant generally is required to exhaust the remedies provided by

31 *Davila*, 542 U.S. at 209.

32 *Ull v. Fire Safety, Inc.*, Case No. 09-cv-509, 2009 U.S. Dist. LEXIS 84226, *7–8 (N.D. Ill. Sept. 15, 2009).

33 *State Dental Ass'n v. Anthem Health Plans, Inc.*, 591 F.3d 1337, 1345 (11th Cir. 2009) (collecting circuit court cases as of 2009 that had recognized *Davila's* two-part test as the proper test for complete preemption under ERISA, including the Ninth, Fifth, Seventh, First, and Third Circuits).

34 *See* 29 C.F.R. § 2560.503–1.

35 *Id.*

> the employee benefit plan in which he participates as a prerequisite to an ERISA action for denial of benefits under 29 U.S.C. § 1132. This exhaustion requirement rests upon the Act's text and structure as well as the strong federal interest encouraging private resolution of ERISA disputes. ERISA requires benefit plans covered by the Act to provide internal dispute resolution procedures for participants whose claims for benefits have been denied. Employee benefit plans must provide adequate, written notice of the specific reasons for such a denial and must afford participants a reasonable opportunity for a "full and fair review" of the decision denying the claim. Congress' apparent intent in mandating these internal claims procedures was to minimize the number of frivolous ERISA lawsuits; promote the consistent treatment of benefit claims; provide a nonadversarial dispute resolution process; and decrease the cost and time of claims settlement. It would be "anomalous" if the same reasons which led Congress to require plans to provide remedies for ERISA claimants did not lead courts to see that those remedies are regularly utilized.[36]

Exhaustion is generally strictly enforced; however, courts have provided for very narrow exceptions, that is, when the administrative remedies would be futile, the remedy is inadequate or when the claimant is denied meaningful access to the administrative review process.[37] Notably, however, plans often include language in the benefit agreement that states the member must exhaust available administrative remedies without any exceptions. In those circumstances, courts have generally enforced the exhaustion requirement without applying the judicially created exceptions. The Ninth Circuit recently explained the rationale as to why:

> ERISA itself does not require a participant or beneficiary to exhaust administrative remedies in order to bring an action under § 502 of ERISA. Instead, ERISA mandates an opportunity for administrative review, and we have treated completion of this administrative review as a prudential exhaustion requirement. We have also consistently recognized three exceptions to the prudential exhaustion requirement: futility, inadequate remedy, and unreasonable claims procedures. Plaintiffs have not shown that we have extended these exceptions to a contractual exhaustion requirement . . . The Supreme Court has explained that the plan, in short, is at the center of ERISA, and accordingly, this focus on the written terms of the plan is the linchpin of a system that is not so complex that administrative costs, or litigation expenses, unduly

36 *Makar v. Health Care Corp.*, 872 F.2d 80, 82–83 (4th Cir. 1989).

37 *Landa v. AON Corp. Excess Ben. Plan*, Case No. 22-cv-21091, 2022 U.S. Dist. LEXIS 150773, *14 (S.D. Fla. Aug. 22, 2022) ("As a result, we strictly enforce an exhaustion requirement on plaintiffs bringing ERISA claims in federal court with certain caveats reserved for exceptional circumstances. Thus far, our circuit has recognized exceptions only when resort to administrative remedies would be futile or the remedy inadequate, or where a claimant is denied meaningful access to the administrative review scheme in place.").

> discourage employers from offering ERISA plans in the first place. While Congress, in enacting ERISA, empowered the courts to develop, in light of reason and experience, a body of federal common law governing employee benefit plans, federal common law doctrines cannot alter or override clear and unambiguous plan terms. When an ERISA plan does not merely provide for administrative review but, as here, explicitly mandates exhaustion of such procedures before bringing suit in federal court and, importantly, provides no exceptions, application of judicially created exhaustion exceptions would conflict with the written terms of the plan.[38]

The judicially created exhaustion requirement is critical to payer-provider disputes as any non-contracted provider that has taken a valid assignment must first ensure that the provider or the participant/beneficiary has exhausted the available remedies. If not, the provider generally cannot bring a lawsuit either in court or arbitration unless an applicable narrow exception applies and the plan itself does not require exhaustion.[39] While the dismissal is often without prejudice, that can pose a problem for providers who sue under ERISA when the applicable limitations period—whether statutory or contractual—has expired.

To be sure, while ERISA does not have a statute of limitations, courts typically either apply the statute of limitations applicable to contracts or a limitations period set forth in the plan or other contract. As explained by the U.S. Supreme Court in *Heimeshoff v. Hartford Life & Accident Ins. Co.*:

> ERISA § 502(a)(1)(B) does not specify a statute of limitations. Instead, the parties in this case have agreed by contract to a 3-year limitations period. The contract specifies that this period begins to run at the time proof of loss is due. . . . Absent a controlling statute to the contrary, a participant and a plan may agree by contract to a particular limitations period, even one that starts to run before the cause of action accrues, as long as the period is reasonable. . . . The principle that contractual limitations provisions ordinarily should be enforced as written is especially appropriate when enforcing an ERISA plan. The plan, in short, is at the center of ERISA. Employers have large leeway to design disability and other welfare plans as they see fit. And once a plan is established, the administrator's duty is to see that the plan is maintained pursuant to that written instrument. This focus on the written terms of the plan is the linchpin of a system that is not so complex that administrative costs, or

38 *Wit v. United Behav. Health*, Case No. 20-17363, 2023 U.S. App. LEXIS 2039, *33–35 (9th Cir. Jan. 26, 2023).

39 *See, e.g. Israel v. Unum Life Ins. Co. of Am.*, Case No. 21-cv-4335, 2023 U.S. Dist. LEXIS 14301, *17–18 (S.D.N.Y. Jan. 27, 2023) ("Section 502 of ERISA entitles recipients of covered benefit plans to enforce rights under the terms of the applicable plan. However, courts may only review ERISA claims brought by individuals who have exhausted the administrative remedies available. If a claimant does not exhaust administrative remedies available, then a court will dismiss an ERISA claim.").

litigation expenses, unduly discourage employers from offering ERISA plans in the first place.[40]

A provider who is able to sue under Section 502(a)(1)(B) also faces other challenges. For instance, there is no right to a jury trial, and the court will review the administrative record as developed in the appeals process. In most instances, the plan grants the plan administrator discretionary authority to determine eligibility for benefits or to construe the terms of the plan, therefore, the court's review will be under an "arbitrary and capricious" standard.[41] In the relatively rare instances when the plan does not grant the administrator such discretionary authority, then the court's review is *de novo*.[42] Although courts articulate the arbitrary and capricious standard in varying ways, it generally means that the court must determine whether reasonable grounds supported the benefits decision. As courts repeatedly recognize, this is a "highly deferential" standard and difficult to overcome.[43]

C. State Surprise Billing Laws and the Federal "No Surprises Act"

In recent years, there has been a tremendous amount of scrutiny over "surprise medical bills," which generally occur when patients are billed for out-of-network services they could not reasonably have anticipated or prevented.[44] An overview of surprise bills was provided in Chapter 4. In most instances, balance billing occurs

---

40 571 U.S. 99, 105–108 (2013) (internal citations and quotations omitted); *see also Med. Mut. of Ohio v. k. Amalia Enters.*, 548 F.3d 383, 390 (6th Cir. 2008) ("When a federal statute contains no limitations period, we normally borrow the limitations period from the most analogous state or federal law. However, choosing which statute to borrow is unnecessary when the parties have contractually agreed on a limitations period and that limitations period is reasonable. Because the contract language clearly states that the parties shall have either two years or three years to bring the claim at issue and MMO did not present arguments indicating that a limitations period of two or three years would be unreasonable, we find no reason to believe that the contractual limitations provision here is unreasonable. Accordingly, we uphold the district court's finding that the limitations provision applies to this case.").

41 *Univ. of N.C. Health Care Sys. v. ITPEU Health & Welfare Plan*, Case No. 4:20-cv-246, 2022 U.S. Dist. LEXIS 177563, *28 (S.D. Ga. Sept. 29, 2022).

42 *Id.*; *see also Firestone Tire & Rubber Co. v. Bruch*, 489 U.S. 101, 109 (1989).

43 *Smith v. Cont'l Cas. Co.*, 450 F.3d 253, 259 (6th Cir. 2006) ("When the plan administrator has discretionary authority to determine benefits, as is the case here, the court reviews a denial of benefits under the highly deferential arbitrary and capricious standard of review."); *see also Fuller v. J.P. Morgan Chase & Co.*, 423 F.3d 104, 106–107 (2d Cir. 2005) ("Where the written plan documents confer upon a plan administrator the discretionary authority to determine eligibility, we will not disturb the administrator's ultimate conclusion unless it is arbitrary and capricious. Under this highly deferential standard of review, this Court cannot substitute its judgment for that of the Plan Administrator and will not overturn a decision to deny or terminate benefits unless it was without reason, unsupported by substantial evidence or erroneous as a matter of law.").

44 Christopher Gorman and Benjamin Chartock, "One in Five Inpatient Emergency Department Cases May Lead to Surprise Bills," Health Affairs, accessed March 19, 2023, https://doi.org/10.1377/hlthaff.2016.0970.

in either the emergency room setting, or when a person receives non-emergency care at an in-network facility but is treated by an out-of-network provider such as a surgeon, anesthesiologist, radiologist or other ancillary provider. Historically, in scenarios where a health plan did not have a contract with a provider, the plan would not pay the entire bill and the provider could balance bill the member for the remaining payment allegedly owed based upon the provider's billed charges. In addition, when a claim was denied in whole or in part and the provider could not recover the balance from the member, the provider was often stuck suing under ERISA pursuant to an assignment of benefits or under common law theories such as unjust enrichment.

However, over the past several years, many states (and the federal government as of 2022) have enacted laws that are aimed at serving the dual purpose of providing protections to patients from surprise medical bills and establishing a framework for payment by insurers to healthcare providers. An entire book could be dedicated to analyzing this subject, but we will cover the sections pertinent to payer-provider disputes because these laws have changed the landscape for resolving out-of-network disputes.

1. *State Surprise Billing Laws*

State surprise billing laws, which generally apply to state-regulated health plans but not ERISA or government-sponsored health plans, vary widely.[45] For instance, some states have broad protections against different types of surprise medical bills, while others have more limited protections focused on a particular care setting such as the emergency room. In many cases, state surprise bill or balance billing laws provide for a methodology to pay out-of-network providers, such as a percentage of Medicare rates or the average contracted rate for the health plan in that region.[46] For instance, Michigan's Surprise Medical Billing law dictates payment for certain out-of-network providers and establishes an arbitration process to resolve disputes.[47] With respect to payment of covered out-of-network providers, the law generally limits payment to the *greater* of: (1) the median in-network contracted rate for the service; or (2) 150 percent of the traditional Medicare fee schedule amount. In addition, applicable providers cannot collect from the patient any amount other than the applicable in-network coinsurance, copayment

45 "Protecting Patients from Surprise Medical Bills," Georgetown University Center on Health Insurance Reform, accessed March 19, 2023, https://surprisemedicalbills.chir.georgetown.edu/state-efforts/.

46 Aliza Gordon, Ying Liu, Benjamin Chartock, Winnie Chi, "Provider Charges and State Surprise Billing Laws: Evidence From New York And California," Health Affairs, September 2022, https://doi.org/10.1377/hlthaff.2021.01332.

47 *See* MCL 333.24501 to MCL 333.24517; *see also* "Surprise Medical Billing Information for Providers, Carriers," Michigan Department of Insurance and Financial Services, accessed March 19, 2023, www.michigan.gov/difs/utilization-review/surprise-medical-billing-information-for-providers-carriers.

or deductible.[48] The law and its implementing regulations allow the Michigan Department of Insurance and Financial Services to review a health insurer's calculation of its negotiated median amount upon a nonparticipating provider's request and to facilitate binding arbitration.[49]

2. *Federal No Surprises Act*

As described in Chapter 4, the Federal No Surprises Act (NSA) was enacted as part of the Consolidated Appropriations Act, 2021 (Pub. L. 116–260) and went into effect January 1, 2022. At a high level, the NSA applies to emergency services, post-emergency stabilization services, nonemergent services provided by certain out-of-network providers at in-network facilities and air ambulance transportation (emergency and non-emergency). While the NSA sets forth numerous requirements that are tangentially applicable to payer-provider disputes, such as restrictions on balance billing, notice and consent requirements and creation of price comparison tools, there are two core components that together have the potential to dramatically change the landscape of these disputes.

First, the NSA establishes a uniform process for claims subject to the NSA to determine cost sharing based upon a "specified state law" or a hypothetical rate called the "qualifying payment amount" or "QPA." A specified state law (SSL) generally means a "state law that provides for a method for determining the total amount payable."[50] Notably, the regulating agencies explained that SSLs are not only "state laws that set a mathematical formula for determining the out-of-network rate," but include laws that "require or permit a plan or issuer and a provider or facility to negotiate, and then engage in a state arbitration process to determine the out-of-network rate."[51] Notably, if a state has an SSL, the cost sharing (and, if

---

48 *See* MCL 333.24507 & MCL 333.24509.

49 *See* MCL 333.24510 & MCL 333.24511.

50 *See* 26 U.S.C. § 9816(I) ("the term 'specified State law' means, with respect to a State, an item or service furnished by a nonparticipating provider or nonparticipating emergency facility during a year and a group health plan, a State law that provides for a method for determining the total amount payable under such a plan (to the extent such State law applies to such plan, subject to section 514 [26 USCS § 514]) in the case of a participant or beneficiary covered under such plan and receiving such item or service from such a nonparticipating provider or nonparticipating emergency facility.").

51 86 Fed. Reg. 36872, 36887 (July 13, 2021) ("The Departments interpret the statutory phrase 'a State law that provides for a method for determining the total amount payable under such a plan, coverage, or issuer, respectively' broadly as referring not only to state laws that set a mathematical formula for determining the out-of-network rate, or that set a predetermined amount for an out-of-network item or service. Rather, the Departments interpret that language to also include, for example, state laws that require or permit a plan or issuer and a provider or facility to negotiate, and then to engage in a state arbitration process to determine the out-of-network rate. Such state laws provide a process for determining the total amount payable, and in such instances, the timeframes and processes under such a state law related to negotiations and arbitration would apply, as opposed to the timeframes and IDR process under the No Surprises Act.").

applicable, the payment) is based upon that SSL. If there is no SSL, cost sharing is based upon the QPA. The QPA is not a payment amount—it is solely used by the plan and provider to determine cost sharing.[52]

Indeed, if there is not an SSL, the NSA allows a health plan to pay any amount for applicable services, but requires the cost-sharing amount to be based upon the QPA to protect members from inordinate cost-sharing amounts and provide uniformity for all members in the plan. In most instances, the QPA for a given item or service is the median contracted rate on January 31, 2019, for the same or similar item or service, increased annually for inflation.[53] There are many factors that affect the determination of the median contracted rate, which we do not need to explore for purposes of this chapter. However, generally speaking, under the NSA, the median contracted rate for an item or service is determined by identifying the contracted rates of all commercial products or plans for a specific payer in the same insurance market,[54] for the same or similar item or service rendered by the same provider type or specialty in the same geographic region, and then calculating the median rate.[55]

Second, the NSA establishes a voluntary but, if invoked, binding process for determining the payment amount for out-of-network claims. Specifically, the NSA requires payment to be at the "out-of-network" rate, which is defined as the rate provided for by any SSL or, if none, then an agreed amount or the amount determined through the independent dispute resolution (IDR) process established by the NSA. Thus, while the NSA does not provide for a specific amount to be paid by the health plan, it establishes an arbitration process for an independent organization to arrive at that amount. The NSA process for payment of applicable out-of-network providers is generally as follows:

1. The plan must make an initial payment at the "out-of-network rate" or give notice of denial within 30 days of receiving the claim.
2. If the provider does not accept the initial payment, it may initiate a 30-day "open negotiation" period where the parties can attempt to reach an agreement on the payment amount.
3. If the parties cannot reach an agreement on the payment amount during the open negotiation period, then four days thereafter either party can initiate the IDR.

---

52 Under the NSA, member cost-sharing is calculated based upon the lesser of the billed charges or the QPA, unless an All-Payer Model Agreement under section 1115A of the Social Security Act or a "specified state law" applies.

53 "Qualifying Payment Amount Calculation Methodology," Centers for Medicare & Medicaid Services, December 2021, www.cms.gov/CCIIO/Programs-and-Initiatives/Other-Insurance-Protections/CAAQualifying-Payment-Amount-Calculation-Methodology.pdf.

54 The insurance market is defined as either the individual market, large group market, small group market or self-insured plans. 42 USCS § 300gg-111(3)(E)(iv).

55 *Id.*

4. IDR is an arbitration process where an independent dispute resolution entity (IDRE) is either agreed upon or appointed, and each party then submits a written submission to the IDRE that outlines what the plan is willing to pay and the provider is willing to accept.
5. The IDRE makes a determination after considering various factors, including the QPA, additional information submitted by parties relating to their respective offers, information on the provider's training, experience, quality and outcomes, the acuity of patient's condition and complexity of services, demonstrations of good faith efforts in contract negotiations and contracted rates between the parties for the previous four years, amongst other things. Notably, the IDRE cannot consider usual and customary charges or the provider's billed charges, nor can it consider public payer reimbursement rates (*e.g.* Medicare and Medicaid).[56]

As is evident, the federal law is intended to provide for a streamlined arbitration process to resolve disputes between health plans and out-of-network providers subject to the NSA, which up to this point was largely unregulated except under any existing state law. This process thus allows providers to seek additional payment without resorting to full-blown, and at times costly, litigation.

However, while this may seem like a straightforward process at first blush, there are several nuances that must be navigated by both providers and plans. For instance, the statute contains several hard-and-fast deadlines that must be adhered to, such as the timeframe in which to initiate an IDR after the close of an open negotiation period. If the provider does not initiate an IDR within that applicable timeframe, then the IDRE will dismiss the IDR as not eligible. In addition, the NSA details what types of claims can be combined (called "batched" or "bundled" claims) in a single IDR, as well as a "cooling off period" after the completion of an IDR. If the provider does not properly batch or bundle the claims, the IDRE will likely dismiss the claims. Likewise, if the provider does not adhere to the cooling off period and prematurely submits another IDR covering the same services, the IDRE will dismiss the IDR.

It is very important that plans and providers understand the interplay between SSLs and the NSA, particularly because the NSA does not apply when calculating member cost sharing or provider payments or to dispute resolution if an SSL applies. And the interplay between SSLs and the NSA is not binary such that if one applies the other does not because there can be instances when an SSL and the NSA will apply to different services in the same dispute. This is because SSLs do not always completely overlap with the NSA. As an example, an SSL may apply to services performed in the emergency room but not to post-stabilization services, whereas the NSA may apply to the post-stabilization services. Therefore, determining whether an SSL applies is extremely important. Thankfully, the Centers for Medicare and Medicaid Services (CMS) has issued guidance to identify

56 *See, e.g.,* 26 U.S.C. § 9816(c).

which states have SSLs and the scope of the SSLs.[57] As an example, in its letter to the State of Illinois, CMS stated the following:

> Illinois does not have an applicable All-Payer Model Agreement that would determine the out-of-network rate. Based on the survey response and CMS communications with the Illinois Department of Insurance staff, CMS understands that 215 ILCS 5/356z.3a is a specified state law that will apply for purposes of determining the out-of-network rate with respect to pathology, anesthesiology, neonatology, radiology, or emergency department services furnished to individuals enrolled in preferred provider organization (PPO) coverage in Illinois by nonparticipating providers at participating hospitals and ambulatory surgical treatment centers. The federal independent dispute resolution process under sections 2799A-1(c) and 2799A-2(b) of the PHS Act and 45 CFR 149.510 and 149.520 will apply for purposes of determining the out-of-network rate with respect to any items and services and nonparticipating providers, nonparticipating emergency facilities, and nonparticipating providers of air ambulance services to which 215 ILCS 5/356z.3a does not apply. CMS will enforce the outcome of the federal independent dispute resolution process for such cases in Illinois.[58]

Both providers and plans need to be fully aware of these letters and the position that CMS has taken with respect to the existence and scope of any SSLs before initiating IDRs so that the proper process is being followed.

III. LEGAL ISSUES RELATING TO GOVERNMENT-SPONSORED MANAGED CARE ORGANIZATIONS THAT IMPACT PAYER-PROVIDER DISPUTES

As described previously, enrollment in government-sponsored managed care organizations such as Medicare Advantage and Medicaid managed care plans has been growing substantially over the past two decades. Given that an increasing amount of money is flowing though these organizations to providers, they are unsurprisingly becoming more entangled in disputes. This section examines some of the key areas of disputes in this realm.

A. Out-of-Network Provider Disputes with Medicaid Managed Care Organizations

In Medicaid managed care, Medicaid MCOs are required under federal law to contract with a sufficient number of providers to establish an "adequate network."[59] An

57 "CAA Enforcement Letters," Centers for Medicare & Medicaid Services, accessed March 19, 2023, www.cms.gov/cciio/programs-and-initiatives/other-insurance-protections/caa.

58 *Id.*

59 *See* 42 C.F.R. § 438.68.

overview of network adequacy requirements was provided in Chapter 4. If a provider and Medicaid MCO enter into a contract, that contract governs the terms of their relationship, including payment amounts. However, providers are not required to contract with Medicaid MCOs. If a provider is not a contracted provider but still renders care to a Medicaid MCO enrollee in emergency situations, federal law mandates that the plan pay the provider, and the provider is required to accept the traditional Medicaid fee-for-service rate unless there is an express agreement for a different rate.[60] Furthermore, many states have implemented regulations or guidance that impose the same requirement with respect to emergency services, post-stabilization services and a variety of other services mandated by state Medicaid programs.[61] Thus, in most instances, when an out-of-network provider renders services to a Medicaid enrollee, the provider will be paid the Medicaid fee-for-service rate. However, this is a developing area of law that will continue to be assessed by courts.

B. Out-of-Network Provider Disputes with Medicare Advantage Organizations

With respect to out-of-network providers, there are two overarching issues that frame disputes with Medicare Advantage Organizations (MAOs): the amount that will be paid and the process by which a dispute may be brought. For out-of-network providers who seek payment from MAOs, federal law and CMS guidance establish the payment as the amount that would be paid under the traditional Medicare program. Specifically, 42 C.F.R. § 214 states, in relevant part, that non-contracted providers "must accept, as payment in full, the amounts that the provider could collect if the beneficiary were enrolled in original Medicare."[62] Thus, any non-contracted provider cannot collect more than the amount that it would be paid under traditional Medicare if it were to bring a lawsuit—a baseline principal that has been established for quite some time.[63] Where the law has been developing over

60 *See* 42 U.S.C. § 1396u-2(b)(2)(D) (stating that any non-contracted provider who render services to a Medicaid MCO enrollee "must accept as payment in full no more than the amounts (less any payments for indirect costs of medical education and direct costs of graduate medical education) that it could collect if the beneficiary received medical assistance under this title other than through enrollment in such an entity.").

61 *See, e.g.*, 1 Tex. Admin. Code § 353.4(f)(2) (requiring Medicaid MCOs to "reimburse an out-of-network, in-area service provider the Medicaid FFS rate in effect on the date of service less five percent, unless the parties agree to a different reimbursement amount.").

62 *See also* 42 C.F.R. § 422.114(a)(2)(i); *see also* "MA Payment Guide for Out of Network Providers, 4/15/2015 Update," U.S. Department of Health & Human Services, April 15, 2015, www.hhs.gov/guidance/document/ma-payment-guide-out-network-payments-0 ("Coordinated care plans, such as HMOs and PPOs, and PACE plans are generally required to reimburse non-contracting providers at least the original Medicare rate for Medicare covered services.").

63 *Glob. Rescue Jets, LLC v. Kaiser Found. Health Plan, Inc.*, 30 F.4th 905, 910 (9th Cir. 2022) ("If the services would have been covered under Parts A and B, the plan is obligated to pay these non-contract providers at least the Medicare-approved rate, 42 U.S.C. § 1395w-22(a)(2)(A); 42 C.F.R. § 422.100(b)(2), and the non-contract provider is obligated to accept the Medicare-approved rate as payment in full. 42 U.S.C. § 1395w-22(k)(1); 42 C.F.R. § 422.214(a)(1).").

the past few years in a way that directly impacts payer-provider disputes, however, is in the context of Medicare preemption and exhaustion.

With respect to Medicare exhaustion, the basic principle is that a Medicare beneficiary and their assignees must first exhaust all of their administrative remedies offered under the traditional Medicare program before bringing suit. While this is generally settled at this point, the path to that conclusion weaves through numerous statutes, regulations and case law over time.[64] In short, the U.S. Supreme Court has interpreted 42 C.F.R. § 405(g) and (h) as requiring any person seeking judicial review over a claim for Medicare benefits to exhaust the available administrative remedies.[65] Building upon that, courts have interpreted this requirement to mean that non-contracted providers must also exhaust their administrative remedies in most circumstances. As the Ninth Circuit recently explained:

> As fleshed out in regulations issued by CMS, administrative review under the Medicare Advantage program involves the same five levels of review, with only slight modifications. The first level of review involves an initial determination by the Medicare Advantage organization itself—called an "organization determination"—as to the benefits an enrollee is entitled to receive under the plan. Importantly for our purposes, organization determinations encompass determinations regarding not only basic benefits (*i.e.*, services that would have been covered under Parts A and B) but also supplemental benefits. The ensuing levels of review include reconsideration by the Medicare Advantage organization, §§ 422.578, 422.582; reconsideration by an independent outside entity, § 422.592; a hearing before an ALJ if the amount in controversy is $100 or more (adjusted for inflation), § 422.600; and review by the Medicare Appeals Council, § 422.608. An enrollee who receives an adverse decision from the Appeals Council may then seek judicial review in federal district court if the remaining amount in controversy is $1,000 or more (adjusted for inflation).[66]

As is evident, courts are concluding that out-of-network providers must first proceed through *all* available administrative remedies, including before an administrative law judge and the Medicare Appeals Council, which can take a long time.[67] As Medicare Advantage continues to enroll more individuals over time,

64 *See, e.g., Heckler v. Ringer*, 466 U.S. 602 (1984).

65 *See, e.g., Glob. Rescue Jets, LLC v. Kaiser Found. Health Plan, Inc.*, 30 F.4th 905, 913 (9th Cir. 2022) ("The upshot: Section 405(g) provides the only avenue for judicial review of a claim for benefits under the Medicare Act, and failure to exhaust one's administrative remedies deprives federal courts of subject matter jurisdiction over claims arising under the Act.").

66 *Rescue Jets, LLC v. Kaiser Found. Health Plan, Inc.*, 30 F.4th 905, 913–914 (9th Cir. 2022) (internal citations omitted).

67 *See also Tenet Healthsystem GB, Inc. v. Care Improvement Plus South Cent. Ins. Co.*, 875 F.3d 584, 587 (11th Cir. 2017) ("If any one of the foregoing parties wishes to challenge any aspect of an organization determination, that party must exhaust its administrative remedies by following a

out-of-network providers need to be acutely aware of this requirement and follow all applicable administrative appeals processes.[68]

C. Preemption and Federal Officer Removal in Medicare Advantage and Medicare Part D

Similar to ERISA, Medicare Advantage and Medicare Part D statutes contain an express preemption provision; however, the case law is not yet as developed for this preemption provision compared to ERISA. The preemption provision for Medicare Advantage states, in relevant part:

> The standards established under this part shall supersede any State law or regulation (other than State licensing laws or State laws relating to plan solvency) with respect to MA plans which are offered by MA organizations under this part.[69]

Notably, the current version was amended in 2003. Prior to that amendment, the preemption provision stated that federal standards would supersede state law and regulations with respect to MAOs only if a state law or regulation was "inconsistent" with Medicare standards.[70] The legislative history demonstrates that the 2003 amendment was intended to increase the scope of preemption, stating that "the [MA Program] is a federal program operated under Federal rules and that State laws, do not, and should not apply, with the exception of state licensing laws or state laws related to plan solvency."[71]

Similar to courts that were first attempting to navigate ERISA preemption, courts have construed this preemption provision both broadly and inconsistently. However, as case law has evolved, the general consensus among the courts is that

---

specific procedure for administrative appeal prescribed by the Medicare Act and its implementing regulations.").

68 Courts have also addressed whether *contracted* providers must first exhaust their administrative remedies and generally held that they do not. *See, e.g., Rencare, Ltd. v. Humana Health Plan of Tex., Inc.*, 395 F.3d 555, 556–557 (5th Cir. 2004) (rejecting argument that a contacted provider needed to exhaust administrative remedies). However, these courts do not generally address whether contracted providers must, at a minimum, exhaust the plans' available remedies before bringing suit, which can be a matter of contract. In addition, similar to how courts found exhaustion to be required under ERISA despite no express exhaustion provision, it is feasible that courts could find contracted providers must also exhaust plan remedies.

69 42 U.S.C. § 1395w-26(b)(3); *see also* 42 C.F.R. § 422.402. This language is similar to the preemption provision of ERISA, when coupled with ERISA's Savings Clause. Although it appears that courts have yet to interpret this language as constituting complete preemption like the U.S. Supreme Court has with ERISA, it is possible that in the future such a conclusion will be reached given the similarities.

70 42 U.S.C. § 1395w-26(b)(3)(A)(2000).

71 *Methodist Hosp. v. Humana Ins. Co.*, 266 F. Supp. 3d 939, 946 (S.D. Tex. 2017) (citing H. Conf. Rep. 108–391 at 557, reprinted in 2003 U.S.C.C.A.N. 1808, 1926 (November 21, 2003)).

most claims against an MAO (or Part D Plan (PDP)) are preempted except claims relating to state licensing laws and laws relating to plan solvency.[72] Like ERISA preemption, Medicare preemption is a powerful tool for MAOs and PDPs that face lawsuits from providers and members alike, as it allows for them to narrow the issues in dispute and claims asserted against them. In any provider lawsuit involving Medicare Advantage or Part D members, preemption should be analyzed closely to determine if it will defeat certain claims.

Notably, despite the preemption clause in Medicare Advantage being similar to the ERISA preemption clause, courts have not recognized complete preemption such that MAOs and PDPs can automatically remove cases to federal court. However, another avenue called "federal officer removal" under 28 U.S.C. § 1442 has emerged. Section 1442 provides a federal forum to "[t]he United States or any agency thereof, in an official or individual capacity, for or relating to any act under color of such office."

Under this doctrine, defendants must show that: (1) they were acting under the direction of a federal officer; (2) a causal connection exists between their actions taken under such direction and the conduct for which Plaintiff sued; and (3) they have a colorable federal defense to Plaintiff's claims.[73] As one court explained:

> Section 1442(a) permits removal only if the defendant was "acting under" an agency or officer of the United States when carrying out the 'acts' that are the subject of the plaintiff's complaint. The words "acting under" are broad, and the Supreme Court has made clear that the statute must be "liberally construed". . . . For the federal officer removal statute to apply to a private person, the "acting under" element "must involve an effort to *assist*, or to help *carry out*, the duties or tasks of the federal superior."[74]

72 *e.g., Uhm v. Humana, Inc.*, 620 F.3d 1134, 1144 (9th Cir. Wash. 2010) (Fraud and consumer protection claims by beneficiary expressly preempted); *Phillips v. Kaiser Found. Health Plan, Inc.*, 953 F. Supp. 2d 1078 (N.D. Cal. 2011) (claims under the California Unfair Competition Law and Consumer Legal Remedies Act are expressly preempted); *General Surgical Associates, P.A. v. Humana Health Plan of Texas, Inc.*, Case No. SA-14-CA-31-RP, 2015 U.S. Dist. LEXIS 54091, at *1 (W.D. Tex. Mar. 17, 2015) (contracted provider's Texas Prompt Pay Act claims expressly preempted); *MHA, LLC v. HealthFirst, Inc.*, Case No. 13-cv-6036, 2015 U.S. Dist. LEXIS 23699, at *1 (D.N.J. Feb. 27, 2015) (non-contracted providers claims expressly preempted by Medicare act), *rev'd by MHA LLC v. Healthfirst, Inc.*, 629 Fed. Appx. 409 (3d Cir. N.J. 2015), *remanded to MHA, LLC v. Healthfirst, Inc.*, 2016 N.J. Super. Unpub. LEXIS 1210 (Law Div. May 25, 2016) (dismissing claims as expressly preempted by Medicare Act); *Mayberry v. Walgreens, Co. et al.*, No. 17 C 1748, 2017 WL 4228205 (N.D. Ill. Sept. 21, 2017) (dismissing as preempted claims alleging that pharmacies billed insulin to Part D rather than Part B in violation of consumer fraud laws); *Haaland v. Presbyterian Health Plan, Inc.*, 292 F. Supp. 3d 1222 (D. N.M. 2018) (holding state law claims preempted by federal regulations that required coverage determinations be made through application of medical necessity standard).

73 *Mesa v. California*, 489 U.S. 121, 131–32 (1989).

74 *Hepstall v. Humana Health Plan, Inc.*, Case No. 18–0163, 2018 U.S. Dist. LEXIS 112727, *7–8 (S.D. Ala. July 3, 2018).

For MAOs and PDPs, the theory is that they are acting under color of federal law when the federal government delegates authority to administer Medicare benefits to them. To date, the fight has largely been at the district court level with mixed results.[75] The one circuit that addressed federal officer removal rejected it under the circumstances in that case. In *Ohio State Chiropractic Ass'n v. Humana Health Plan Inc.*, the Sixth Circuit examined a situation where an MAO recouped overpayments from a non-contracted provider who sued for their recovery.[76] The MAO removed the case to federal court under the federal officer doctrine and then moved to dismiss the case for failure to exhaust administrative remedies, which the district court granted. On appeal, the Sixth Circuit examined whether removal was proper and concluded "the relationship between CMS and MAOs is not so unusually close that Humana may wield the officer-removal statute." Interestingly, the court looked at the relationship between CMS and MAOs and concluded that CMS had not delegated Medicare administration to MAOs, despite the extensive regulatory oversight and program requirements and in one interesting passage stated:

> But do MAOs perform a job that the government would have to perform itself if it did not contract with private firms? We think not. If no health insurer chose to contract with CMS as an MAO, it is doubtful that the government would get into the business of offering its own MA plans. It certainly doesn't *have* to. More likely, it would fall back on traditional fee-for-service Medicare—which it must provide regardless.

In attempting to distinguish the myriad lower court decisions that, up to that point, generally found federal officer removal proper, the court commented that they "did not engage with the question whether the MAO relationship to the federal government is akin to a delegation."[77] Notwithstanding that decision, in recent years the pendulum seems to be shifting toward allowing federal officer

75 *Glob. Rescue Jets, LLC v. Kaiser Found. Health Plan, Inc.*, 30 F.4th 905, 917 (9th Cir. 2022) (while concluding that an MAO "qualifies as an officer or employee of the United States or the Secretary, as those terms are used in the third sentence of § 405(h)" for exhaustion purposes, the court expressly declined to determine whether the same was true for federal officer removal purposes).

76 *Ohio State Chiropractic Ass'n v. Humana Health Plan, Inc.*, 647 Fed. Appx. 619 (6th Cir. 2016).

77 *See, e.g., Inchauspe v. Scan Health Plan*, Case No. 2:17-cv-06011, 2018 U.S. Dist. LEXIS 23056, at *1 (C.D. Cal. Jan. 23, 2018) (finding removal proper); *Goncalves By & Through Goncalves v. Rady Children's Hosp. San Diego*, 865 F.3d 1237, 1249 (9th Cir. 2017) (FEHB claims and finding removal proper); *Ohio State Chiropractic Ass'n v. Humana Health Plan, Inc.*, 647 Fed. Appx. 619 (6th Cir. 2016) (finding removal improper); *Assocs. Rehab. Recovery, Inc. v. Humana Med. Plan, Inc.*, 76 F. Supp. 3d 1388, 1391 (S.D. Fla. 2014); *Rudek v. Presence Our Lady of Resurrection Med. Ctr.*, No. 13 C 06022, 2014 U.S. Dist. LEXIS 152025, at *1 & n.1 (N.D. Ill. Oct. 27, 2014); *Einhorn v. CarePlus Health Plans, Inc.*, 43 F. Supp. 3d 1268, 1270 (S.D. Fla. 2014); *Mann v. Reeder*, No. 1:10-CV-00133, 2010 U.S. Dist. LEXIS 134821, at *2 (W.D. Ky. Dec. 21, 2010); *Beaumont Foot Specialists, Inc. v. United Healthcare of Tex., Inc.*, 2015 U.S. Dist. LEXIS 170755, at *4 (E.D. Tex. Dec. 14, 2015); *Woodruff v. Humana Pharmacy Inc.*, 65 F. Supp. 3d 588, 590–91 (N.D. Ill. 2014).

removal for cases against these types of plans.[78] For instance, in a recent case, a California district court examined the case law and concluded that the "unusually close relationship existed between MAOs and CMS such that MAOs fulfill a basic governmental task" by administering Medicare benefits.[79] As such, the court found removal proper.

As we move forward with this doctrine, and as enrollment in Medicare Advantage and Part D continues to increase, courts will continue to analyze federal officer removal and whether it allows these types of plans to seek jurisdiction in federal court. If the history of ERISA offers any insight, it seems that the policy considerations underlying removal in that context are equally applicable for Medicare Advantage and Part D, namely, to have a more uniform application of federal law. In any event, health plan attorneys need to be cognizant of the potential for removal of cases brought against MAOs and PDPs and act swiftly if it may apply.

IV. CONCLUSION

In the multi-trillion-dollar world of healthcare, payer-provider disputes happen every day. While at times these disputes can seem technical or (gasp) boring from an outsider's perspective, the reality is that they can present highly complex legal and factual issues that are continuing to evolve through the courts. As a result, practitioners, both new as well as experienced, who are involved in this area need to fully understand the issues that permeate each case. This chapter looked at many of the issues that arise between payers and providers to give practitioners a general understanding of these disputes and some of the key issues that arise in them, including common types of contractual disputes and emerging legal issues impacting this type of litigation. As the industry evolves, plan and provider counsel need to stay abreast of both the legal and industry developments so that they can most effectively represent their clients.

78 *Hepstall v. Humana Health Plan, Inc.*, Case No. 18–0163, 2018 U.S. Dist. LEXIS 112727, *13–14 (S.D. Ala. July 3, 2018) (collecting cases and examining their outcomes); *see also Body & Mind Acupuncture v. Humana Health Plan, Inc.*, 2017 U.S. Dist. LEXIS 22267, at *5 (N.D. W. Va. Feb. 16, 2017) (collecting cases).

79 *Escarcega v. Verdugo Vista Operating Co., LP*, Case No. 19–9478, 2020 U.S. Dist. LEXIS 61977, *21–22 (C.D. Cal. Apr. 8, 2020).

CHAPTER 9

Payer-Provider Disputes from the Provider Perspective

Mackenzie Wallace

I. INTRODUCTION

This book has described the relationships (and the agreements related thereto) between health care providers, health care plans and their patients/members that form the basis of managed care. And we have learned throughout the book, reimbursement by health care providers is a complex process that incorporates multiple agreements, parties and often disputes. The purpose of this chapter is to analyze such reimbursement disputes from the provider perspective. As was described in Chapter 8, a provider's ethical and legal duty to provide healthcare services to patients arises out of contractual and non-contractual obligations in a tripartite service relationship involving the patient, the provider, and the payer (e.g., health plan).

Managed care litigation refers to disputes regarding the provision of healthcare services to patients in exchange for reimbursement or fees paid for by one or multiple payers. The involved parties may include a combination of provider, payer and patient, though the most heavily litigated disputes generally involve a provider and a payer.

The primary difference between provider/payer and patient/payer litigation is the type of governing contract. For example, the governing contract between the provider and the payer or health plan may be the Hospital (or Provider) Services Agreement, which describes the fees that the health plan will pay to the hospital in exchange for medically necessary services. On the other hand, the Health Benefit Plan (also called the Evidence of Coverage), which includes the summary of benefits the health plan member or enrollee is entitled to receive, governs the relationship between the patient and the health plan.

II. THE ROLE OF CONTRACTS

Reimbursement of health care providers often incorporates multiple agreements. The most important agreement is the agreement between the payer and the provider, if it exists.

A. Contract Formation

Contractual disputes between payers and providers arise out of agreements described above,that is, where the provider agrees to perform healthcare services in exchange for fees paid by the payer. Sophisticated drafting of contracts often yields provisions reaching far beyond just the exchange of fees for services, however. Furthermore, contracts need not be in writing in order to exist between payers and providers. In situations where the terms are not in writing, the parties' actions are crucial to determining whether a contract exists and what payment the provider should receive for the services performed.

1. *Written Contracts*

A written contract is one of the most powerful tools for both the provider and the payer. In in-network reimbursement disputes—that is, cases where a contract such as a "Provider Services Agreement" governs the relationship between the provider and the payer or health plan—the principal purpose of such an agreement is for the provider to deliver healthcare services to the health plan's members at agreed-upon rates. Equally relevant to reimbursement rates, however, are myriad provisions controlling the circumstances under which a provider will be paid for the services they perform. For example, carefully written terms control what constitutes "medical necessity,"[1] what is required for a "clean claim,"[2] procedures under which the provider may be required to submit a clean claim, the timeframe for a payer's obligation to pay claims, circumstances under which a payer may perform utilization review, procedures for disputing unpaid and underpaid claims and the forum for formal dispute resolution.

It is critical for both providers and payers to avoid ambiguity in these types of contract terms because disputes regarding interpretations of such ambiguities can quickly result in costly litigation. Though boilerplate templates for provider service agreements often include provisions that are commonly litigated in managed care, it is vital to tailor these provisions to the individual needs of the parties. Time spent on legal review of provider service agreements is time well spent.

If ambiguous terms do become the subject of dispute, there are a number of tools that may be used to assist with contract interpretation. For example, parol evidence,[3] which may include precontract drafts, emails and financial models used during contract negotiations, and other written communications might be used to show what the parties intended. Robust record maintenance is a good

1 "Medical Necessity" means health care services that a physician, exercising prudent clinical judgment, would provide to a patient.

2 "Clean Claim" is a term usually defined in the Agreement and typically is defined as a claim that has no defect, impropriety or lack of required substantiating documentation.

3 Parol evidence is any agreement that is not contained within the written contract.

practice for both providers and payers, as written documentation created at the time of contract negotiation may serve as critical evidence.

2. *Oral Contracts*

One commonly overlooked contract is an oral contract between a provider and payer. This is generally formed during the preauthorization stage of healthcare service delivery. To obtain preauthorization, a provider typically calls a patient's insurance company (the payer) to request that a particular service be approved (i.e., preauthorized) prior to rendering the service. Where the formation of a contract requires an offer, acceptance and consideration, the act of the provider calling the payer may constitute an offer in a preauthorization situation. The act of the payer preauthorizing the service may constitute acceptance. The consideration is the provider performing a service or treating the patient in exchange for a fee.

In an oral contract formed during preauthorization, the fee typically becomes the most frequently disputed element. If a written contract exists between the provider and the payer, the parties might default to the applicable rate schedule or fee schedule if one exists. If there is no written contract, several options exist for determining the rate, such as the "usual and customary" (see Chapters 5 and 6) rate for the service, the Medicare rate, or some other agreed-upon rate between the provider and the payer.

Even where an oral contract is formed between a payer and provider, it is good practice to follow up with written documentation that includes the precise service approved (including relevant DRG or CPT codes), the dates of service approved and the approved level of care. This can minimize the risk of disputes.

3. *Course-of-Conduct Contracts (Implied-in-Fact Contracts)*

Providers and payers often have longstanding relationships whereby they agree to exchange services at particular rates. As such, these types of relationships may have been formed initially with or without a contract. If there is no written contract, the parties' actions might create a course-of-conduct contract.

B. Actions Precedent to Contract Formation

Actions precedent to the formation of a course-of-conduct contract might include the parties' mutual exchange of services at a particular rate over a long period of time or the parties' continued exchange of services at a certain rate following the termination of a written contract due either to contract lapse or an affirmative act. A course-of-conduct contract might also form when there is an existing agreement, but the provider performs certain services or the payer pays certain rates outside of strict provisions of the contract, and neither party protests the actions.

For example, a course-of-conduct contract might emerge out of a situation where emergency services are performed at an out-of-network hospital and the patient requires additional post-emergency inpatient care. If the patient is stabilized but still requires additional care, the hospital will generally contact the payer to request authorization for continued services. Once the payer authorizes inpatient care at the out-of-network hospital, a course-of-conduct contract can exist between the payer and the provider. However, even though a contract exists, the rate the provider will receive for medically necessary services can become a contentious issue in the absence of written terms for payment.

C. Actions Subsequent to Contract Termination

The parties' actions in the absence of a written contract or following the termination of a written contract are crucial. The strongest way a provider might object to a payer's underpayment of contractually agreed-upon rates is to cease doing business with the payer until the payer reimburses agreed-upon rates. However, ceasing to perform medical services often is impractical or impossible, particularly when the provider is in-network or in emergency situations. Thus, sending a demand letter or other type of written request for payment can signal that the provider will not tolerate extra-contractual actions.

D. State Law Governing Requisite Degree of Protest

State laws govern the requisite degree of protest that parties may be required to make to avoid being bound by a course-of-conduct contract. During the pendency of a payment dispute, the provider might be permitted to accept partial payments while still reserving the right to recoup full payment under a quantum meruit[4] theory. Most payers recognize that paying nothing for services legitimately provided can create an egregious pattern of unfair payment. Furthermore, there is no reason for a payer to withhold undisputed portions of a claim. However, payers often withhold full payment of a claim until the dispute is resolved; therefore, it is a best practice for the provider to dispute underpayments and denials of claims as soon as possible.

III. IN-NETWORK DISPUTES

Commonly litigated causes of action in in-network disputes include claims for breach of contract, quantum meruit, unjust enrichment and violations of state prompt pay laws.

Claims for breaches of contract arise out of violations of the Provider Services Agreement, which principally requires the insurer to timely pay for the services

4 Quantum meruit is an equitable theory of recovery whereby a provider is entitled to fair payment for the services provided.

the provider performs. When a health plan receives the benefit of having the healthcare obligations to its members discharged and the members receive the benefit of having medical care provided to them, the payer might be unjustly enriched for refusing to adequately reimburse the provider. A provider might also accept partial payment while still reserving the right to recoup full payment under a quantum meruit theory. Some courts will determine the quantum meruit rate by balancing the plan's in-network rate with that of the industry's customary rates.

State prompt pay statutes typically require insurers to pay a healthcare provider's claim within 30 days of receipt of an electronically submitted clean claim. Prompt pay statutes might also require the insurer to pay interest for late-paid claims.

A. Fee-for-Service Compensation Contracts

Fee-for-service arrangements, whereby the provider receives a fee in exchange for each service rendered, have historically been the most common reimbursement approach. Notwithstanding the trend in value-based arrangements (see Chapters 4, 5 and 6), fee-for-service reimbursement is also the most common approach at issue in managed care disputes.

1. *Methods Used to Set Provider Fees*

In fee-for-service arrangements, reimbursement to a provider is often based on:

> (1) standard procedure charges, which may be based on Current Procedural Terminology (CPT) codes, Diagnosis Related Group (DRG) codes, the Medicare rate or some other agreed-upon contractual rate for each covered service; (2) a per-diem rate, which is based on fixed daily charges for specific services or groups of services; or (3) a fixed percentage of the provider's billed charges.

B. Authorizations

Most payers require authorization as a prerequisite to coverage of certain services. The payer may require the provider to request authorization prior to the service being performed (i.e., preauthorization), or the payer might allow for post-authorization if obtained within a certain timeframe of performance of the service. Lack of authorization is one of the most common reasons payers cite for denying payment of a claim.

Failure to obtain authorization is not always fatal to a provider's ability to recover payment for services performed, however. Retroactive authorizations might be permitted where the plan would have authorized the service had preauthorization been requested. Furthermore, if the service was medically necessary, a provider may successfully argue that the failure to request authorization was harmless. Physicians in practice may disagree over the medical necessity of a service. Thus, when a payer denies authorization of a service because the service was not medically necessary, a provider can challenge medical necessity in a reimbursement dispute and engage its own medical expert.

Emergency Exception

Payers sometimes incorrectly deny a claim for lack of authorization in emergency situations, where preauthorization is prohibited by federal or state law. Under the federal Emergency Medical Treatment and Active Labor Act (EMTALA),[5] a provider must screen and stabilize any individual who presents in an emergency room without regard for the individual's ability to pay or the provider's ability to receive payment. Many states have adopted laws similar to EMTALA that prohibit payers from requiring preauthorization in emergency care situations. The Affordable Care Act (ACA) also prohibits use of prior authorization related to emergency care.[6] In emergency situations, therefore, payers should be advised not to deny claims based on lack of authorization.

Course-of-Conduct Transactions in Authorizations

Preauthorization and retroactive authorization can also give rise to enforceable course-of-conduct contracts. For example, if the payer authorizes surgery with two days of inpatient care, but complications arise out of the surgery and the physician indicates the patient needs to stay for an extra day, the plan may be required to pay for the extra day of care. Furthermore, if the payer has a history of retroactively authorizing a certain service because it is medically necessary, a provider can reasonably argue it was not required to request preauthorization because the payer historically authorized the service retroactively. Ambiguous contract terms regarding retroactive authorization in provider/payer contracts may be interpreted against the drafter, which often is the payer.

Retroactive Denial of Authorization

A payer may retroactively deny authorization on the basis of a member's ineligibility. This occurs when a member's enrollment in a health plan lapses (typically due to unpaid premiums) or when the member is otherwise not covered under the plan. When a provider detrimentally relies on preauthorization and performs the service, there are a number of reasons a payer may be required to pay.

For example, the payer may have negligently authorized a service despite what it knew or should have known about the member's eligibility status. In this type of circumstance, the payer might be bound by a course-of-conduct contract or equitable theories of recovery such as quantum meruit. In addition, a disenrollment

5 42 U.S.C Section 1395dd.

6 29 CFR Section 2590.715–2719A.

provision in the parties' contract might require the payer to pay benefits for ineligible members, which may or may not require the provider to first seek payment from the ineligible member. State law may also prohibit payers from retroactively denying authorization that the provider relied upon after the service has been provided.

C. Timely Filing

As providers know, timely submission of claims (or timely filing) is crucial to ensuring claims are paid on time. But even where a provider submits a claim on time, a payer may deny the claim, asserting that the claim was received after the timely filing deadline. This often occurs with paper or manual claims, which are sometimes necessary even though most claims today are filed electronically. Providers can rebut payers' arguments that claims were not properly submitted with strong evidence of established timely filing practices.

Proof of Submitted Claims

Payers generally contest receipt of payment rather than the time the claim was sent. In response, providers can apply the "mailbox rule," which is an established principle providing that an item was sent on the day it was mailed. The mailbox rule is best paired with additional methods of proof, and alternatively, providers might consider submitting claims via certified, registered or overnight mail. Providers also are advised to develop and maintain strong internal policies and internal evidence of claim submission, which can be supported with training materials and verified with internal claims processing notes indicating dates that claims were submitted. In addition, evidence of follow-up phone calls or correspondence with the payer regarding the claim acknowledge receipt of a claim. These policies and processing notes can be the strongest evidence of a timely claim submission and receipt of the claim by the payer, particularly when offered as evidence by a representative who is well-versed in the provider's procedures and can verify robust practices of timely submission and routine follow-up correspondence with the payer.

Justifications for Untimely Claim Submission

The consequence of alleged untimely claim submission can result in full denial of a claim. However, certain justifications for untimely claims submission can result in an arbitrator or judge finding that the provider should still be reimbursed for the services rendered because the provider may have good cause for not submitting the claim on time. For example, a patient may provide incorrect insurance information, resulting in a lengthy process whereby the provider bills the wrong payer and is unable to bill the correct payer until it receives the proper information. Worse, a patient may die during the course of treatment before the provider is able to obtain their insurance information, when providers are typically more focused on treating patients in these situations than on billing patient's insurance.

A prohibition on punitive "liquidated damages" clauses might also preclude payers from enforcing claim submission deadlines if doing so would constitute a penalty. Such a contract provision would preclude the payer from receiving an excessive sum that is not related to the provider's failure to meet certain contractual requirements. This is because the benefits a payer would receive from denying claims after the provider upheld its primary obligation to provide healthcare services could constitute a windfall to the payer and a penalty to the provider. Many state laws also prohibit parties from enforcing punitive contract provisions.

Even in the absence of these justifications, payers often have an unconvincing form-over-substance argument when it comes to proving damages. This is particularly so when a payer authorizes a claim and would have been required to pay it anyway. Equitable doctrines support the notion that providers should receive compensation for performing authorized services for a payer's members and should not be penalized for technicalities of untimely submission of claims.

Where providers seek reimbursement for untimely claims in managed care disputes, their arguments are the strongest when they can show compliance with other contractual requirements, such as clean claim submission and appeals. Additionally, compliance with the statute of limitations for the underlying cause of action is further evidence of a practice of timely behavior.

D. Medical Necessity

Payers sometimes deny claims on the basis that a service was (in the payer's opinion) not medically necessary. This is an area where providers have unique credibility in managed care disputes because they directly interact with patients to render appropriate and often live-saving care. Providers need not accept a payer's rejection of physicians' medical judgment, especially where a payer's denial was generated from automated programs, nonphysician reviewers or physician reviewers without recent experience in the practice area at issue.

Definitions of Medical Necessity

The American Medical Association provides the following definition of "medical necessity" that is widely accepted by medical authorities and is often used in contracts between providers and payers:

> Health care services or products that a prudent physician would provide to a patient for the purpose of preventing, diagnosing or treating an illness, injury, disease or its symptoms in a manner that is: (a) in accordance with generally accepted standards of medical practice; (b) clinically appropriate in terms of type, frequency, extent, site, and duration; and (c) not primarily for the

> economic benefit of the health plans and purchasers or for the convenience of the patient, treating physician or other health care provider.[7]

Furthermore, federal statutes and state statutes recognize a "prudent layperson" standard for emergency medical conditions, including the following language in the EMTALA law:

> A medical condition manifesting itself by acute symptoms of sufficient severity (including severe pain) such that a prudent layperson, who possesses an average knowledge of health and medicine, could reasonably expect the absence of immediate medical attention to result in: a) placing the patient's health in serious jeopardy; b) serious impairment to bodily functions; or c) serious dysfunction of any bodily organ or part.

Payers often include restrictive definitions of medical necessity and may allow themselves wide latitude to deny payment for failure to meet certain medical necessity criteria and care guidelines such as those contained in the Milliman Care Guidelines.[8] However, a plan's definition may violate the prudent layperson[9] standard in emergency care situations. Furthermore, reasonable physicians may differ in their judgment of a patient's course of treatment, and the physician who treated the patient has a strong argument for deference over a non-treating physician who retrospectively reviewed the claim.

Length of Stay and Level of Care

Rather than deny an entire service or procedure for lack of medical necessity, payers might seek to narrow their medical necessity denials to include only the length of stay or level of care. For example, if the treating physician ordered three days of inpatient care, but the plan believes the patient only required two days of inpatient care and one day of observation, the payer may deny the third day of care or pay only the observation rate. Hospital levels of care include inpatient, outpatient (including observation), intensive care unit (ICU), telemetry, medical/surgical care and subacute care.

---

7 American Medical Association, Health Policies, H-320.953 (2016).

8 The Milliman Care Guidelines and Interqual Guidelines are evidence-based knowledge and best practices relevant to patients in a broad range of care settings used by providers and insurance companies.

9 The prudent layperson standard requires payers to provide coverage for emergency care based on symptoms, not final diagnoses. The Prudent Layperson language, adopted individually by most States, defines an emergency medical condition as: A medical condition manifesting itself by acute symptoms of sufficient severity (including severe pain) such that a prudent layperson, who possesses an average knowledge of health and medicine, could reasonably expect the absence of immediate medical attention to result in: a) placing the patient's health in serious jeopardy; b) serious impairment to bodily functions; or c) serious dysfunction of any bodily organ or part.

Inpatient Care	Care provided in a hospital or other type of inpatient facility where the patient is admitted.
Outpatient Care	Any healthcare consultation, procedure, or treatment that is administered without admission to inpatient care in a hospital or medical facility.
ICU	Provides the critical care and support for acutely ill and injured patients.
Telemetry	A portable device that continuously monitors patient ECG, respiratory rate, and/or oxygen saturations while automatically transmitting information to a central monitor. Patients in telemetry are stable but require constant monitoring.
Medical/Surgical Care	Preoperative, perioperative, intraoperative, postoperative, and post-discharge care related to a surgery.
Subacute Care	Subacute care is comprehensive inpatient care that does not require intensive care or invasive procedures.

While guidelines such as Interqual[10] and Milliman can be used as tools to help determine appropriate levels of care, the proper treatment of a patient demands physician judgment under real-time circumstances. Treating physicians should be advised to keep detailed medical records supporting treatment and level of care decisions.

Regarding length of stay, a hospital can only discharge a patient with a physician's order, and the hospital must continue providing care until a patient is discharged. But even when a physician believes a patient can be discharged, the discharge process can become challenging when a patient needs to be transferred to a nursing facility or post-acute rehabilitation center and there are no available beds. For example, if a hospital seeks transfer of a patient to a skilled nursing facility, but there is no bed available for the patient, the hospital must continue to

10 Similar to the Milliman Care Guidelines, Interqual also provides clinical decision support for payers to help ensure clinically appropriate medical-utilization decisions.

provide care because it cannot discharge the patient to their home. In this type of situation, the hospital generally assumes the burden of contacting facilities until an available bed can be located. When this occurs, the provider has a strong argument that the continued level of care is excused and that it should receive payment from the plan for the care provided.

E. DRG Downgrades

In recent years, some payers have denied claims after initial claim submission or after an audit based on DRG coding. There are typically three types of such denials: (1) disputes strictly stemming from disagreement over the DRG coding itself, (2) disputes stemming from disagreement over the clinical diagnoses underlying the coding or (3) some combination thereof.

MS-DRGs

As described in Chapter 3 and previously in this chapter, many commercial health plan agreements provide for reimbursement based on Medicare-Severity Diagnosis Related Groups (MS-DRG). The MS-DRG system groups patients with similar clinical characteristics who are expected to require similar levels of hospital resources, and payments are made on a per-discharge basis, that is, one payment for each inpatient hospital stay. See Chapter 1 for a detailed explanation of the MS-DRG payment calculation. Payment rates based on MS-DRGs in commercial health plan agreements are typically calculated in one of two ways:

- Multiplying a hospital-specific MS-DRG base rate by the applicable MS-DRG weight; or
- Per diem rates based on MS-DRG per-discharge amounts, which are equal to the number of days in the per diem period(s) multiplied by the per diem rate(s) in the agreement.

Disputes Regarding DRGs

At various stages of claim adjudication, payers may reduce the amount paid on a claim based upon a DRG disagreement. For example, a payer may "downcode" the MS-DRG code by removing a "CC" or "MCC" designation[11] and may cite to the secondary diagnosis not supporting an increase in the length of the hospital stay or the level of treatment provided. In so doing, the payer interprets the agreement, and a dispute may ensue between the provider and payer regarding the agreement. At issue may be applicable coding procedures, appropriate coding levels and the existence of clinical diagnoses to support codes used. In cases of downcoding on a claim, a payer may contend that the diagnosis assigned was incorrect or invalid,

11 CC stands for "complication or comorbidity" and MCC stands for "major complication or comorbidity." See Chapter 1 for more information.

or a payer may simply disagree with the DRG coding on the claim. Disputes may ensue as a result of disagreement regarding the diagnoses, the DRG coding or both.

F. Line-Item Charge Denials

Payers sometimes deny line-item charges[12] that they deem routine or believe should be bundled or packaged with other items on a claim. For example, a payer may deny line-item charges for supplies such as gauze, sponges, or surgical kits on a surgery claim, contending that these items are included in the room charge or the procedure charge. Payers may also deny line-item charges for oxygen provided in the ICU on the grounds that patients who are admitted to the ICU typically require respiratory care. In some cases, payers have denied charges for venipuncture, indicating that it should be included in laboratory test charges, and denied charges for saline solution as being included in medication charges.

There are no state or federal laws or regulations regarding the classification of items or services on commercial or Medicare claims. Therefore, hospitals can structure their charges for these items and services as they see fit. For example, a hospital can separately charge $300 for a procedure and $25 for oxygen, or it can simply charge $325 for the procedure. While a hospital can choose to bundle charges for certain equipment, supplies and other items into a procedure charge, regardless of whether the patient uses the items, from the provider's standpoint, it is appropriate to identify the line-item charges separately because (1) it would be inappropriate for bills to reflect items that patients do not use, and (2) it is easier to track inventory based on actual usage of items.

Medicare claims may be denied based on National Correct Coding Initiative (NCCI) edits.[13] For example, Medicare may deny charges for procedures if coding modifiers are not used. However, NCCI edits are not considered the industry standard for billing commercial claims.

G. Contract Changes through Revised Policies

Payers may also seek to change contract provisions regarding claim submission procedures, appeal and grievance requirements, reimbursement rates or other material aspects of a claim through unilateral policy changes. These may include revised policy manuals, bulletins that are published online, memos or letters that

12 The Claim Form (or UB-04) includes the "Total Charges" but also includes line-by-line detail with CPT codes for individual line items that correlate to items on the bill. See Chapter 1 for more information regarding claim forms.

13 The National Correct Coding Initiative (NCCI) is a government program to promote national correct coding methodologies and reduce improper coding, with the overall goal of reducing improper payments on Medicare and Medicaid claims. National Correct Coding Initiative (NCCI), Centers for Medicare & Medicaid Services (CMS), www.cms.gov/medicare-medicaid-coordination/national-correct-coding-initiative-ncci#:~:text=The%20National%20Correct%20Coding%20Initiative,Part%20B%20and%20Medicaid%20claims.

are circulated to providers, changes implemented as a result of updated claims processing software and other policies. For example, a plan might circulate a letter to a provider requiring that certain procedures be billed with coding modifiers that were not part of the original Provider Services Agreement.

If a provider receives notice of a unilateral policy change, the provider should object in writing. This is the clearest way to protest the change. If a provider does not protest the change and allows the payer to deny or underpay the claims for a long period of time, the payer might point to these actions as evidence of nondispute and further argue that the provider's inaction supports a contract modification that was accepted through the provider's course of conduct.

Generally speaking, unilateral contract changes that lack express provider approval are unenforceable. Such policy changes might also violate integration clauses in the contract that require both parties to sign before they can be enforced. A payer may attempt to rely on contract language that permits such unilateral changes via policy manuals, bulletins or other methods, but these changes may also be unenforceable. For example, contracts in many states require a covenant of good faith and fair dealing that prevents material changes to the contract's terms. Unilateral changes might also be deemed illusory for lack of definitive terms, particularly where the updated policies are vague or contradictory. Finally, policy changes might be struck for lack of consideration, as most states generally require contract changes to include new or additional consideration.

H. Contract Termination

Contract termination is a concern of both providers and payers at the outset of any dispute. The type of termination determines the procedural resolution process and available remedies. While contract terminations can occur from either side, this section will describe a payer's termination of its contract with a preferred provider.

The responsibilities, amounts owed and legal implications for payers and providers determine the mechanism by which a contract ends. A contract can terminate with cause, without cause or by the contract's own terms.

1. Termination with Cause

The basis for termination with cause usually involves negligence, fraud or tortious misconduct. Due to the severity of such charges, the provider is usually afforded remedies in the form of an appeal and hearing. Contracts will sometimes limit the administrative remedies available by inputting a waiver of such appeal; however, depending on the state where the provider is located, this language may be invalid, and the provider will still be entitled to an appeal. A contractual clause limiting an appeal may also turn on the charge itself, as courts may enforce the clause in medical negligence actions but not for billing irregularities. During the appeal process, the provider's status will remain as a participating or in-network provider until further notice, unless the underlying conduct implicates an unacceptable standard of care provided or risk for patients' well-being.

Sometimes a payer will end, or threaten to end, a relationship with a provider for referring patients to out-of-network providers, stating that these referrals constitute a breach of contract. Specifically, a payer in this situation may believe it is in the best interest of a member to remain within the plan's network. But these restrictions can spur uncertainty, especially if the member has a plan that specifically allows for reimbursement of out-of-network services.[14] Restrictions can also run afoul of the law because while payers want members to use in-network providers, they must comply with their state's adequate-coverage standards.[15]

2. *Termination without Cause*

A contract termination without cause allows either party to end the contractual relationship for any or no reason, as long as reasonable notice is provided. This type of termination does not usually afford a provider the same administrative remedies as in a for-cause action. But once again, this depends on the state where the provider is located. Some state courts do not require a payer to provide a hearing, appeal or even a reason for the termination while others, such as California and New York, find that a provider is entitled to notice, a hearing (comprising at least three members) and a prompt decision.

3. *Expiring Contracts*

Typically, two issues arise with regard to expiring contracts: (1) whether the provider's rates in a newly negotiated contract will apply retroactively, and (2) how the provider's rate is determined when the contract expires and the parties are still negotiating, but ultimately do not form a new contract. Some contracts contain a provision stating that the same rate will continue until the contract's termination. If the contract is silent on this issue, the parties could agree to apply the rate from the expired contract (though this option is less likely). A payer may try to pay lower rates under an expired contract; however, the provider in this case would likely push back and argue that the payer assumed the risk by continuing to negotiate.

I. Alternative Dispute Resolution

Managed care disputes are not always resolved in courtrooms. In an effort to save costs, payers and providers might opt for alternative dispute resolution such as arbitration, mediation or administrative procedures. Indeed, most Provider Services Agreements include a mandatory arbitration clause, which may dictate the arbitration forum, parameters for arbitrator selection and prerequisites to pursuing arbitration such as exhausting administrative remedies or attempting to settle the dispute informally between the parties.

---

14 Such as a Preferred Provider Organization (PPO) plan.

15 These vary by state but at a minimum require EMTALA compliance.

1. *Arbitration*

Arbitration generally arises through a contractual requirement. The process resembles a traditional court proceeding in many ways, including providing for written discovery, depositions, dispositive motions and a hearing on merits. The matter is decided by a single arbitrator or panel of arbitrators, rather than by a judge and jury. Furthermore, arbitration generally allows the parties more flexibility in the procedures for resolution by limiting the number of depositions, limiting the number of interrogatories or requests for deposition and even agreeing to methods such as statistical sampling to limit the number of claims. A number of forums are available for selection, including the American Arbitration Association (AAA), Judicial Arbitration and Mediation Services (JAMS) and the American Health Lawyers Association (AHLA).

While arbitration generally is viewed as a cost-saving method of dispute resolution, arbitration can still be expensive. The forum where the arbitration occurs can have a significant impact on costs, as the association selected might require nonrefundable fees in the thousands of dollars to initiate a matter. In addition, individual arbitrators may have high hourly rates and/or cancellation fees if a hearing is canceled due to settlement. Finally, arbitrators often are reticent to grant dispositive motions, which may force parties to incur significant costs to proceed to the final hearing.

In some cases, providers may find that arbitration clauses are not advantageous. For example, some providers feel that payers feel pressure to settle court cases in order to avoid negative public relations or bad legal precedent. On the other hand, state and federal privacy rules such as HIPAA may provide an incentive to keep some matters out of public court systems where the parties could incur significant costs to redact patient names, anonymize evidence and exhibits and file motions under seal. Because arbitration proceedings are not publicly available, these types of privacy concerns are not an issue. Thus, arbitration may be a better choice. Nearly all aspects of arbitration are confidential; however, once an arbitration proceeds to hearing and an award is issued, the award might not remain confidential should one party then seek to enforce the award in court. Therefore, settlement is the most effective way to ensure the arbitration remains confidential.

a. Scope of Arbitration

Arbitration clauses may include a broad arbitration provision covering all disputes "arising out of, relating to or concerning" the Provider Services Agreement. This sweeping provision has been found to cover not only contractual disputes, but also tort disputes and even statutory disputes. Limiting the scope of arbitration in a contract can help to specifically identify what is covered and what is outside the parameters of arbitration. Disputes can occur where the contract is ambiguous regarding scope. An ambiguous arbitration clause may ultimately be enforced after a party first pursues a case in state or federal court, incurring potentially significant expense, only to have a judge order arbitration based on their interpretation of the arbitration clause. Providers and payers alike should therefore carefully review such clauses and reach a mutual understanding of their meaning in practice.

b. Remedy Limitations

Arbitration clauses may also significantly limit the remedies available to the prevailing party, including punitive damages, noneconomic damages and consequential damages. In contexts outside of managed care, these limitations have been found contrary to public opinion and void. Those seeking to avoid arbitration should carefully review these provisions and state laws, as such provisions could invalidate an entire arbitration clause. Payers might be reluctant to agree to such limitations if they will risk striking the entire arbitration provision.

c. Multiparty Disputes

Arbitrations where there are multiple parties involved—such as those where not only a provider and health plan are involved, but also a health plan's third-party delegated payment entity—may become particularly complex (see Chapters 5 and 6 for more information on third party administrators and delegated entities). Often, an arbitration clause applies only to the provider and the payer while the third party either has no contract or a contract that does not require arbitration.

Adjudicating a matter in both an arbitration forum and in court can yield inconsistent results. Thus, parties typically will attempt to try an entire matter in one forum. While payers and providers may have individual reasons for preferring one forum over the other, providers often opt for litigation in state or federal court while payers may opt to enforce an arbitration provision. State laws applicable to multiparty, multi-contract disputes determine whether a judge has discretion to deny enforcement of an arbitration clause where a case involves both arbitrable and non-arbitrable issues.

d. Class-Wide Arbitration

Another question courts have considered is whether arbitration provisions prohibiting class-wide arbitrations are enforceable. In class action cases alleging price fixing and unfair competition against health plans, some courts have found such provisions unenforceable and void as against public policy. Other courts in the consumer context have found contractual class arbitration waivers unenforceable. Yet other courts have enforced such arbitration provisions, creating a scenario where courts are precluding class arbitration while simultaneously enforcing arbitration provisions.

Conflicting court decisions highlight the importance of carefully analyzing the meaning of the language in arbitration clauses. For example, parties should consider whether the phrase "class action" appears, and even if it doesn't, whether a class action arbitration may be implied with sweeping language allowing any claim brought to be arbitrated.

2. *Mediation*

Mediation is another form of alternative dispute resolution that can aid parties in reaching early settlement. Mediation typically involves one or multiple meetings with a neutral party such as a judge, attorney or other professional to discuss the parties' positions and attempt to find a common ground on which to settle their differences.

Parties typically are able to decide whether or not they will engage in mediation. In arbitrations, for example, the parties might agree to a mediation deadline as part of the scheduling order. In other instances, mediation may be compelled by a court order or by contract. Mediation is low risk because it is non-binding, though it may be less appealing because it requires parties to "show their cards" to the other side. Furthermore, parties sometimes opt not to engage in mediation when they know there are fact issues to be determined and seek to adjudicate the merits of the case. On the other hand, where the parties' aim is to settle early and save costs, mediation can be a powerful tool to facilitate resolution.

3. *Administrative Procedures*

Payers increasingly require exhaustion of administrative remedies before a provider may file suit or an arbitration demand. Such administrative remedies generally require the provider to follow the payer's grievance process for appealing underpaid and paid claims. These appeals processes are often complicated and often conflicting.

For example, a payer might require different appeals processes for medical necessity denials versus other types of denials. The "grievance" provision of the Provider Services Agreement might contain little to no instruction about the grievance procedure itself and instead direct providers to appeals instructions in bulletins, websites, and/or other external resources, any of which might have differing instructions or be updated without substantial notice to providers. Furthermore, a payer may find an appeal inadequate for failure to attach specific grievance forms created by the payer.

A provider may successfully argue that they exhausted administrative remedies requirements by substantially complying with appeals procedures. Alternatively, a provider may argue that an appeal would have been futile because of a payer's history and practice of ongoing denial of claims without explanation after multiple appeals. In addition, when a provider submits multiple appeal letters, has their representative follow up with a payer regarding the status of payment, and/or otherwise shows protest of a claim denial or underpayment, a judge and/or arbitrator may find that the payer is emphasizing form over substance and that the provider substantially complied with the spirit of the appeal requirement. Providers are advised to implement robust policies and procedures to appeal claims in writing immediately upon learning that a payer has denied or underpaid a claim.

J. Medicare and Medicaid Claims

Medicare and Medicaid claims adjudication is different from commercial claims adjudication. Providers and payers alike should be aware of Medicare and Medicaid reimbursement rates, regulations and procedures for dispute resolution. This includes Medicare Advantage and Medicaid managed care plans as well.

IV. OUT-OF-NETWORK DISPUTES

Out-of-network disputes can occur when a provider has no express contract with a payer. As nonparticipating providers, out-of-network providers have no pre-existing agreement to accept particular rates from a payer as payment in full. If an out-of-network provider did not agree to any particular rate, the provider will typically seek the "usual and customary" rate, "reasonable and customary" value or some variation thereof depending on the state law and applicable patient health plan. Out-of-network disputes often arise in the emergency room context.

A. Types of Claims

Out-of-network disputes often include claims arising out plans subject to the Employment Retirement Income Security Act of 1974 (ERISA). In an ERISA claim, providers will seek to enforce rights to recover ERISA benefits that are assigned to the provider via patients who are insured under ERISA plans issued, insured and/or administered by the health plan. As we have learned in previous chapters, there are two primary types of ERISA plans: (1) fully insured ERISA plans, which are employer-sponsored health insurance plans where the employer insures the policies through an insurance company; and (2) self-funded ERISA plans, which are employer-sponsored health benefit plans where the employer underwrites (pays for) the benefits, and a third-party administrator administers the plan.

Health plans may be required under ERISA, state contract law and various equitable principles to properly pay claims to out-of-network providers, but the type of ERISA plan dictates the causes of action available to the provider. For example, claims pursuant to fully insured ERISA plans are subject to state law, and thus state contract and statutory causes of action can apply without any ERISA preemption analysis required. Claims under self-funded ERISA plans require an ERISA preemption analysis to determine which causes of action may apply. In self-funded ERISA plans, a claim for denied ERISA benefits is still appropriate.

Non-ERISA claims can include claims for quantum meruit, unjust enrichment, breach of implied contract and violations of state statutes, including state emergency care statutes and state prompt pay laws. Several states have adopted laws requiring insurers to pay out-of-network providers for delivering emergency care.[16]

B. Obligation to Pay a Reasonable Amount

Where no agreement governs the relationship between the payer and the provider, the next step is to analyze what, if anything, governs the payments made by the payer to the providers.

1. *Agreements to Pay Usual and Customary Amounts*

Where no written agreement (network contract) exists, a patient's insurance plan (e.g., the benefit plan or subscriber agreement) or the state insurance code specifies the amount a plan is required to pay a provider for providing emergency or non-emergency services. Benefit plans may require coverage of medically necessary out-of-network services at the "usual and customary rate" or at a rate derived therefrom. The "usual and customary rate" may refer to comparable charges for similar services or procedures in the same geographic area where services or procedures were provided.

2. *Assignments of Benefits*

As a general policy, providers typically obtain assignment of benefits from patients during the patient intake stage.[17] Assignment of benefits is the process where a patient assigns the provider the right to receive payment for services rendered directly from a payer. The assignment may also expressly assign the right to recover self-insured ERISA benefits. Under a valid assignment of benefits, the provider "stands in the shoes" of insureds whose services the health plan agreed to cover and is entitled to any amounts for which the insureds would be entitled to reimbursement.

C. State Laws Requiring the Usual and Customary Rate

While some health benefit plans may require payment of the usual and customary rate, some state laws may also require payment of the usual and customary rate. In California, the Knox-Keene Health Care Service Plan Act of 1975, along with EMTALA, requires hospitals and other medical providers to perform "emergency [medical] services and care to persons who are in danger of loss of life, serious

16 *See, e.g.*, Tex. Ins. Code 1271.155; *see also*, *e.g.* Nev. Rev. Stat. 439B.

17 When the patient arrives to the provider and is stable, the provider seeks information regarding the patient's insurance and payment information.

injury or illness."[18] The Act also specifies that when a hospital or other medical provider does not have a contract with a health plan, the plan must reimburse the provider at the "reasonable and customary value [of] the [emergency] health care services rendered."[19] The "reasonable and customary value" takes into account the following factors:

- The provider's training, qualifications and length of time in practice;
- The nature of the services provided;
- The fees usually charged by or paid to the provider, including rates paid by both commercial and governmental payers;
- Prevailing provider rates charged and paid by both commercial and governmental payers in the general geographic area in which the services were rendered;
- Other relevant aspects of the economics of the medical provider's practice;
- Any unusual circumstances in the case.[20]

Other state laws also require health plans to pay the usual and customary rate. For example, in *In re North Cypress Medical Center Operating Co., Ltd.*, 559 S.W.3d 128 (2018), the Texas Supreme Court provided guidance for determining the usual and customary rate to be paid by commercial health plans: "[W]e do not hold, that the rates negotiated between North Cypress and any particular insurer govern the reasonableness of its charges to uninsured patients."[21] The court further explained that "[t]hese cases demonstrate at least the **potential connection** between reimbursement rates and the reasonableness of billed charges" (emphasis added). Moreover, the court recognized that "**many considerations** go into negotiated rates that may explain a discount applied to a particular insurer" (emphasis added).[22] Texas statutes also contain language regarding payment of the usual and customary rate for HMOs.[23]

Generally, providers will point to either state law or the benefit plan as governing the reasonable amount to be reimbursed. This amount depends on various state laws and requires analysis of the same depending on the location of the provider.

18 Cal. Health & Safety Code § 1317(a).
19 Cal. Code Regs., tit. 28, § 1300.71(a)(3)(B).
20 *See* Cal. Code Regs., tit. 28, § 1300.71(a)(3)(B).
21 559 S.W.3d at 136.
22 *Id.*
23 Tex. Ins. Code Ann. § 1271.155(a): "A health maintenance organization shall pay for emergency care performed by non-network physicians or providers at the **usual and customary rate** or at an agreed rate" (emphasis added). Relating to Exclusive Provider Benefit Plans, the statute states: Tex. Ins. Code Ann. § 1301.0053(a): "If an out-of-network provider provides emergency care as defined by Section 1301.155 to an enrollee in an exclusive provider benefit plan, the issuer of the plan shall reimburse the out-of-network provider at the **usual and customary rate** or at a rate agreed to by the issuer and the out-of-network provider for the provision of the services and any supply related to those services" (emphasis added).

D. Determination of a Reasonable Amount

Payers may pay out-of-network providers rates that are lower than in-network rates on belief that these rates are reasonable amounts. However, providers need not accept a payer's unilateral decision regarding the reasonable value for the services provided. In disputes regarding reasonable value, both parties will typically engage experts to opine on the value of the services provided. Selected approaches for determining reasonable value are described below.

1. Fair Market Value

Some experts may look to the "fair market value" to determine the reasonable value of claims at issue in an out-of-network dispute. Fair market value is defined as the "price that a willing buyer will pay and a willing seller will accept in an arm's-length transaction."[24] Similarly, under Federal Stark Law, fair market value is defined as "mean[ing] the value in arm's-length transactions, consistent with general market value. General market value means . . . the compensation that would be included in a service agreement as the result of bona fide bargaining between well-informed parties . . . the compensation that has been included in bona fide service agreements with comparable terms."[25]

Central to these definitions of reasonable value is an acknowledgment that payers define benefit plans and configure provider networks to financially incentivize plan members to use certain providers. In exchange for payers directing their members to them, providers typically offer discounted rates. Payers may decide to pay rates on out-of-network claims that are equal to or less than their contract rates (which are sometimes lower than Medicare rates), based on the premise that such rates are the reasonable values.

However, an out-of-network provider would maintain that in these situations the plan does not provide value (in the form of member direction) that warrants discounts from the provider's prices. In other words, provider discounts agreed to in in-network arrangements (i.e., contract rates) are the result of a bargaining process between providers and payers whereby health plans offer significant value to participating providers in exchange for discounted rates. In out-of-network situations, no such bargaining occurs.

2. Comparable Payment Data

In order to evaluate the reasonable value, experts typically review market rate data, including (1) comparable out-of-network data, (2) the provider's charges, (3) adjusted in-network data and (4) other categories of data depending on

24 Smith, T. and Dietrich, M. "The BVR/AHLA Guide to Healthcare Industry compensation and Valuation," 2010, page 130.

25 42 CFR Section 411.351.

availability. Experts typically analyze large amounts of data to determine and calculate the market rate. From the provider's perspective, the provider's billed charges should also be considered when evaluating the reasonable value, while a payer's will point to the in-network rate for the services. Providers would typically agree that in-network rates can be used as a data point in the calculation of reasonable value but must be adjusted to consider the elective benefit impact on such a negotiated rate.

IV. CONCLUSION

The relationships between healthcare providers, healthcare plans and their patients/members are complex and involve many agreements and processes. One of the goals of managed care is to improve the quality of and access to care for patients, but the intricacies of the processes related to the delivery and reimbursement of healthcare services can result in complex administrative procedures for providers. In turn, these complexities can trigger underpayments and claim denials that can impact providers' ability to provide access to high-quality patient care. Ensuring fair and accurate reimbursement to providers is important to ensure that quality and access are not undermined.

A Look to the Future

The future of contracting, reimbursement and compliance is likely to vary across different geographic areas of the U.S. For hospitals and physicians operating in a geographic area where capitation reimbursement or other risk-based models are not prevalent, the future may not bring dramatic changes in reimbursement and contracting approaches. While there may be incremental adjustments in network composition, these adjustments are unlikely to materially impact hospitals and physicians in the absence of mergers or acquisitions that disrupt a market and create potential network realignments.

Current hospital reimbursement methodologies such as per diem, DRG and case rates are likely to continue, with potential expansion of case rates for specific cardiac, neurological and orthopedic procedures. Package or bundled hospital rates may not become widespread among commercial plans but are likely to continue for certain types of services in the Medicare program.

Value-based arrangements, incentive payments and other alternative payment models are likely to continue where there are opportunities to track and reward quality and positive patient outcomes.[1] One unanswered question is whether these types of programs will achieve the health plan's goals of earlier detection of disease and better management of chronic conditions.

The largest potential change would likely be driven by providers in specific markets who enter into risk-based arrangements where historically such arrangements did not exist. This could create opportunities for HMOs, for example, to enter these markets or increase market share.

1 Data for these types of initiatives may be collected through the Healthcare Effectiveness Data and Information Set (HEDIS), which is maintained by the National Committee for Quality Assurance (NCQA) and the Uniform Data System (UDS).

For hospitals and physicians operating in mature markets with a balance of HMO and PPO benefit plans, network changes will likely be focused on implementation of narrow networks anchored by Centers of Excellence[2] for specific surgical or medical treatments. It is likely that health plans will continue to pursue value-based arrangements, case rates and package rates for specific surgical procedures as well.

In terms of compliance, states that already have robust regulatory oversight programs are likely to continue to expand, with increasing focus on patient access to care. In states where health plan oversight has not been as robust, it is likely that organizational distress or patient complaints regarding access to care will drive regulatory agencies to increase requirements.

In terms of price transparency, it is not clear how or when enforcement of CMS requirements will be addressed by regulatory agencies. The argument that transparency in pricing will help consumers better spend their healthcare dollars has not yet been borne out. Some also argue that price transparency will undermine the basic foundation of managed care, which has been volume discounts. It is also possible that the hospital price transparency and payer transparency requirements will be a focus of potential discussions regarding anti-trust and the ways in which markets may be negatively impacted by transparency reporting requirements.

Another potential disruptor is private equity. Private equity firms have purchased hospitals, physicians' organizations and other healthcare providers in recent years, usually focusing on specialists in specific geographies.[3] However, some private equity firms have started to evaluate IPAs, including those that hold HMO licenses.[4] To date, the author has not observed any impact on contracting, reimbursement or compliance as a result of private equity ownership of providers.

Ultimately, providers and payers need each other. Although these entities have had relatively volatile relationships that have sometimes caused each side to be suspicious of the other's motives, consumers and regulators may demand that they strive to be better partners for the benefit of their patients.

2 A center of excellence typically refers to a hospital with a specialized program for a specific treatment (i.e., cardiac bypass) where the hospital and physicians apply industry best practices and have significantly better outcomes in patient care.

3 Gretchen Morgenson and Emmanuelle Saliba, "Private equity firms now control many hospitals, ERs and nursing homes. Is it good for health care?" NBC, May 13, 2020, www.nbcnews.com/health/health-care/private-equity-firms-now-control-many-hospitals-ers-nursing-homes-n1203161.

4 David Carnevali, "Carlyle seek to line up bid for urgent care provider Heritage," Reuters, November 15, 2022, www.reuters.com/business/healthcare-pharmaceuticals/exclusive-carlyle-seeks-line-up-bid-urgent-care-provider-heritage-sources-2022–11–15/.

Index